Frederic Janes

The Janes Family

A Genealogy and Brief History of the Descendants of William Janes...

Frederic Janes

The Janes Family
A Genealogy and Brief History of the Descendants of William Janes...

ISBN/EAN: 9783337073985

Printed in Europe, USA, Canada, Australia, Japan

Cover: Foto ©ninafisch / pixelio.de

More available books at **www.hansebooks.com**

THE

JANES FAMILY.

A

GENEALOGY AND BRIEF HISTORY

OF THE

Descendants of William Janes

THE

EMIGRANT ANCESTOR OF 1637,

WITH AN

EXTENDED NOTICE OF BISHOP EDMUND S. JANES, D.D.,
AND OTHER BIOGRAPHICAL SKETCHES:

BY THE

Rev. FREDERIC JANES.

"INQUIRE, I PRAY THEE, OF THE FORMER AGE, AND PREPARE THYSELF
TO THE SEARCH OF THEIR FATHERS."—*Job*, viii, 8.

NEW YORK:
JOHN H. DINGMAN, 654 BROADWAY:
(C. SCRIBNER & CO)
1868.

J. MUNSELL, PRINTER,

ALBANY, N. Y.

PREFACE.

I purpose in these pages to give a simple line of narrative of the descendants of William Janes, following down through the different generations in the several branches, describing more or less minutely the character of persons whose names are well known to the public, having figured in their day, prominently before the world, and achieved more or less success upon the field of human endeavor, and also, shall speak of many others, less conspicuous, humble yet earnest individuals, of different generations, though I fail to do them the fullest justice.

It is but a token of love and grateful acknowledgment of the noble deeds of our progenitors to take their names from the perishing records of the present, and place them in durable form for affectionate remembrance as fragrant family memorials.

The history of the Janeses in the old world, their Norman or French extraction, and the valorous entering of Guido de Janes into England with the Norman Baron, afterward Henry II of the English throne, and his having allotted to him the manor of Kirtland as a reward of bravery and military prowess as a general, and the success of his grandson in the Crusades, for the recovery of the Holy Land from the infidels will be briefly narrated.

The line of connection between this ancient family and William Janes, the emigrant, has not been established and fortified by complete and satisfactory evidence; but numerous circumstances, pointing in this one direction, render such a fact in a high degree probable.

A feeling of pride may justly accompany the remembrance of worthy ancestors, the early founders of the nation: men perhaps, more noble than the lineage of royal lines, who scrupled not to cast out our fathers from their early homes, and compel them to venture the treacherous ocean, and the greater treachery of the savages of the forest, to work their way as best they could in a new country on an untried theatre of action.

In them, how has the old and the new world met, and what an era then and there begun in the history of nations.

To exhibit the virtues of such men we only need to record their deeds, and give a true expression of the principles that called forth those deeds to the observation of mankind.

The early conquest in which they were engaged under the French Barons, their part in the drama of the Roman Catholic and Protestant conflict, in different centuries, and their activities in the exciting scenes of Puritan reformation and the Pilgrim emigration to the New World, their early conflicts, struggles and victories, can hardly find space in this limited volume, beyond some simple allusions.

Our more immediate concern is with the descendants who lived and acted in that brief space of time, from William Janes the emigrant, down to the present blessed era of freedom.

We make up our humble tale from many disjointed fragments, and all our efforts to weave in so many fugitive rehearsals, legends and anecdotes of the personages who have appeared upon the stage, in a systematic manner, we fear will be impossible.

The gathering of these statistics is an enormous task, which fact can be better appreciated by one who has made the effort.

Pressing and constant cares in a new country and the busy scenes through which all are crowding in the passage of life, will be a fair excuse for some neglect of the records, by our fathers, not appearing to them of any immediate importance, though of great literary value to their posterity.

Between the past and the present generations how soon time draws a veil too thick to allow us to look beyond the records themselves, however imperfect.

In completing such a work, one which demands so wide a range of research over centuries, so vast a sweep in its geographical lines, so many generations, past and present, come into retrospect, we find

difficulties formidable and perfection hopeless; but not appalled at
the fear of unkind criticism we venture to submit the following pages
to the public, for the perusal of all who are immediately or remotely
interested, while we are well aware that further research, more time
and more expense would eventuate in the production of a volume of
still greater interest and more satisfaction.

GENEALOGY signifies the line of descent, or list of a persons' ancestors.
The Hebrews expressed it by Sepher-Toledoth, the "Book of Generations." How careful were the Jews to preserve their genealogies. The
sacred writings contain their genealogies extending backward three
thousand five hundred years. The genealogy of our Saviour is
drawn out by the Evangelists from Adam to Joseph and Mary, through
a space of over four thousand years. Matthew gives the line of descent
through Joseph, his reputed or legal father, and Luke through Mary,
his mother. In searching them we notice that the Messiah was restricted
by divine appointment, to the posterity of Abraham to the family
of David, to the existence of the second temple; and our Lord was
of the *direct* line of the *elder* branch of the royal family, in truth the
very person, who, had the dominiou continued in the family of David,
would have legally sat on the throne. *Gen.*, xlix, 10; *Acts*, ii, 35–36.
It is a praise-worthy and pious work to search out the links that connect
us with those who have passed away, the honored representatives of our
name and line of being, the noble heroes of many endeavors and
many struggles for grand achievements. We have noticed of late
great activity and commendable zeal in this direction.

We were as happy as surprised to notice so many volumes on the
shelves of our printer whose monogram appears on our title page; to
see how many of them were issued under his immediate supervision;
the Hyde, the Clark, the Hall, the Whitmore and the Macy genealogies,
etc. Some of them large elegant volumes, showing the zeal and
earnest effort put forth by thoughtful, reverent children of the Pilgrims. There are numerous others on the passage for the press, which
may please or astonish. Our friends Dr. D. P. and Mrs. F. K. Holton
of 12 West 54th street, New York city, are preparing a quadruple

mammoth work on the descendants of their four grandparents, the Far-
wells, the Parsons, the Holtons and the Winslows combined, as *per will*
of Miriam Holton, who, in her passing away from time, was deeply
impressed with the Christian duty of devoting more attention to this
interesting subject to secure the records that might irredeemably
perish.

There is a zest in the perusal of so many works and in bringing before
our minds so many peculiarities of different generations.   But we cannot
promise that our arrangement is more philosophical or more commendable than others, or that our history will excite peculiar pleasure
Some, even, may be displeased with minuteness, and some may be tried
for want of minuteness in their particular case ; but we venture the
volume will find readers wherever the family name exists.

From worthy motives to achieve something for the good of the
present age and something to benefit posterity, the writer has devoted
many hours of tedious and perplexing labor, and deprived himself of
many midnight hours of rest.   May others as faithfully toil to reclaim
the records of their fathers and put them in durable form for preserva-
tion and not fail to receive a better — a higher reward.

JANES FAMILY COAT OF ARMS.

The Coat of Arms which has been in the Janes family for several generations.

Arms, argent (white); a lion rampant, azure (blue), between three escallops, gules (red). Crest out of a ducal crown, *or* (gold), a demi lion rampant, blue, holding between the paws an escallop shell, red.

Motto — *Ex Virtute Bonos.*

The lion rampant, in the arms, was given from an ancestor having, whilst in command, won a battle. The escallop shells indicate the having made pilgrimages to Jerusalem. The ducal crown was given to those who held command under the sovereign duke of the ancient French confederation.

ELM STREET

Market Place has disappeared, the large green is occupied as public ground, surrounded by elms; the churches and State House on the west.

CHURCH STREET

| No. 9. An Elder. 1¼ acres. | No. 10. Jasper Crane. 1¼ acres. | No. 1. Mr. Davenport. 2¼ acres. |
| No. 8. Mr. Rowe. 2 acres. | No. 2. Richard Malborn. 2 acres. | |

Market Place.

No. 7. Matthew Gilbert. 2 acres.	No. 6. 2 acres.	No. 3. John Nash. 1½ acres.
		No. 5. John Chapman ½ acre.	No. 8. John Nash.
		No. 4. John Benham. ½ acre.

STATE STREET

CHAPEL STREET

Cutler's Cor.

Thomas Gregson.

139 ft.	235 ft. William Janes.	170 ft.	288 ft. Rd. Hull.	220 ft. William Preston.
139 ft.	461 ft. John Budd,			
354 ft.	Mr. Illckock.			
133 ft. John Brocket.	Robert Seely.	Thomas Jeffrey.		
138 ft. Roger Alling.	140 ft.	120 ft.		

A copy of the earliest Map of New Haven, as plotted by the original settlers.

GEORGE STREET

INTRODUCTION.

The compiler of these pages did not expect, when he commenced tracing the line of his ancestry, running back in some respects beyond the first immigrant of the name, to bring anything before the public.

But some years of research brought forth so much interesting matter in this relation, and the number of the families of the name being so much more numerous than was anticipated, and so many facts clothed with great interest appeared, that the subject was pursued amid many other cares to its present issue, and many of the family were anxious for the publication of the result of this long continued and very tedious research. It contains little of interest to any outside of the family represented, unless, perhaps, to some antiquarian lovers of genealogical lore.

The research, amid many discouragements, impresses deeply the conviction that much remains unrecorded which should have found page room; and much valuable information and many important facts to perfect a suitable genealogy exist in various family records and

other manuscripts scattered through the country which
should appear in this connection.

All this amount of matter particularly requested
would have been furnished had proper attention been
given to the many kind requests made to different
persons to send forward a brief family record, with
remarks of any interest, which would have cost but a
few hours, perhaps but a few minutes, of labor.

The compiler has spared no pains to give a perfect,
though not a full record, of the families here named;
but as the work is assumed personally, without numerous assurances of patronage and remuneration, much
interesting matter is omitted that might, under other
circumstances, have been added for the gratification
of those interested; but the cost forbids any large
venture. Perplexity and toil are incident to such an
effort beyond all calculation, and may well discourage
any attempt. So much labor, so much correspond-
ence, so many letters unanswered, unnoticed, so many
folios searched in vain, so much travel, and expense of
time and money would not be undertaken a second
time, ordinarily if ever. But we shall be satisfied if
we can satisfy others, and see those who have encou-
raged the work and those who have a desire to obtain
it, and those who feel that a family good has thus
been accomplished, exhibit the magnanimity to bear
their part of the burden, and own a copy of a record
which they may leave behind them as a valued legacy
to their children.

Many persons of whom the author had no knowledge

and who are in distant parts of the country, would no doubt have gladly aided in this endeavor; and gratitude is due to many kind friends in and out of the family for their prompt assistance, and we can but regret that some of them have already passed away from earth to higher relationships.

The copying of records by so many different parties, and the liability to mistake figures or miscopy them, must be the apology for any evident errors.

We regret that so many families have been so separated from their friends in the eastern states that they cannot now be traced with any degree of perfection; and that so many of the younger families can only be named — their record being neglected, or uncopied in season — after all the effort that has been made to collect them through verbal and written communications.

Many facts of valuable history might have been put in durable form for the entertainment or improvement of others; but the general impression prevailing, that little importance is to be attached to such a history or genealogy, sometimes even those, who should be interested in the publication, prove themselves indifferent to the task.

The author would have been glad if he could have had sufficient time and met with sufficient encouragement to spend other months in searching out a full history of all that was interesting in the old country as well as in these states. It would have been of material benefit if all who had known the true design of this work had done their part to make it a full and correct publication of what it purports to be; but much effort, much importunity has called forth too limited an amount of statistical facts. Such needless embarrassments must furnish the apology for some of these deficiencies.

The heroic examples of virtue and pious endeavor which are mirrored before us, should stimulate the present generation to greater fidelity and truer self-denial, and fill them with courage to emulate the great excellencies of our worthy ancestors, who loved civil and religious freedom, and devoted themselves to the securing of its perpetuity.

It is certainly desirable to place in a permanent and readable form the records and registries of the families who so early came to this pilgrim soil, and took such a prominent part in moulding the infant institutions under which their children were to thrive and enjoy whatever is excellent in culture and sweet in fruitage.

Mankind are much more strongly inclined to deal with the present than with the past. But we cannot ignore the past without ignoring historic manhood.

We are but the children of those who pushed through the mysterious experiences of the past; and from these marvelous experiences of other generations of men, we should be stupid not to profit. The character of our ancestors, stamped upon their children, determined the part they were to act on the great theatre of life amid providential revolutions, moral and political.

The Puritans of New England were in a large sense constructors of society. They were the founders of that mighty edifice which they and their children were to fashion and complete, and render imperishable.

The vine, dug from the storm riven bowers of persecution, planted in a genial soil, grew and spread itself over the land, and now millions enjoy its luxuriant shade which so defends them, and it will be ever cherished as a blood-bought legacy purchased by the toils and tears of a noble race who knew how to prize civil and religious freedom.

Those noble sufferers for conscience sake should not be forgotten by an ambitious and ungrateful posterity. We should honor the memory of those who, as to the earthly, gave us our being and launched us upon the tide of life for its struggles and its conquests.

It is hoped the plan of the work will be easily understood. By numbering each person in their order in Arabic or common figures, and the order of births in the family by Roman letters — both of which are given again as a caption to biographical notices of such as had issue — biographical descriptions can be readily found. This arrangement will enable one to trace his line backward. Each one is supposed to know the branch with which he is connected, and, by referring back to the preceding generation in his branch, he will follow back the line of his ancestry. Where the two numbers correspond the birth of his parent will be found; so on back to his earliest progenitor. Single figures (1), (2), indicate the different marriages of the same

person. Letters also to indicate the different denominations, as (B) for Baptist, (C) for Congregationalist,
(E) for Episcopal, (M) for Methodist, (P) for Presbyterian, will be found convenient when we find it
important to speak of denominations.

HISTORICAL.

Most of the settlers of New Haven came with Mr. Davenport and Mr. Eaton in the ship Hector to Boston, arriving there June 3, 1637, where they tarried awhile on board of their chartered vessel. Nash, in the *History of his Fathers*, says, concerning this company : " On the 26th of July, 1637, from the ship Hector, and another ship not named, a company landed at Boston composed principally of merchants of London whose wealth and position prepared them to come over under better auspices than any company which had preceded them. They were mostly members of the Rev. John Davenport's church and congregation of Coleman street, London. They were provided with men skilled in various arts, and with whatever an infant colony would prospectively need.

" They were urged to settle in the vicinity of Boston ; but being resolved to plant a new colony of a higher and better grade than the others that sprung from necessity, they sought a new field on the shores of these American wilds where they could evolve the new ideas then struggling for birth and growth in the bosom of their souls.

" With lofty aims they felt impressed with the duty of
finding a quiet resting place to carry out the purpose
of their mission. A committee was sent forth to
search a location for a settlement, and they, in due time,
decided upon Quinnipiac (New Haven) then owned
by a small tribe of Indians. Near the last of March
the whole company sailed from Boston, and in
little more than two weeks (April 16) they reached
their new harbor, and commenced to prepare their new
homes. In November they entered into an agreement
with the chief Momaugin and his councillors for the
purchase of the lands. They spent the first summer
and winter in laying out their lands, in building their
rude dwellings, and preparing for a permanent
residence."

On the 4th of June, 1639, they held their famous
meeting in Mr. Newman's barn, and drew up their
fundamental agreement for the regulation of the civil
and religious affairs of the colony.

The whole number who then, or soon after, signed
the covenant, was 419. They were a people of sterling
integrity, and were moved by an unshaken confidence
in the promises of God.

The leading spirit of this new enterprise was Rev.
John Davenport, who had, for his religious opinions
and faith, left London for the continent, to be, if
possible, more useful in the service of his Master.

Finding no door of usefulness now open before
him in Holland — in this land where so many of the
Puritans, for a short time, had found refuge — Mr.

Davenport soon after returned to his native country—
England—for the purpose of emigrating to America.

For some years he had been familiar, chiefly through
his personal friend Rev. John Cotton, with the weighty
affairs that were going on in New England. He had
taken an early interest in the formation of the Massachusetts colony, and contributed £50 towards the
procurement of its charter. He was present at the
meeting of the company in London, March 23, 1629,
and also at those of March 30, April 8, August 28–29,
and those of November and December following.

He now resolved with his friend Theophilus Eaton,
to collect a band of colonists whom, under God, they
might lead out of spiritual Egypt — the house of bond-
age and oppression — into the distant land of promise.
Many of those who had formerly enjoyed the ministry
of Mr. Davenport in Coleman street, were ready to
join them.

He who divided the Red sea before the Israelites
gave this little company as safe a passage across the
ocean. They arrived in Boston in the Hector, and
another ship, on the 3d of June, 1637. Among other
passengers who came with this expedition was Edward
Hopkins, son-in-law of Governor Eaton, and himself
for many years governor of Connecticut colony. By
his will he became a distinguished benefactor of Har-
vard College and several other institutions of learning
in New England. With these came also Lord Leigh,
son and heir of the Earl of Marlborough, a youth of
nineteen, humble and pious, who came merely to see

3

the country, and returned to England a few weeks
after in company with Sir Henry Vane. Mr. Davenport was heartily welcomed by Mr. Cotton and his
associates, and more particularly as his assistance was
now required in helping to stay the prevalence of anti-
nomian error, which seemed at the time, through the
fanaticism of Ann Hutchinson and others, to have
threatened the peace and purity of the churches.

His preaching, and also his counsels in the synod of
that year, evidently had a favorable influence in the
suppression of those dangerous errors.   At the request
of the synod he closed the proceedings by a sermon on
the text, Phil. iii, 16.   In this discourse he declared
the result of the assembly, and " with much wisdom
and sound argument urged to unity and harmony."
These difficulties being in a good degree removed, it
became an object with Mr. Davenport and his company
to fix upon a place of settlement.

The wealth, intellectual endowments and moral worth
of this newly arrived company of emigrants, made it
very desirable with the already organized colonies of
Plymouth and Massachusetts to retain them among
them, and to this end very liberal offers were made.

" The refusal to accept which," says Mr. M'Clure,
" was regarded as almost an unkindness by those who
coveted this accession to their strength."   It was thought
that Mr. Davenport's residence in Massachusetts, might
draw down upon that colony the speedier wrath of
Laud, who loved them not before.   When he heard ,
Mr. Davenport had fled to New England, to avoid the

storm of prelatical indignation, the persecuting archbishop had boldly said, *My arm shall reach him there.* It
was supposed that the scattering of those who were
obnoxious to Laud into different places might lessen
the motives for stretching out his potent arm against
them. Although he obtained a commission from the
king to carry out these designs, yet the political excite-
ments by which they were surrounded at home, obliged
him and his monarch, Charles I, to confine their
activity to resisting a revolution which eventually re-
sulted in the overthrow of their own power. As John
Cotton expressed it, " God rocked three nations with
dispensations to procure some rest for those shaking
infant churches."

Another probable reason why Mr. Davenport and
Mr. Eaton wished to form an independent colony beyond
the limits of any existing grant or patent, was, that
they might carry out their peculiar views in regard to
a civil state. They seemed to have desired the formation of a community in some respect different from any
that existed elsewhere, one more thoroughly *scriptural*,
more in accordance with the ancient Jewish system,
one fashioned throughout in the strictest conformity
to the rules of the Bible.

In the fall of 1637, Mr. Eaton and others of the
company made a journey to Connecticut to explore the
lands and harbors on the coast. They came to a place
lying at the head of a harbor which sets up about four
miles from Long Island sound. Its Indian name was
Quinnipiac. The explorers were much taken with the

beauty and fertility of this tract of country, and most of them being Londoners and accustomed to commercial pursuits they deemed it a desirable site for the establishment of a commercial town. This place was therefore fixed upon for the location of their colony. On what is now the south side of Church and Meadow streets they erected a hut, in which a few men remained for the winter to make preparations for the commencement of the settlement, while the rest returned to Massachusetts.

Early in the spring the colonists prepared to remove to their new homes in the wilderness.

After taking an affectionate leave of their friends, and gratefully acknowledging the many kindnesses they had there received, the company sailed from Boston for the place of their destination on the 13th of March, 1638.

This band of pilgrims reached Quinnipiac, the future New Haven, on the 14th of April, 1638. Mr. Davenport was then forty-one years of age.

The next day is the Sabbath. A drum beats in the rude and hasty encampment. The armed men, with their wives and children, gather at this signal under a branching oak. They meet to consecrate to God a new region reclaimed from heathen darkness. For the first time the aisles of that forest temple resounded with the praises of the Most High. Here are men nurtured in the halls of Oxford and Cambridge, and women used to all the elegant refinements of the British metropolis. They are gathered under the

oaken tree. Why are they here? Why this change
in their condition? Why are they here, far from the
haunts of civilization, confronting privations and
suffering in every form? It is for conscience, to keep
that sacred thing unspotted — it is for posterity — for
eternity — for God.

> What sought they thus afar,
>   Bright jewels of the mine?
> The wealth of seas? the spoils of war?
>   They sought a faith's pure shrine.
>
> Ay, call it holy ground,
>   The soil where first they trod;
> They have left unstained what there they found —
>   *Freedom to worship God.*

Surely angels rejoiced while infinite love smiled
upon the scene. Mr. Davenport preached from the
text, Matthew iv, 1. At the close of these services Mr.
Davenport remarked that *he had enjoyed a good day.*
Soon after their arrival at Quinnipiac, at the close of
a " day of fasting and prayer," these exiles formed and
subscribed what they denominated a *plantation covenant.*
By this instrument they engaged " that as in matters
that concern the gathering and ordering of a church, so
also in all public offices which concern civil order, as
choice of magistrates and officers, making and repealing laws, dividing allotments of inheritance, and
all things of like nature, they would all of them be
ordered by the rules which the Scripture held forth to

them." This may be considered the original civil constitution of the New Haven colony.

It may here be stated that the planters of this colony
did not disregard the rights of the Indians. The
most ancient record in existence at New Haven is, as it
ought to be, the record of two treaties with the ab-
original proprietors by which the soil was purchased,
and the relations thenceforward to subsist between the
Indians and the English were distinctly defined.
These treaties commenced thus, "Articles of agreement
between Theophilus Eaton and John Davenport and
other English planters at Quinnipiac, on the one party,
and Momaugin, the Indian Sachem of Quinopiocke
and Sugcogism, Wesaucucke, and others of his council, on the other party, made and concluded the 24th
day of November, 1638, Thomas Stanton being inter-
preter."

These treaties were held in good faith by both parties,
and the colony lived in much peace and security from
the hostile attacks of the surrounding tribes. By these
treaties the Indians considered themselves under the
protection of the English, while they retained the right
to hunt in their forests, to fish in the streams, with
the pledge not to disturb the corn fields or pastures of
the English, or to interrupt their trade.

More than a year after their arrival was spent in
erecting their dwellings, and in clearing their lands.
During this period Mr. Davenport prepared his *Discourse about Civil Government in a New Plantation, whose
Design is Religion.*

This treatise was published many years after in 1673. It was a vindication of the practice long maintained by our fathers of allowing the rights of voting and holding office to only such as were members of the church.

Having given themselves time for mature deliberation and wise counsel, and practically recognizing the principle that "Governments are instituted among men, deriving their just powers from the consent of the governed," "all free planters"—by which was meant all who were engaged in planting the colony—on the 4th of June, 1639, convened in a large barn of Mr. Newman, and in a formal manner proceeded to the organization of a civil government. "No reference, direct or indirect," says Professor Kingsley, "was made by those concerned in this transaction to their native country, as at the time the colonists signed their plantation covenant, so now they seem to have supposed that since they were in fact beyond the actual control of any existing sovereignty, they had a perfect right to constitute a government for themselves."

The business of the occasion, in conformity to the views of those assembled and the propriety of the case, was opened with prayer, and Mr. Davenport is said to have preached a sermon from Prov. ix, 1.

Mr. Davenport then proposed several queries to the planters, and urged them " to consider seriously in the presence and fear of God, the weight of the business they met about, and not to be rash or slight in giving their votes to things they understood not, but to digest fully and thoroughly what should be propounded to them, and without respect to men, as they should be satisfied and persuaded in their own minds, to give their answers in such sort as they should be willing should stand upon record for posterity." They then unanimously resolved " that the Scriptures do hold forth a perfect rule for the direction and government of all men in all duties, which they are to perform to God and men as well in families and commonwealth as in matters of the church."

After this they renewed their assent to their plantation covenant, and mutually bound themselves, not only in their ecclesiastical proceedings, but also in the choice of magistrates, the making and repealing of laws, the dividing of inheritances, and in all civil matters to submit themselves to the rules held forth in the Word of God.

Then, as the record informs us, Mr. Davenport declared to them by the Scriptures what kind of persons might best be trusted with matters of government, and, by sundry arguments from Scripture, proved that they were such men as were described in Exod. xviii, 21, Deut. i, 13, with Deut. xvii, 15, and 1 Cor. iv, 1, 6, 7.

After some further consideration, the company, among other fundamental regulations, adopted this: " That church members only should be free burgesses, and that they only should choose magistrates and officers among themselves, to have the power of transacting all public civil affairs of the plantation, of making and repealing laws, dividing inheritances, deciding differences that may arise, and doing all things and business of like nature."

Having founded their civil commonwealth they proceeded to the organization of their church.

On the twenty-second of August, 1639, *seven persons*, chosen out of their number, among whom Mr. Davenport was one, entered into a covenant with one another, and with Christ, and thus was constituted the first church of New Haven. Being thus organized, they proceeded to admit others of the company to their fellowship.

Shortly after the church was instituted Mr. Davenport was chosen pastor. He was ordained by the hands of two or three of the lay brethren through Mr. Hooker and Mr. Stone. The reverend pastors of the church in Hartford were present, and one of them made the prayer. This ceremony was not used, because the validity of his ordination in the Church of England was doubted, it being in fact but an *installation* or solemn recognition of his new relation to a particular church.

His pastoral relations were satisfactory, and his labors greatly blessed by winning many of the "heirs of the grace of life."

Soon after the organization of the church, the general court, called the "seven pillars," proceeded to constitute the body of freemen and elect their officers. Mr. Davenport expounded several passages of Scripture, describing the character of civil magistrates as given in the sacred oracles. Theophilus Eaton, the excellent statesman and counseling friend of Mr. Davenport, was

4

chosen their governor, and everything was as harmo-
nious, successful and prosperous as it could be possibly
expected. So much we record to show the excellency
of purpose, and the stability of the men who composed
this new colony with which William Janes had as-
sociated himself in matters, temporal and spiritual,
of the highest moment, and in which he was so prominent an actor.

THE JANES FAMILY.

The family of Janes is of Norman or French origin.
Guido de Janes, as a general of the French Confederation, accompanied Henry II lawful heir to the English
throne, when he went over to assume the sovereignty
(1154), instead of his mother Matilda, empress of
Germany, daughter of Henry I, and appointed by him
to be his successor.

This Norman baron, heir to the throne, having established himself firmly as the English sovereign, the first
of the Plantagenets, conferred upon Guido de Janes the
manor of Kirtland or Kirtling in the county of Cam-
bridgeshire, for his valor as a general in his service, and
as an acknowledgment of military prowess. We cannot
yet obtain the particulars of his family, but his grandson
Geoffry de Janes (about 1200 or 1204) took up arms
with Baldwin, count of Flanders, in his successful effort
to obtain Jerusalem, and was one who contributed to
make Baldwin king of Jerusalem. Geoffry, after his
return to England, made with his son Guy or Guido
three pilgrimages to the Holy Land. Hence the escallop shells in the coat of arms which commemorate
those events.

Before his death, he acquired through his wife Eleanor, the heiress of Sir Richard Penruddock, the lands of Botalock in Cornwall, upon which he erected a chantry for four Cistercian monks, which he dedicated to " St. Mary of Grief." These chantries, or chanting singing places, were in connection with the cathedrals and chapels of worship, and were popular in those superstitious days, and gave a great name to the wealthy, benevolent souls, who contributed their wealth to build them, and the soul of the patron was especially supposed to be prayed out of purgatory. The Roman Catholic religion, it is hardly needful to say, was the religion of that dark period.

For a few centuries chantries were quite flourishing. Great numbers connected themselves with them, but in the 37th year of Henry VIII's reign these endowments were confiscated to the crown, and any failing to come into his possession were taken by his successor Edward VI.

The family name, Janes, is still in Kirtling, and, by a rare fortune, these estates mentioned are still in the family name.

From this family came William Janes or Jeanes in 1637 with the John Davenport colony which remained eight months in Massachusetts, in or near Boston, before they set sail for New Haven, their chosen abode, for a settlement.

The generations between Geoffry de Janes and William the emigrant are not yet transmitted to the compiler. We know little of *their* history. Henry

Janes, born 1611, graduated at Oxon hall, and was greatly esteemed for his many good qualities of mind and heart, as an ornament to the church for which he ministered till called to his account. We suppose him an elder brother of William our ancestor.

The name in French we find de Jeanne. It was Anglicized by dropping the *de* and afterward one of the *n*'s, adding an *s* for euphony, or to show of what family. The first *e* was retained and used in many early records. On the Springfield, Massachusetts, records we have Abell Jeanes. William Jeanes so signed his on the plantation covenant. I think he dropped the first *e* afterward, and his family followed the same orthography. Our ancestors paid less attention to the spelling of their names than those at the present day. We find Jane, Jene, Jeans, Jayne, Joan, Jeanes, and Janes—all may have come from the same French Jeanne.

In these published pages some links are still wanting to make the connections certain between some of the families, as will be seen by the reader; but a degree of perfection is reached by full copies of many different records in various parts of the country.

From their great multiplication they must be considered a prolific race, obedient to the command " Multiply and replenish the earth." They claim no distinction for heroic deeds or ancestral renown, or what the world may mark as the glory of the human race.

They have no higher or surer schemes for the acquisition of wealth than others. But if fidelity, honest and stable, unquestionable piety be worthy of note, then, in the history of their fathers, there is cause for devout reverence. Like the majority of the Puritans[1] who fled from Europe—from England—for the sake of their faith, for freedom in way and spirit of worship, their ancestors were particularly a religious people. They were distinguished for their lofty aims and for their spirit of · self-denial. Their descendants have mainly followed in the way these ancient worthies trod. They have pushed on diligently in a career of usefulness and prosperity in a measure worthy of their sires. They may truthfully be called a respectable, industrious and prosperous race. Without very many preeminent distinctions they have filled many posts of honor and trust. They have stood high at the bar, and have been honored on the bench, in the halls of congress, in the pulpit, at the marts of commerce and in the department of agriculture.

---

[1] Soon after the commencement of the reformation in England (1534), the Protestants were divided into two parties, one the followers of Luther, and the other of Calvin. The former had chosen gradually and almost imperceptibly, to recede from the church of Rome; while the latter, more zealous, and convinced of the importance of a thorough reformation, and at the same time possessing much firmness, and high notions of religious liberty, were for effecting a thorough change at once. Their consequent endeavors to expunge from the church all the inventions which had been brought into it since the days of the apostles, and to introduce the " Scripture purity," derived for them the name of Puritans.

WILLIAM JANES.

In relation to our progenitor, William Janes, who emigrated to this country in 1637, we have left us only the briefest items of history. The veneration and respect his name inspires in our hearts, creates in us a wish to learn, if possible, some other things concerning his history which at this period could not well be found, though there are some interesting traditions. He was a man of sterling character and great moral force, rendering himself essentially useful in his profession. He was among the early settlers of the country, with John Davenport and his coadjutors.

He was born in Essex, England, during the reign of James I, about the year 1610, when the Puritans were suffering a fearful persecution from powerful and bitter foes.

In the year 1637 when he came to this country with other companions of persecution and adventure, anxious admirers and ardent lovers of liberty, Charles I was the reigning monarch, and Bishop Laud, the religious tyrant, was in his glory as high commissioner of religion and of conscience. The times were indeed stormy and fruitful in the development of strong faith among Christians. These crises stirred the masses with a mighty purpose to achieve their freedom and that of their posterity.

This was the class of men who planted the New Haven colony, among whom William Janes acted a prominent part. For about seventeen years he was a conspicuous citizen and beloved teacher, moulding and training the minds of the young and in educating the rising generation of the colonists to the utmost extent their facilities would allow, and in imparting the best intellectual culture and the highest moral tone to all the youth of the infant colony. He was a teacher of the rudiments of education, and a teacher of the doctrines of the Bible. Vigorous, systematic, resolute and true to every instinct of manhood, he was beloved and respected by all who knew him.

The records show that this new colony paid him the small sum of £10 per annum, and the more prosperous and wealthy parents made a further compensation personally.

In the year 1652 the people of Wethersfield, a colony near Hartford, invited him to remove among them as their teacher, which he finally engaged to do, but only " by consent of the brethren."

But he returned to New Haven during the same year and resumed his former position, leading the younger members of the colony in their social, political and religious aspirations, and as a teaching elder the minds of others to clearer views of the doctrine of redemption.

His homestead he built on his allotment of land

which he received October, 1639, on the corner of
Chapel and Church streets, known as Cutler corner,
and now covered by a costly pile of brick buildings.
This lot, at the corner of the now beautiful green,
measured 139 feet on Church street and 235 on Chapel
street.[1]

An early valuation of the property of the colony
made his considerably above the average, but not large.
In the New Haven colony records William Janes is
named: 1. as signing the plantation covenant, which
shows his autograph. 2. In 1643 he makes returns of
5 persons in his family and an estate of £150. 3. In .
1648 he is a member of the general court. 4. In the
latter end of the year, viz: March, 1648 – 9 he "pas-
seth over to John Meggs, his house and lot lying at
the corner over against Mr. Gregsons betwixt the
house of John Budd and the highway." (See Map,
8th page).

About the year 1656, with other pioneers of liberty,
he went higher up the Connecticut valley to the west
of Holyoke, about eighteen miles above Springfield,
to a place they called Northampton. Here, in the
wilderness, others began to lay the foundations of
good government. Here they planted a high toned,
moral and religious colony. Here they enjoyed the

---

[1] The lot is now worth nearly two hundred thousand dollars
including the buildings. On this lot William Janes built his first
house — here lived with his young family the hope of future generations. He had in 1643 only two or three children — the record of
births seem to be wanting except in case of Ruth, b. February 15,
1650, so that we have an imperfect record of the remaining children.

5

blessings of civil and religious freedom. The votes
on the town record of Northampton will show his
status there :

"Voted 25th of June, 1657, that William Janes
become an inhabitant. 10th January, 1658, town
voted that William Janes be recorder of lands and
so for ensuing years. Voted 19th February, 1660, to
agree with William Janes, to transcribe the old records. Voted 17th June, 1660, that he have a house
lot of two acres." [Voted 11th January, 1662, town
grant to Elisha Janes, four acres land, on condition he
build a house thereon within a year. One month
from that time Elisha died suddenly at Springfield.]

Here William Janes practiced his teaching art.
The town early voted him £10 town stock per year
for teaching, and besides four-pence per week for
teaching the primer, and six-pence per week for teaching to cast "accompts." If any did not come every
day, in their case the charge should be made so as to
reckon three school days one week. He was the recorder of lands for many years, and the Northampton
records show hundreds of pages of his bold autograph. Here he was a teaching elder, and, in the absence of the minister, conducted the religious services
of the Sabbath. Here he built his new house on the
spot, some years later occupied by the grandfather
of Gov. Caleb Strong, who died a century and a
quarter afterward.

The Connecticut River rail road company purchased
of the Strong family, and now occupy the spot for

their grounds and depot, over which thousands pass and repass, which in his early day would indeed have seemed marvelous.

Here, in the house built by him, he parted from the wife of his youth, the mother of his early children, who died like a Christian heroine, committing her mourning family to God, and leaving behind her a record of purity and maternal devotedness worthy of her position and her profession.

These early Christians established an influence in behalf of morality and practical religion to be coveted by later generations. Prayer and self-abnegation and self-sacrifice were the characteristics of these. pioneers which gave society a mould that was permanent in its sweet perfume of spiritual blessings.

Notwithstanding the many Christian virtues, the spirit of self-denial and the high toned piety of the New England fathers, they had their imperfections. Their many trials and crosses must have soured their temper in relation to the conduct of prodigal youth and other companions of their heroic struggles.[1] Want

---

[1] LAW REGULATING DRESS. — Sumptuary laws restraining excess of apparel in some classes were common in England and other nations for centuries. Massachusetts enacted such a law in 1651, ordering that persons whose estates did not exceed £200, and those dependent on them should not wear gold or silver buttons, gold or silver lace, bone lace above 2s. per yard, or silk hoods or scarfs upon penalty of 10s. for each offense. Any person wearing such articles might be assessed in country rates as if they had estates of £200.

The first attempt to have this law observed in Hampshire, was made in 1673. At the March court, twenty-five wives and five maids

of prudence and foresight vexed their souls when laboring so industriously to maintain a livelihood, since fire and sword, the tomahawk and death was constantly imaged before them.

The Connecticut valley was the theatre of vast tragical events; but providence designed their settlement and occupancy for a superior race.

The lands bordering on Connecticut river, which are now in the towns of Northampton, Hadley and Hatfield, were first known by the Indian name *Nonotuck*. It was as early as the 6th of May, 1653, that a number of persons petitioned the general court of Massachusetts to grant them liberty to plant, possess, and inhabit the place on *Conetiquot* river above Springfield, called *Nonotuck*, as their own inheritance, representing that the same was a place suitable to erect a

---

belonging to Springfield, Northampton, Hadley, Hatfield and Westfield, were presented by the jury as persons of small estate, who "use to wear silk contrary to law." Six of these belonged to Hadley, viz:

Wife of John Westcarr was acquitted.
"   Joseph Barnard was fined 10s. and cost, 2s. 6d.
"   Thomas Wells, Jr., was admonished.
"   Edward Grannis was admonished.
"   Joseph Kellogg·was acquitted.
Maid Mary Broughton was admonished.

Of the thirty, only three were fined, and the fines were remitted at the next court.

At the March court, 1674, the wife of Edward Grannis was again presented for wearing silk. Her silk hood and scarf were brought into court, and "though somewhat worn, they had been good silk." She was fined 10s.

At the March court, 1676, the jury presented sixty-eight persons from five towns, viz: thirty-eight wives and maids, and thirty young men," some for wearing silk and that in a flaunting manner, and

town for the furtherance of the public weal, and the propagating the gospel, and which promised, in an ordinary way of God's providence, a comfortable subsistence, whereby they might live and attend upon God in his holy ordinances without distraction.

There is a tradition, that one English family came to this place in 1652, and lived here during the next winter, on land which lies east of what is called *Hawley street*. However this may be, in the year 1653, a number of the petitioners took possession of the township, in consequence of the liberty given them by the government.

Selectmen, or townsmen, as they were then generally called, were chosen in the year 1655. It is presumed from this, as well as from other circumstances, that the town was incorporated in the year

others for long hair and other extravagances." Two were fined 10s., and many of the others were ordered to pay the clerk's fees, 2s. 6d. each. There were ten from Hadley, viz: Joseph Barnard and his wife Sarah, and his sister Sarah, William Rooker, Thomas Crofts, Jonathan Wells, Joseph Grannis, Nehemiah Dickinson, wife of Mark Warner; and the wife of Thomas Wells, Jr., who was fined 10s. Nine were admonished and ordered to pay the clerk's fees. Several of the sixty-eight presented were wives, daughters or sons of men of good estate. Two unmarried daughters of Elder John Strong of Northampton were of this number.

In March, 1678, eight females of Northampton, Springfield, etc., were complained of for wearing silk contrary to law in this day of calamity and trouble. Two were fined 10s., some paid clerk's fees, and some were referred to another court. The boldest of these females was Hannah Lyman, sixteen years of age, daughter of Richard Lyman of Northampton, deceased. She was presented September, 1676, "for wearing silk in a flaunting manner in an offensive way and garb, not only before, but when she stood presented, not only in ordinary but in extraordinary times." She was fined 10s. January, 1677.

1654. But it is said the act of incorporation cannot now be found.[1]

The Indian title to the land had been purchased in 1653, from a number of Indians, who claimed to be the owners of it; and a deed was given by them accordingly, to the use of the settlers. But on the 28th of September, 1658, the sachem, *Umpanchela*, complained to the commissioners, assembled to hold a court at Northampton, that he had not received so much for his part of the land as he expected. It was thereupon agreed by the inhabitants to satisfy his demand; and the sachem executed a new deed, in the presence of the court, releasing to the inhabitants of Northampton, all his right and title to the township.

For the space of twenty-two years after Northampton was settled, the first settlers lived in peace with the Indians.

There was frequent intercourse between them and their English neighbors, the Indians often coming into the village for traffic and other purposes, and the salutation of *Netop* (my friend) was often heard in the street.

Indian men and women, young men, maidens and small children in their scanty dresses, were every day sights, and excited no especial curiosity. The men sold furs and venison, and the women made and sold baskets and other things.

---

[1] It was probably burnt, with the records, in the great fire in Boston in 1711, or afterwards, when the court house was burnt.

Among these laborious Indian women were some that were mild and kind hearted. The western Nipmucks continued to be pagans.

As to the others, though complaints were sometimes made of their petty thefts, and of abuses committed when they were in a state of intoxication, yet they remained here in peace and friendship with the English, until the war commenced in 1675, called *Philip's* war, in the course of which they left this part of the country, and none of them have ever since had a settled residence here.

At the beginning of Philip's war, the Indians about Springfield, Northampton and Hadley seemed inclined to join the English, or at least to remain neutral; but they were soon induced by the emissaries of Philip to unite with him and the other hostile Indians. The combination was so general and extensive, as to endanger the existence, not only of the settlements on Connecticut river, but of the whole colony. The Indians frequently assaulted the towns on the river, and in some instances did great mischief to the inhabitants, killing their cattle and destroying their property, when they were unable to take their lives.

On the 25th of August, 1675, the Indians killed *Samuel Mason,* in this town, and on the 28th of September in the same year, they killed *Praisever Turner* and two other persons. About the middle of October following, seven or eight men, venturing to bring in some of their harvest from *Pynchon's meadow,* were suddenly attacked by the Indians, and the greater part, being destitute of arms, as the enemy had observed where they were deposited and seized them, they were glad to flee with their horses, which they took from their carts. One of them, however, got possession of his gun, and killed one of the Indians, and then escaped with the rest. At the same time the Indians burnt four or five houses, and two or three barns, that stood at some distance from the principal settlement. On the 29th of the same month, the Indians killed *Thomas Salmon, Joseph Baker,* and *Joseph Baker Jr.*, as they were at work in the meadow, and attempted to burn the mill, but it was so well defended that they were unable to effect their purpose.

To guard against a surprise, the inhabitants made a kind of barricado about the town, by setting up pallisados, or cleft wood about eight feet long, to check the force of any sudden assault. This must have been a weak defense against a warlike enemy, but it proved to be of great use against the Indians; for though on the 14th of March, 1676, a large number of them broke through the pallisados at the lower end of the street, now called *Pleasant street,* in three places, yet as a company of soldiers had arrived in town the evening before, the Indians met with a warm reception, and as soon as they began to be repulsed, they fled with precipitation through the breaches, and never afterwards, during that war, adventured to break into this or the neighboring towns, that were so secured. In this attack, they killed *Robert Bartlet,* and *Thomas Holton,* and two other men and two women, and set fire to four or five dwelling houses, and as many barns. Many of the Indians, it was supposed, were killed.

In the attack, made upon the Indians at Deerfield, near Miller's Falls, on the 19th of May, 1676, by upwards of one hundred and fifty men, who had been collected from Northampton, Hadley and Hatfield, and which has been called the *Fall fight*, several of the inhabitants of this town lost their lives, with *Capt. William Turner*, who commanded them. Of those who marched from Northampton, fifteen were killed.

The pallisados, before mentioned, were kept up several years; but having gone to decay, the people in March, 1690, considering themselves in danger of being assaulted by the enemy, encompassed a great part of the town with pickets, near the place where the former stood in Philip's war. This kind of defense was maintained for a number of succeeding years.

On the 13th of May, 1704, old style,[1] the Indians

---

[1] OLD STYLE. — The number of days in a year was determined in ancient times, by the *styles*, which cast a shadow on a plain surface. The shortest was on the day of the summer *solstice*, and its return in 365 days completed the civil year. Julius Cæsar made a reform in the calendar, forty-six years before Christ. His solar year consisted of 365 days and six hours, and the six hours were taken into account by making every fourth year of 366 days. This manner of computing time is old style. There was an error in it, the true solar year being eleven minutes and some seconds short of 365¼ days, and this difference made a whole day in about 129 years, and before the year 1582, the vernal equinox occurred on the 11th of March, thirteen or fourteen days sooner than in the time of Cæsar. Pope Gregory XIII introduced the new style in 1582, by taking out ten days from the month of October, which corrected the calendar back to the council of Nice 325 years after Christ. To countervail in future the excess of eleven minutes and twelve or fifteen seconds in a year it was determined to

attacked the village of Pascomac. They had been to Merrimac river; but meeting with no success they then directed their course toward Westfield; but Westfield river was so high they could not pass it. At this time they were in almost a famishing state: but being near to Paskhomuck, of which they had learned something the year before, and hoping to obtain provision to satisfy their hunger, they changed their route for that place, *intending*, as they afterwards declared, to resign themselves up, if they could obtain no food otherwise. In the evening before the 13th of May, the Indians went upon Mount Tom, and observed the situation of the place. As the meadow was then covered with water, they supposed the village might be taken, and that no aid could come seasonably from the town, on account of the intervening flood.[1] A little before day light, the Indians attacked the village. The house of Benoni Jones was encom-

omit three days in four centuries, by making common years of three leap years, viz: 1700, 1800 and 1900. Some English philosophers and others objected to this imperfect reform of the calendar, this going back to the council of Nice instead of the Christian era, and there were other objections, and England continued to follow the old style until 1700, and eleven days after that year. By an act of parliament, eleven days were taken from the old calendar in 1752, the 3d of September being reckoned the 14th, and England and her colonies conformed to the new style.

[1] The season at that time was remarkably backward; for though so late in the year, being the 24th of May, according to the present style, the trees and bushes had not budded; and the year was so far advanced before the flood subsided from the meadow, that many persons doubted whether it was expedient to plant their corn; but notwithstanding, as there was no frost till late in the season, the crop of corn proved to be uncommonly good.

passed with pickets. The Indians procured flax and other combustibles, and set them on fire, which was communicated to the house. A young woman, named *Patience Webb*, was awaked, and, looking out of a window, was shot through the head. The .people surrendered, and all the families I have mentioned were · killed or taken prisoners. Some of the prisoners were afterwards rescued by people from the town: but one of the number, Benjamin Janes, having fallen a little in the rear, effected his escape by running to the water, through a hollow, encompassed with bushes, near the residence of Mrs. Phineas Clark, and springing into a skiff he knew to be lying there, he headed it for Northampton, and, with the blessing of heaven succeeding his efforts, was soon there; and hence was preserved, and was also the first to inform the people of the attack of the Indians upon Paskhomuck village and of the horrors his eyes had witnessed. The people of the town were at once upon the alert to intercept, if possible, the enemy, and to recapture the captives: and those of them who were under the command of Capt. Taylor went round by Pomeroy's meadow, and met the Indians between Mount Tom and Westfield road, on the farm, now in possession of ·Messrs. Waites, when a skirmish ensued, in which the captain was killed.[1] Of the five families belonging to the

---

[1] A post was sent to Hartford, and the next day Major William Whiting came up with 192 dragoons; they pursued the Indians at first on horseback and next on foot on account of mountains and swamps, but did not overtake them.

village, the Indians killed the following persons: Samuel Janes,[1] his wife and three children; Benoni Jones and two children, and the young woman before named; John Searle and three children; Moses Hutchinson and one child; and four children of Benjamin Janes — the whole number nineteen. The wife of this Benjamin Janes was taken to the top of Pomeroy's mountain, and was there knocked in the head and scalped. The people from Northampton found her in this situation, and perceiving that she was still alive, carried her with them, on their return, to the town; and she recovered and lived until she was more than eighty years old. The wife of Moses Hutchinson was taken prisoner, but soon made her escape. John Searle's wife was also taken and severely wounded, but was afterwards rescued from the Indians. Benoni Jones's wife, and Elisha, the son of John Searle, were taken prisoners to Canada: of the *former* of these I have learned no particulars beyond what I have given; but, of the *latter* it is a pleasure to state, that, after living some years in Canada, he returned to his few surviving friends, passed among them the residue of his days, and at length died "*in a good old age.*"[2]

---

[1] Samuel Janes lived where the house of Mr. Obadiah Janes now stands; John Searls, where his son Elisha and his grandson of the same name afterwards dwelt; Benjamin Janes, where Captain Philip Clark lives; and Moses Hutchinson, near the place where Mr. Solomon Ferry's house stands.

[2] Elisha Searle was a small lad when captured. He was conducted a prisoner to Canada, where his mind was thoroughly imbued with the superstitions of the Romish religion. When he became a young man, he, with a company of Indians, made arrangements to enter on

Another party of Indians on the road leading to
Westfield, killed one, and took two prisoners; but
others of our men, coming up, retook the prisoners
and killed two of the Indians.

July 9th, 1708, *Samuel Parsons* and *Joseph Parsons*
were killed in Northampton by the Indians.

On the 10th of August, 1711, *Samuel Strong, Jun.*,
was killed, and his father taken prisoner.

August 26th, 1724, *Nathaniel Edwards, 2d*, was
killed by the Indians, in the road near Bartlet's mill,
and another person was wounded.

In the year 1745, the town, considering themselves
in danger of an invasion from the French and Indians,
agreed to take measures to fortify themselves. For
this purpose the town was divided into fourteen sections, in each of which one house was forted and
guarded with flankers, to be a place of refuge for the
women and children: they also erected mounts or

a hunting and trapping expedition, along the great Western lakes,
for the purpose of obtaining fur. As no priest was to accompany
them, he went to his priest, and with much concern inquired what he
should do, as there would be no priest to whom he could confess, and
he might die on the journey? The priest told him that it would be
just as well to confess to a tree as to a priest; and then sent him
away. This declaration struck Elisha very forcibly, and he did not
forget it. He revolved the idea in his mind until he became convinced
that the whole system of Romanism was a deception.

After his return, he refused to confess his sins to a priest, and soon
visited the place of his nativity. He related this account to his pious
friends and relations, and became an enlightened and exemplary professor of the Protestant religion. He never returned to Canada, but
married, reared up a family, was a worthy citizen, and maintained a
reputable standing in the church of God. Some of his descendants
still remain in this region.

watch houses in divers' places, particularly in the extreme parts of the town. Before the end of that war, on the 27th of August, 1747, *Elisha Clark* was killed by the Indians, when he was threshing in his barn, in that part of the town, which is now Southampton. At another time, in the course of the same war, *Noah Pixley* was killed in the road, in the same quarter of the town.

In the war, which commenced in 1755, no injury was done by the French or Indians in Northampton. The people, however, thought themselves in danger, and for some time, at the commencement of the war, a watch was maintained in the night time, in divers parts of the town. A number of soldiers were also stationed at Southampton for the defense of the inhabitants of that district.

We have heard of other instances of mischief done in this place by the Indians, but have not learned the particulars. From the first settlement of the town it was an exposed frontier, until after the conquest of Canada in the year 1759. Settlements had been gradually extended northward upon Connecticut river, but fear of the French and Indians prevented improvements at any considerable distance west from the river. The country to the west and northwest, between this place and Canada, was a wilderness for more than a hundred years after the town was settled.

Among the earliest transactions of the people of this place, we find that measures were taken for the settlement of the gospel ministry among them. On the 7th of June, 1658, it was agreed in town meeting, by unanimous consent, to desire *Mr. Eleazer Mather* to be a minister to them in a way of trial in dispensing his gifts. In December of that year, the town voted that a rate of one hundred pounds should be levied for building a house for the ministry; and on the 4th of January then next following, they agreed to lay out eighty acres of meadow for the ministry.

The Rev. Eleazer Mather was the first settled minister in the town. He was a son of the Rev. Richard Mather of Dorchester, and was born at that place May 13th, 1637. When a church was gathered at Northampton, he was ordained the pastor of it on the 18th of June, 1661, and was greatly esteemed as a man of talents and piety. Soon after the ordination of Mr. Mather, *Mr. John Strong* was ordained *ruling elder* of the church. On the 23d of November, 1662, the people unanimously expressed their desire to settle *Mr. Joseph Elliot* among them as a *teacher*. This appears to have been also the desire of Mr. Mather, the pastor; for on the 30th of December of the same year, the church voted unanimously, that two teaching officers were appointed as ordinances of Christ Jesus in his church, and that it was the duty of every church to do what in them lay, that they might be furnished with two teaching officers. In the language of the *Cambridge platform*, which they seem to have adopted, the office of pastor and teacher was distinct. The *pastor's* special work was to attend to exhortation, and therein to administer a word of wisdom. The *teacher*

was to attend to doctrine, and therein to administer a
word of knowledge. The *ruling elder* was to join with
the pastor and teacher in acts of spiritual rule, in
admitting members, ordaining officers, and excommu-
nicating offenders, and to feed the flock of God with
a word of admonition. The same distinction of offices
had then been generally adopted in the colony; but
soon after, it gradually ceased, and there is now, perhaps, no instance of its being preserved in any of the
Congregational churches.

It appears from the records of the town, that Mr.
Elliot assisted Mr. Mather in the ministry for a year
or two, and a settlement and salary were offered him
by the inhabitants, who agreed to build him a house;
but he was never ordained as a public teacher in the
town.

On the 12th of July, 1661, the town voted to build
a meeting-house forty-two feet square. At the same
time a committee was chosen to carry on and finish
the work, which they afterwards completed accordingly.

The town had agreed in the year 1658, that the
burying place should be on the meeting house hill, near
the ground on which the present meeting house stands.
But in October, 1661, they voted, that the place of
burial on the meeting house hill should be altered, and
a committee was chosen to find a more convenient
place. At the next meeting in May, 1662, the committee reported in favor of the place, which has ever
since been used for that purpose.

The first English inhabitants in Northampton formed their settlement in a wilderness when the savages were numerous, and when, excepting the town of Springfield, there were no white inhabitants of the state within eighty miles of this place.[1] Several of the first planters were of those who came from England in 1630, and first settled at Roxbury; some of them had moved in 1636 from Roxbury to Springfield. But it appears that many of the early settlers of this town were of the company, which sailed from Plymouth in England, March 30, 1630, and arrived at Nantasket on the 30th of May following. They first began a settlement at Dorchester. Their ministers were Mr. Warham and Mr. Maverick. In 1635 and 1636, Mr. Warham, and the greater part of his church, moved from Dorchester to Windsor in Connecticut.

Previous to Mr. Mather's settlement here, viz: on the 28th of April, 1661, he took a dismission from the church at Dorchester, and at the same time several others, who had moved to this town, and were members of the church in Dorchester, were dismissed from it, to join in gathering a church in Northampton. A number had also come from Windsor to settle here, who had accompanied Mr. Warham from the time he left England. From these men, who came from Windsor and Dorchester, and who were persons of exemplary virtue and piety, it is presumed that most

---

[1] At that time the nearest English settlements in this state, except Springfield, were at Concord and Sudbury. In a short time afterwards Marlborough was settled.

7

of the present inhabitants of Northampton, Southampton, Westhampton and Easthampton are descended.
The three last were originally part of Northampton.

Mr. Mather died on the 24th of July, 1669. By
his wife, who was daughter of the Rev. Mr. Warham
of Windsor, he left one daughter, who married the
Rev. Mr. Williams of Deerfield, and was killed by the
Indians, when that town was destroyed in February,
1704. In a publication of Dr. Increase Mather of
Boston, who was a younger brother to Mr. Mather of
this town, he is said to have preached at Northampton
eleven years.   It appears, therefore, that from the time
he was invited to preach on probation in June, 1658, he
continued to preach here three years before he was
ordained.   In the year 1671 a treatise was published
under the title of "*Serious exhortations to the present
and succeeding generation in New England, earnestly calling
upon them all to endeavour that the Lord's gracious presence
may be continued with posterity ; being the substance of the
four last Sermons preached at Northampton by the Rev.
Eleazer Mather.*"

Soon after the death of Mr. Mather, *Mr. Solomon
Stoddard* was invited to preach in this town ; and on
the 4th of March, 1670, the town voted unanimously,
that they hoped by the blessing of God to give Mr.
Solomon Stoddard, on condition of his settlement
among them, one hundred pounds yearly, as long as he
continued among them, and carried on the work of the
ministry alone.   Mr. Stoddard continued to preach
here, and on the 7th of February, 1672, he wrote a

letter, addressed "to the Rev. John Strong, ruling elder of the Church of Christ in Northampton," accepting their call. In this letter, after referring to the invitation of the Church and people that he would undertake to be their pastor, he says, "Without eyeing that power and grace which God has treasured up in Jesus Christ, it were altogether vain for me to attempt such an undertaking. The best is, that when we have the command of God for our warrant, we have his promise both for assistance and pardon. I do therefore venture to declare, that it is my intention, sometime this next summer, to answer your desire in accepting of your invitation, giving up myself the residue of my days to the service of the house of God in this place; beseeching you, who are not altogether unacquainted with the difficulties, temptations and burdens of such a work, nor wholly strangers to my unfitness, to bow your knees to the Father of our Lord Jesus Christ, earnestly begging that he would fit me by his spirit for so solemn a charge, and make me a blessing unto you and your posterity; that I may be enabled to be a faithful steward, and that my labor may not be in vain; that light, and peace, and the power of religion may be continued in this plantation." Mr. Stoddard was accordingly ordained on the 11th of September, 1672. He married the widow of the Rev. Mr. Mather, and was an eminent and useful minister of the gospel in this place until his death, which happened on the 11th of February, 1729, in the eighty-

sixth year of his age. His son, the Hon. John Stoddard was several years a member of the council, and
held other important offices. The Hon. Joseph Hawley, who was his grandson, was also distinguished in
public life, and was a liberal benefactor to the town.

In the life time of Mr. Stoddard, on the 29th of
August, 1726, the town voted to invite *Mr. Jonathan
Edwards*, whose mother was Mr. Stoddard's daughter, to assist the Rev. Mr. Stoddard in the work of
the ministry; and on the 21st of November following,
he was invited to settle among them in that office, and
was ordained on the 15th of February, 1727.

On the 6th of November, 1735, the town voted to
build a new meeting house, and raise and cover it by
the end of the then next summer. This new meeting
house was placed northeasterly from the old, and as
near to it as might be; it was not finished until December, 1737. Before it was completed, viz: on the
13th of March, 1737, the front gallery of the old meeting house fell, when the people were assembled on the
Sabbath for public worship; but through the goodness
of God, though great numbers were upon and under
the gallery, no one was killed or mortally wounded.

The Rev. Mr. Edwards continued in the ministry in
this town more than twenty-three years, and was
highly and universally esteemed and respected; but at
length an unhappy disagreement arose between him
and the major part of his people, concerning the
qualifications for admission into the church, and in consequence of it, the pastoral relation between Mr.

Edwards and the church was dissolved on the 22d of June, 1750.

Some seventeen years later when another new colony was started by the people of Northampton and Hadley for some untried section further up the valley, they proposed to William Janes to go with his influence, his talents and his property, and to be their religious teacher, and counsellor in their expected perils. He consented, as he loved his mission of doing good and planting religion in every part of the new country so soon to be settled. He was the leader among this younger band of pilgrims and bold pioneers who gladly go forth to carry and spread the institutions of education and religion in their path.

He preached his first sermon on the Sabbath after their arrival under the spreading branches of a large oak tree.[1]

Time passed on, and after the outbreak of King Philip's war, the savages carried fear and havoc among the white people thinly scattered over New England, and this small company so far out on the frontier suffered most bitterly from this cruel and savage foe. Being suddenly assaulted by a large and overwhelming number, eight of their men, having already been waylaid and killed, they could only have hope of life by a strong defense in their stockade fort. But here they would sooner or later be de-

---

[1] This tree is supposed to be the one near the centre of the street at the lower end of the village, which must be a number of centuries old, and looks much like the ancient and former Charter oak of Hartford.

stroyed, if no outward force could come to their aid. One of their bold young men ventures in the night to run the perilous gauntlet for thirty miles and inform their friends at Northampton and Hadley. Soon a company of young soldiers come to deliver them if possible from their alert and watchful foe. The Indians had posted themselves about a mile and a half from the fort in a formidable ravine where this company must pass to their friends.

Waylaid, while in the foot path of the forest, without any suspicion of danger, they were suddenly fired upon by the murderous savages, of whom a sufficient number had come from guarding the fort, to thwart the purpose of the whites, who were coming to the relief of their friends.

Capt. Beers, finding that the stealthy savages had him to great disadvantage, and that they might soon be entirely cut down, orders a retreat, and they flee at once to a rise of ground a mile nearly from this spot, now called Beers mountain, where they continue to defend themselves from the savages till Capt. Beers himself falls and all hope fails them as so many of their comrades are now weltering in their blood. Some twelve of them not killed or seriously wounded, flee on horseback or on foot as best they can for some possible retreat of safety. It is reported that in the chase one fell into a gully filled with the dry leaves of autumn, which so suddenly covered him that he considered himself comparatively safe, and in the quiet of the evening he ventured out and climbed a tree to see if possibly there might be any light of the fort which would serve to guide him in finding these white friends. He saw the light and followed in its direction on the bank of the river till he came near and gained the fort and reported the terrible disaster. The few soldiers who escaped to Northampton roused their friends to send out a more formidable and cautious band, who drove and scattered the Indians, and in carts brought away those who could not walk in their homeward travels.

These waiting Christian pioneers were sustained by an unfaltering faith in the power and kind providence of God. These earnest pilgrims — about twenty-five families — were safely conducted to Northampton and Hadley, their former homes. Among the persons killed by the Indians during their first stay in Northfield were Ebenezer and Jonathan Janes, sons of William, young lads of about seventeen and eighteen years of age.

Ten years later, 1685, they made another attempt at settlement, and continue for some five years in subduing the forest and building their rude habitations with little interruption. William Janes, it is believed, was in this second endeavor, venturing the perils of the times in company with only eight families, who were to enjoy only a short season of peaceful industry. Again were they driven away, losing almost all their earthly substance.

After this last attempt William Janes spent the remaining days of his life in Northampton, dying at

a good old age, leaving behind a name revered,
untarnished and imperishable.

In after years some of his children and grandchildren returned to this town (Northfield) and settled
on the identical spot allotted to William in the first
settlement, and the writer of this genealogy takes
pride in saying he venerates the place made sacred
by those early sacrifices, and lovely as the spot where,
first he breathed the vital air.

The early history of the town will be further known
and understood by republishing a letter of Rev. John
Hubbard, who was their third minister, and settled
in 1750, some thirty-seven years after that last and successful attempt to occupy and cultivate these northern
fields.

NORTHFIELD, *Sept.* 1, 1792.

In the year 1672 the township was granted to
Messrs. Pinchon, Peirsons and their associates, the
Indian name *Squawkeague*, laid out on both sides of
Connecticut river, six miles in breadth, and twelve in
length.

In the year 1673 settlers came on, planted down
near one to the other, built small huts, covered them
with thatch, near the centre made one for public
worship, and employed one Elder Janes as their
preacher, also ran a stockade and fort around a
number of what they called houses, to which they
might repair in case they were attacked by the enemy.
These first settlers were a set of religious congre-

gational people, emigrated from Northampton, Hadley, Hatfield, etc.

Probably in about five or six years, an Indian war broke out, a large army came suddenly upon them, killed some in their houses, others as they were coming out of the meadows; the rest of this distressed people, men, women and children fled to their fort, unable to sally out and repel the enemy, in the utmost distress, and no present relief could be afforded them. The Indians in the meantime kept around them, killed their cattle, destroyed their grain, burnt up the houses that were without the fort, and laid all waste. The dead bodies of their neighbors were unburied. The people full of fear lest the Indians would break into their fort. A number of days and nights were they in this distressed condition. In the meantime one of their brave men got out of the fort in the night and ran to Hadley near thirty miles.

A certain Captain Beers, with his company and a number of teams were ordered to go and bring off the distressed people. But when they had got within two miles of the settlement, on the 4th of September, were way-laid, almost all the company killed; and the teams taken. The few that survived this bloody carnage fled back to Hadley; then Captain Treat with a larger body of men, and more teams were ordered out, and fetched off the distressed inhabitants.

Thus long did these poor people continue in fear and jeopardy every hour. At length they arrived to the place above mentioned. The Indians soon returned

8

and destroyed their fort and everything that remained.
All was now desolate and waste, and continued so for
about five or six years, the war ending. In 1685,
settlers came on again, continued ten or twelve years,
built mills and some convenient houses, and carried
on their husbandry to a good degree, and introduced
mechanics.   The settlement flourished, however had
not arrived to such ability as to settle a minister,
though they began to hire some preaching.   But alas!
another Indian war breaking out the people were drove
within their forts, which they had erected.

Government afforded them some protection, notwithstanding the Indians pressed hard upon them,
killed some and took others captive, and the hearts
of the rest of the people were dismayed and discou-
raged, and in council on the 2d of September, in 1690,
having lost seven or eight men, determined it was best
to return to the lower towns.   This they did, late in
the fall or beginning of winter, when the Indians had
withdrawn.   The next spring the Indians came on,
burnt up a second time, laid the settlement waste.
This brings us to the year 1700 or more, a little
before Deerfield was destroyed.

In the year 1713 the proprietors petitioned the
general court to grant them a committee to ascertain
and fix the boundaries of their home lots, meadow
lots, etc.   The committee were the Hon. John Stoddard of Northampton, Eleazer Porter of Hadley,
Henry Dwight of Hatfield, Esqrs.   Settlers came on
very much together, rebuilt their mills, houses, and

soon proceeded to set up a house of public worship, and were now incorporated into a town by the name of Northfield, as it was the northernmost town in the county of Hampshire and colony of the Massachusetts, on Connecticut river.

About the year 1718 — were gathered into a distinct church, invited and settled Mr. Benjamin Doolittle of Wallingford in Connecticut, who continued in the ministry about thirty years, died 1748, aged fifty-four years. He began with the people in their third settlement, where not more than thirty-five families lived, to see them increase almost to a hundred and to a good degree of opulence and wealth, though oft worried with distressing wars, it being very much a frontier. It was in Mr. Doolittle's [1] day that the province line was run between New Hampshire and Massachusetts, which cut off one-third part or more of the original town, and is now Hinsdale. In the year 1750 the people invited and settled Mr. John Hubbard of Hatfield, who has continued in the ministry more than forty years. We are not more than a hundred and twenty families at this present time.

The air is salubrious, and the soil tolerably fertile. No Indians nor any of their monuments appear. Northfield is southward of the centre of the settlement of Connecticut river. The people are all furnished with Bibles and other good books, in their houses, but no social library. Generally a grammar and other

---

[1] Town laid a road in Pschoug meadow up to a pile of rails where Mr. Doolittle's horse died.

good schools exist in town. The most of the people pursue husbandry; it is an excellent township for raising wheat and other kinds of grain. Commerce has flourished, and is now again reviving. It has a number of good buildings, an elegant house for the worship of God. Of late, a curious *still-house* has been set up for making gin; this I fear will be of no public utility.

The people are pretty well united in faith, worship and Christian discipline. No sectaries.

JOHN HUBBARD.

The year 1662 was an eventful year to William Janes. In January he lost his son Nathaniel, in February he lost Elisha next older, in April he lost his first wife Mary, and in November of the same year he married (2) Hannah Broughton.

Also the year 1675 was a similar year in affliction. In September, his two sons, Ebenezer and Jonathan, were killed by the Indians in Northfield: Jacob died 28th of October in New Haven, and Jeremiah died the 1st March previous, and during the fall of the same year the father and small colony at Northfield were driven from their settlement and despoiled of most of their goods.

With a servant of old he could say, " All these things are against me." Like other suffering pilgrims, "he fought a good fight and kept the faith."

We have not a full record of deaths and afflictive occurrences, and know not what other trials were

bravely and heroically met and with fortitude sur-
mounted. Faint glimpses only are seen when there
are brief upliftings of the curtain.

William Janes preached the first sermon at Northfield under the shade of an oak, the year 1673, the first
Sabbath, the first colony arrived, believed to be the
first Sabbath of June. Rev. Benjamin Doolittle, a
surgeon as well as a divine, native of Wallingford,
son of John, who was son of Abraham Doolittle, was
born 10th July, 1695, graduated at Yale College 1716.
He was engaged 15th August, 1718. He signed a
new agreement 10th March, 1738. He died suddenly
9th January, 1748, thirtieth year of his ministry, æ.
fifty-four. His epitaph expressed the combination of
the two professions, of spiritual and natural healer.
A large posterity of Doolittles[1] are his descendants.

Rev. John Hubbard was engaged 5th March, 1749.
He was highly esteemed among his people, and
exerted considerable influence during a long ministry
of forty-five years; he died 28th March, 1794, æ.

---

[1] Children of Rev. Benjamin and Lydia Doolittle:
Oliver, October 28, 1718.
Lydia, August 24, 1721, m. John Evans.
Charles, July 31, 1722.
Eunice, July 24, 1724.
Susannah, June 13, 1726, m. Seth Field, Esq.
Lucius, March 10, 1728, was the father of Mrs. Major Elisha
    Alexander.
Chloe, March 4, 1730.
Lucy, February 27, 1732.
Thankful, January 20, 1734.
Amzi, November 15, 1737.

eighty-nine. The first stockade fort was built on a
gentle rise of land four or five rods above the Oliver
Mattoon house, the most suitable location in the immediate vicinity.

The writer well remembers the foundation stones
before they were removed or covered with earth. It
was at first surrounded with a compact paling of sharpened poles for a barricade and some other rude defense,
and within the inclosure was a number of small
dwellings for the convenience of different families.
Some of the proprietors came to Northfield as early as
1673.

The Indians gave deeds of lands, which they claimed.
The colony took a right from the general court of a
tract of twelve miles by six; that is, from Miller's river
to Ashuelot river, and three miles east and three west
from the Connecticut river. This was afterward materially reduced by laying out new towns and by running
the state line of New Hampshire.

In the second settlement, 1687, John King and
William Clark came up and made arrangements with
the Indians — who were then in à friendly mood —
for the proprietors who lived in Northampton and
Hadley.

Beside the sons of William Janes, killed by the
Indians, Joseph, Samuel and Benjamin are on record
as land holders. Samuel was killed at Northampton.
His son Jonathan, who met with so narrow an escape
at the time, being only eight years of age, had arrived
to manhood when the third settlement was made,

and then, or soon after, perhaps 1717, came to Northfield as the only representative of the family at that
time.

In 1725, his Uncle Benjamin came from Coventry,
Conn., to abide for a time, and to adjust his claims as
coheir with others of the family. He owned by allotment or purchase the lot north and adjoining the old
homestead which was originally assigned to William
Janes; but soon after the third and final or successful
settlement possessed by Jonathan Janes, his grandson,
who was the writer's great-grandfather. This Jonathan had an older brother, Samuel, who had with him
escaped the tragic death struggles at Pascomac, who
was with him a joint owner of lands in Northampton and Northfield. They made a settlement, Samuel
relinquishing the father's and uncle's rights, which
inhered now in these two brothers. Jonathan's quit
claim deed to lands in Northampton was doubtless in
substance the same as this of Samuel's, which we here
insert, being executed one hundred and thirty-four
years ago.

To All Chriſtian People to whome Theſe preſents Shall
come Greeting. Know Ye That I Sam¹ Janes of Northampton In the County of Hampſhire & Province of the
Maſſachuſett Bay In New England for divers good cauſes
and Conſiderations me moving have Remiſed Releaſed and
for Ever quit Claimed and by Theſe preſents for My Self,
& my Heirs do fully, Clearly and Abſolutely remiſe, re-
leaſe and for ever quit claim Unto my Brother Jonathan

Janes of Northfield within f[d] County (in his full and peaceable poffeffion and Seizen) and to his Heirs and Affigns for ever ; all the Eftate right, Title, Intereft, Ufe, Claim and Demand Whatfoever, as I the faid Samuel Janes, now have or had, or ought to have in or to all the Meffuage Tenements, and Lands Whatfoever that are Scituate In the Town of Northfield In Said County that was the Eftate of my Honoured Father Samuel Janes late of Northampton Deceafed & y[e] Eftate of my Uncle Jofeph Janes of Northampton Difceafed. To Have and To Hold all the Said, Meffuage, Tenements, and Lands, Unto the f[d] Jonathan Janes, His Heirs and Affigns for ever, to the only Ufe, Difpofall and behoof of the Said Jonathan Janes His Heirs and Affigns for ever, So that neither I the Said Sam[l] Janes nor my Heirs, nor any other perfon or perfons for me or them, or in my or Their Names, or in the right or Stead of any of them Shall or will by any way or means hereafter, have, Claim, Challenge or Demand any Eftate right or Title or Intereft in or to the premifes or any part or parcell thereof: But from all and every action, Right, Eftate, Title, Intereft and demand of in or to the premifes, they and every of them fhall be Utterly Excluded and barred for Ever by thefe prefents : and alfo the Said Sam[l] Janes & his Heirs & affigns, the Said Meffuage, land & tenements and other the premifes with the Appurtenances to the Said Jonathan Janes, to his Heirs and Affigns, to his and their own proper Ufe, Difpofall and poffeffion In manner and form above Specified Againft their Heirs and affigns and every of them shall warrant and for Ever defend by Thefe prefents. In Witnefs Whereof I hereunto Set my Hand & Seal This fourth Day of March Anno Domini 1729|30, and in the third year of yᵉ Reign of our Sovereign Lord King George the Second &c

SAMˡˡ JANES

Signed Sealed and DD In prefence of

PRESERVED CLAPP

SAMˡ MATHER.

Hampfhiʳ Northhamton March 4 17$\frac{29}{30}$.

Samuell Janes the fubfcriber to the Inftrument on the other fid appeared and acknoledged the fame to be his act and Deed before me.

JOHN ASHLEY Jus peas.

Hampfhʳ fs Springfᵈ Sepʳ 24ᵗʰ: 1734.

Recᵈ: and Recorded in the Records of Deeds for faid County Libᵒ G: Folᵒ 543.

℈ JOHN PYNCHON Regᵗ.

We love to have pictured upon the canvas the scenes of other days, the memories of our fathers' trials and triumphs, the histories of their conflicts, their successes, or their misfortunes. We love to linger around the dear old hearthstone the reminiscences of our progenitors, the histories of their civil, military and religious acts, the heroic struggles through which their deep and unshaken faith has carried them. We love to speak of their virtues and dwell upon their revered names, and note their works and ways and varied transactions; especially when we remember that they were of the same blood; that because they were, we are also.

9

Our hearts may be filled with sadness when we recount the many sorrows that filled the stricken hearts of a few brave men and courageous women, huddled together for a number of days in a frail, ill contrived fort, with hideous savages around them, outnumbering them ten to one. Perhaps a greater sadness comes over us as we rehearse the tragic fate of Captain Beers and most of his bold comrades who valiantly met, but unsuccessfully struggled with a more stealthy and a more numerous foe. William Janes, in this rude fort at Northfield, with his weeping but hopeful companions, thus saw and felt their danger; yet a beam of joy lightened their sadness, as their faith lifted them up to a full trust in the covenant keeping God. Two of his sons had been slain by the roamers of the forest, and there were probably one or two others in the fort, with this distressed company, sharing a common sorrow.

But long before Northfield was settled, the older sons of William Janes were living apart from their father, commencing life for themselves, and laying the foundation for social, religious and intelligent society, and shaping, each for themselves, their way for gaining a livelihood among men.

We might have written more minutely about William Janes, our progenitor, whose life stretches over a comparatively brief but marked period[1] of the

---

[1] During the eventful life of our progenitor, most of which was spent in this country? many important events transpired in these colonies and in Europe. We call this schedule only a fraction:

world's history. We might have written more fully of the places he helped to settle and of his labors as a registrar, a copyist, a secular, moral and religious teacher. He was called Elder Janes, and was truly a teaching and preaching elder in distinction from a ruling elder, which was fully understood at that period. His secular labors were not remitted, and it was not expected he would forego any opportunity to push forward the laudable endeavors of this new and anxious colony. The last few years of his life were

---

1620. The Pilgrims, persecuted English dissenters, settle Plymouth; they sign the first written constitution of America before leaving their vessel.

1620. Richelieu unites with the hero of Sweden, Gustavus Adolphus.

1621. He stirs up war against the Huguenots.

1625. Charles I succeeds his father James I, who died 1st January.

1625. Swedes and Flemish settled Delaware.

1626. 9 April, Sir Francis Bacon died.

1628. Salem is settled.

1629. Charles contends with parliament, anxious to be himself absolute monarch.

1630. Boston is settled.

1631. 19 March, Connecticut patent executed.

1632. Maryland settled by Catholics under Lord Baltimore.

1633. Archbishop Laud accedes to ecclesiastical power, and persecutes the Puritans to great extremities.

1635. Thomas Parr died (born 1483), aged 152 years.

1636. Hartford and Providence are settled.

1638. The solemn league and covenant formed in Scotland against English kingly tyranny.

1638. John Hampden takes his noble independent stand against the English crown.

1639. New Haven settled.

1640. November 3, the long parliament assembled.

1640. Thomas Wentworth and Laud are impeached.

1640. Montreal founded. Jesuits go out to Christianize the Indians.

1641. 12 May, Wentworth executed on Tower-hill.

spent in Northampton among old and tried friends; where there was little fear of sudden and ferocious intrusion of savage hordes, that could not be easily repelled; where were many of the comforts and joys of a settled society; where the power of religion was working like leaven among the mass of society; where some of his sons resided and could give him a cheerful welcome, after being bereaved of so many of his children and so much of his real property; where he enjoyed the preaching and the pious counsels of the

---

1642. The king attempts to take five members of parliament, fails and civil war ensues.

1644. The famous battle of Marston Moor in which the·royalists are defeated by Cromwell and Fairfax.

1644. Charter for New Jersey 23d June.

1645. At Naseby Charles commands in person and is totally defeated.

1648. Becomes a prisoner to Cromwell and beheaded 30th January.

1649. Cromwell subdues the royalists of Ireland.

1650. 15th July, Charles II lands in Scotland and is proclaimed king.

1651. Cromwell defeats the Scots, and Charles II escapes by disguising himself: is concealed in an oak.

1653. Cromwell turns out the Rump parliament at the point of bayonet.

1653. Naval war between England and Holland.

1654. Christiana (daughter of Gustavus Adolphus) resigns the crown of Sweden to Charles Gustavus.

1657. Charles X (Charles Gustavus) conquers John Casimir of Poland.

1658. Dunkirk conquered from the Spaniards by the French and the English sent by Cromwell to their aid. It is yielded to the English.

1658. August 12th, Oliver Cromwell died.

1660. Charles II being brought back by General Monk, is peaceably received as king of Great Britain. This period is called the "Restoration."

1661. Charles shows his faithlessness to the Scots.

1662. Winthrop, son of Governor Winthrop of Massachusetts, pleases Charles II and obtains a liberal charter for Connecticut.

eminent Rev. Solomon Stoddard, who was the minister of that church from 1670 to 1726; where he had buried his Mary (in 1662), who periled with him the ocean and the wilderness, and the savage tenants of the forest.

His honored dust mingles with many as noble in life as he — the Mathers, the Stoddards and Edwardses, and multitudes whose bones are crumbling in the lovely cemetery of Northampton, their spirits having "part in the first resurrection."

1664. Charles makes war with the Dutch. New York taken, from the Dutch governor Stuyvesant, by Colonel Nichols.

1665. Terrible plague in London, 100,000 people die.

1666. September 2, 3, 4 and 5, 13,000 buildings consumed by fire in London.

1667. Charles II gives to Monk and Shaftsbury the southern section of the American republic.

1673. Marquette sails down the Wisconsin to the Mississippi; discovers the mouths of the Illinois, Missouri, Ohio, Arkansas, etc.

1675-6. Great distress in New England on account of King Philip's war.

1682. William Penn founds Philadelphia.

1682. Peter the Great becomes czar of Russia.

1683. 15th December, Isaac Walton died.

1683. Lord Russell and Algernon Sidney suffer death for opposing tyranny.

1685. Charles II succeeded by James II.

1685. James II sends Sir Edmund Andros to be governor general in New England.

1687. Lima destroyed by an earthquake.

1688. The new revolution in England. The people reject James II and call William III Prince of Orange, denying the divine right of kings and declaring the sovereignty of the people.

1690. The year of William Janes's death, Schenectady is destroyed by the French and Indians; immense suffering, being in dead of winter.

"Peace to the just man's memory; let it grow
Greener with years, and blossom through the flight
Of ages; let the mimic canvas show
His calm benevolent features; let the light
Stream on his deeds of love that shunned the sight
Of all but heaven, and in the book of fame
The glorious record of his virtues write,
And hold it up to men, and bid them claim
A palm like his, and catch from him the hallowed flame."

When the war began, Hampshire county contained
the following towns and plantations: Springfield — including West Springfield and Long meadow — Westfield, Northampton, Hadley, Hatfield, Deerfield, Northfield, Brookfield and Suffield. The people at Suffield
soon left the place, and if there were any settlers at
Swampfield (Sunderland), they did not long remain.
September 2d, they set upon several men that were gone
out of the fort at Squakheag; they slew eight of our
men, not above one of them being slain that we know
of; but made no attempt upon the fort. The next day,
(September 3d), this onset being unknown, Capt. Beers
set forth from Hadley with about thirty-six men and
some carts to fetch off the garrison at Squakheag, and
coming within less than two miles of the place, the
next morning (September 4th), were set upon by a great
number of Indians from the side of a swamp, where
was a hot dispute for some time. They, having lost
their captain and some others, resolved at last to fly, and
going to take horse, lost several men more, I think
about twelve. The most that escaped got to Hadley

that evening. Next morning another came in, and at
night another that had been taken by the Indians, and
loosed from his bonds by a Natick Indian. He tells
that the Indians were all drunk that night; that they
mourned much for the loss of a great captain; that the
English had killed twenty-five of their men. Six
days after, another soldier came in, who had been lost
ever since the fight and was almost famished, and so
lost his understanding that he knew not what day
the fight was on. On the 5th day of September (Thursday), Major Treat set forth for Squakheag with above
a hundred men. Next day coming nigh Squakheag
his men were much daunted to see the heads of Capt.
Beers's soldiers upon poles by the wayside. After they
were come to Squakheag, some were fired upon by
about fourteen Indians. Major Treat was struck upon
the thigh, but not harmed. Coming to the fort, he concluded forthwith to bring off the garrison, so they came
away the same night (September 6th), leaving the cattle
there, and the dead bodies unburied; since which
seventeen of their cattle came a great part of the way
themselves, and have since been fetched into Hadley.

Mather says the men fought till their powder and
shot were spent, and the Indians killed above twenty,
and only thirteen escaped. A cart with some ammu-
nition fell into the hands of the enemy. According
to Hubbard, Capt. Beers went up with supplies for
the garrison, and they were set upon very near to the
town, out of the bushes, by a swamp side, and Capt.
Beers and about twenty of his men were slain.

The swampy ravine south of the village of Northfield, where the Indians were in ambush, and Beers
Plain, across which the soldiers retreated to their
horses, are well known at this day. Men now living
have found bones and bullets near where the fighting
took place.

About 1823 two entire skeletons were seen wholly
uncovered from the blowing and shifting of the sand
upon the Reuben Smith plain, which was the battle
ground of the first struggle Captain Beers had with
the enemy. The sons of Simeon Holton saw them
after a severe wind, and their father told Dr. Charles
Blake, who took them away for anatomical purposes.

The writer himself has seen many of the different
bones of a human body, particularly the skeletons of
human heads, when a youth he passed and repassed
that way to go to his father's pasture and return. A
monument·should have been, and we hope will yet be
erected in memory of the heroes, who so early fell in
defending their friends from ferocious enemies.

Mr. Russell, in his list, reports only sixteen slain at
Squakheag, September 4th, and gives the names of
eleven, viz: Capt. R. Beers, John Chenery, Ephraigh
Childs, Benjamin Crackbone, Robert Pepper, George
Syruss, John Gatchell, James Miller, John Wilson,
Joseph Dickinson (of Northfield), William Markham,
Jr. (of Hadley, an only son; he was with a team), Robert
Pepper, erroneously numbered among the slain, was
taken, and was with the Indians when Mrs. Rowland-
son was a captive. Capt. Beers was from Watertown,

and was in the Pequot war thirty-eight years before. His widow died June 19th, 1706, aged 92.

Hubbard says, one man if not more, was found with a chain hooked into his under jaw, and so hung upon the bough of a tree. It was feared that he was hung up alive. Cattle often fled from the Indians and sought the protection of the English. When Major Willard came near Brookfield, the cattle which had been frightened away by the yells and firing of the Indians, fell into his rear, and followed him and his company into the village. In this, and later Indian wars, the people were always alarmed when the cattle ran furiously out of the woods to the village.

After Major Treat left Northfield, September 6th, the Indians destroyed this small village. This was the second place in Hampshire county that was laid waste. It had been settled only two or three years, but contained nearly as many families as Brookfield. Most of them were from Northampton. They had no minister or meeting house, but William Janes, a competent person, used to pray and exhort in pleasant weather, under a broad-spreading tree.

The Nipmucks and Wampanoags, whom the English captain had long sought after in vain, first showed themselves upon Connecticut river on the 1st day of September, and made an attack upon Hadley. As our river Indians were engaged the same day at Deerfield, these must have been the Indians which came from the east. And it can hardly be doubted that they killed the eight men at Northfield,

10

September 2d, attacked Captain Beers, September 4th, and fired upon Major Treat, September 6th. They exulted in their success; and, after Northfield was deserted, lived upon the good things which the English had left. They seemed not to have crossed the river and united with the river Indians until about the middle of September. Every town had to entertain soldiers, and the upper villages had families from Deerfield, Northfield and Brookfield. The people of Hampshire were able to supply all with food.

Eleven Indians appeared near Northfield, and some of them were recognized as Indians who formerly lived in these parts. On the 16th of August, three men, two women and a girl were killed at Northfield, and it was believed that they were murdered by these Indians. Major Pynchon sent soldiers to Northfield, and thirteen men were sent up from Hartford. By order of Governor Andros, in November sixty Connecticut men were posted at Northfield under Captain Jonathan Bull during the winter. The destruction of six persons at Northfield is not noticed by any historian, and their names cannot now be found.

The tears, fears and groans of the broken remnant of Northfield is the beginning of a petition from that place to the general court, dated June 27, 1689, in the hand writing of Rev. John Russell of Hadley. They say that they had twenty-five families before the six persons were slain by the Indians, and that half had since deserted the place, and only twelve families remained.

They ask for advice and help. Peter Tilton, Samuel Partridge and John King were appointed to order matters at Northfield. About seventy souls, of whom only fifteen were men, remained in the place until the spring of 1690, when Northfield was abandoned the second time, and remained desolate twenty-five years. Hadley was again the most northern town on the east side of the river.

A new fort and garrison were added in February, 1724.

On the 3d of that month Timothy Dwight with soldiers, carpenters and teams left Northampton and went up the river, and in a few weeks they built a block house named Fort Dummer, on the equivalent land, a mile or two below the present Brattleborough, which cost £256. This was the first building erected by civilized beings in Vermont. Captain Timothy Dwight[1] commanded the garrison at this fort till the close of 1726. Captain Joseph Kellogg, a native of Hadley, commanded at Northfield; Captain Samuel Barnard, and afterwards Lieutenant Timothy Childs, commanded at Deerfield. Captain Benjamin Wright, formerly of Northampton then of Northfield, was always ready to fight Indians, and he was at the head

---

[1] He was a lieutenant colonel in the militia; brigadier general in the expedition against Louisburgh in 1745; a number of years a member of the council; speaker in the lower house of representatives; judge of the court of common pleas for the county of Worcester, from 1745 to 1750; and after his removal to Great Barrington, was appointed in 1761, judge of the county court, and probate judge for that county.

of several scouts and expeditions up the river and towards Lake Champlain, in this war.

We have now traced our first progenitor,[1] the emigrant, from the place of his origin to his settlement in New Haven, where he resided about eighteen years, giving a condensed view of the primitive condition of that early and prosperous colony; thence to Northampton, Mass., where he spent the most active period of his earthly pilgrimage, giving the early history of that, then frontier town; thence to Northfield, the northernmost attempted settlement, for many years, the gloomy scene of many tragic conflicts; where William Janes went with the first bold adventurers of the day, and where he probably went a second time, ten years later than the first venture; where the fire and the tomahawk made sad devastation among his noble sons, and wasted most of his estate; where he preached under the shade of the noble old oak still standing; where his life was frequently periled and miraculously preserved; where his descendants at a

---

[1] In the lifetime of William Janes there was no newspaper published in America.

The year of his decease, (20th of September, 1690), one small sheet was worked off upon a hand press at Boston, by Richard Pierce, printer, on the 25th of September, five days after William Janes's recorded death. This insignificant little sheet was condemned by the authorities as containing "reflections of a high nature," and its publication pronounced contrary to law. The unfortunate little intruder was strangled, and has had a perpetual lock jaw among the unseen state papers of the state department in London. Such an honor poor Pierce did not dream of, when he ventured boldly to utter by such means the public sentiment.

later period settled on lands selected by him or allotted to him, when the storm of Indian war was abated; giving a brief history of this well known township of trying memories, where some of the family of the Janeses have had a residence from the commencement.

These brief allusions we are constrained to make,'as we close this account of this beloved man, our ancestor, and the short sketch of the towns where his influence was spent and his principles displayed; and the scenes through which he passed as a self-denying, cheerful pilgrim, were enacted.

> Can ye lead out to distant colonies
> The o'erflowings of a people, or your wrong'd
> Brethren, by impious persecution driven,
> And arm their breasts with fortitude to try
> New regions; climes though barren, yet beyond
> The baleful power of tyrants? These are deeds
> To which their hardy labors will prepare
> The sinewy arm of Albion's sons.—*Coleridge.*

> Yes, in the desert there is built a home
> For Freedom. Genius is made strong to rear
> The monuments of man beneath the dome
> Of a new heaven; myriads assemble there
> Whom the proud lords of man, in rage or fear,
> Drove from their wasted homes.—*Shelley.*

*

SECOND GENERATION.

WILLIAM JANES, the emigrant, m. Mary ...., in England. They came to America in 1637. One or more of their children were born in England. He died 20 Sept., 1690. She died 4 April, 1662.

CHILDREN.

1 I.   JOSEPH, born 1636; ? unmarried; died 26 Feb., 1694.
2 II. ELISHA, born 1639; ? died 25 Jan., 1662.
3 III. NATHANIEL, born 1641; ? died 11 Feb., 1662.
4 IV. ABEL, born 1644; ? married Mary Judd; died 1718.
5 V.   ABIGAIL, born 1647. ?
6 VI. RUTH, born 15 Feb., 1650; baptized 24 March, 1650; married John Searl, (2) Nathaniel Alexander.
7 VII. JACOB, born 1652; ? died 28 Oct., 1675.
8 VIII. WILLIAM, born 1654; ? married Sarah Clark, 1685.
9 IX. REBECCA, born 1656; ? unmarried; lived with William.
10 X. JEREMIAH, born 1658; ? died at Northampton, 1675.
11 XI. EBENEZER, born 1659; ? and
12 XII. JONATHAN, born 1661; ? were killed on the same day by Indians, at Northfield, 2 Sept., 1675.

NOTE. Elisha, Nathaniel, Abel and Abigail were baptized 19 March, 1648, by the Reverend John Davenport, and printed in the *New England Historical and Genealogical Register*, as children of Thomas James; but in calling the attention of Henry White to the subject who got it copied for the *New England Historical and Genealogical Register*, he reexamined the record and saw it written, " children of Bro. James; " still a mistake by the original writer or transcriber, who should have written " of William Janes."

In looking at the records in Springfield, we find that " Nathaniel Janes of Northampton who sojourned here a little tyme, fell sick and dyed ye 22d day of Jany., 1662. Elisha Janes, an elder brother, also fell sick here and died, ye 11 Feb., 1662."

William married (2) 20 Nov., 1662, Hannah Broughton, widow of John Broughton, who died March, 1681.

13 XIII. SAMUEL, born 9 Oct., 1663; married (1) Elizabeth
Smead, (2) Sarah Hinsdale.
14 XIV. HEPZIBAH, born 13 Feb., 1665.
15 XV. HANNAH, born 5 Oct., 1669.
16 XVI. BENJAMIN, born 30 Sept., 1672; married Hannah .....

The Grand Divisions.

Preliminary to the introduction of the succeeding
generations, it is proper to remark, that only four of
the eleven sons of William Janes married and raised
up families. The others died early, or were killed by
the Indians, except Joseph. .We shall find it convenient to constitute *four grand divisions* with the families
of these four married sons, viz : *Abel, William, Samuel*
and *Benjamin.* We designate the *first* division as the
line of *Abel.* The *second* as the *line* of *William.* The
third as the *line* of *Samuel,* and the *fourth* as the *line* of
Benjamin.

In examining the book and in tracing back the ancestral *line* of any individual, the whole printed plan
will present itself like a *chart* to the mind, and be easily
comprehended.

It is well to notice the remarks on the last page of the
Introduction, and by keeping in mind the *line* with
which any one is connected, the arrangement will seem
plain to any person, and further simplification appears
to be wholly unnecessary.

THIRD GENERATION.

4 (IV) ABEL, SON OF WILLIAM.

Abel Janes, b. about 1644, m. Mary Judd, dau. of William Judd, of Farmington, Conn., 4 Nov., 1679, and resided, as it appears, most of the time in Northampton, till the year 1706. He moved to Lebanon about this time; and, as his children were born previously, we looked for the date of their birth, without success, in the records of Northampton. We have found most of the names of their children, doubtless, but not all, we fear.[1]

He was an early pioneer to this town, and was highly esteemed as an intelligent father, friend and

---

[1] Deacon Thomas Judd emigrated from England, 1635. His children were

    Elizabeth.
    William. m. Mary, dau. of John and Mary Steele.
    Thomas.
    John.
    Benjamin, and three others.
William and Mary Judd's children were
    Mary, m. Abel Janes.
    Thomas.
    John.
    Rachel.
    Samuel.
    Daniel.
    Elizabeth.

counsellor, leading a respectable family of influential
children and grand-children in the paths of virtue and
true religion. When he died, 18 December, 1718, he
left behind him the legacy of a good name, that his
children might profit by his example. From him and
his children has come down an influence for morality,
for patriotism, and pure religion, which will continue
to extend and bless other generations.

His son William, and five of his grandsons, moved
from Lebanon to Brinfield, Mass., purchased five
hundred acres of land, became wealthy farmers, and a
number of the descendants still remain in the town and
in the vicinity, while numbers have gone with virtuous
and patriotic principles to distant towns and cities
throughout the Union.

There is a deed on record at Springfield, dated 28
May, 1705, Abel Janes is mentioned then as resident of
Northampton. In the latter part of this or the next
year, he moved to Lebanon.

Another deed was made of Northampton lands, and
recorded in Springfield, 1716; he was then living in
Lebanon.

A quit claim deed from Samuel and Jonathan, the
compiler's great-grandfather, dated 28 March, 1716, to
Abel, says, " These presents witnesseth that we, Samuel
Janes and Jonathan Janes of Northampton, county of
Hampshire, in the province of Massachusetts bay, in
New England, for and in consideration of a certain
instrument bearing date with these presents, receive of
our uncle, Abel Janes of Lebanon, etc."

11

ABEL'S EPITAPH.

Here Lieth the Body of Mr. Abel Janes

yᵉ Hufband of Mrs. Mary Janes, who

Died December yᵉ 18 1718 in yᵉ
73 year of his age

Leet Heavens Bleffings reft upon
yᵉ Derling of my youthful dayes
& alfo one my children yong
To keep them all in wifdom's wais

—::—

MARY'S EPITAPH.

Here lyes yᵉ Body of yᵗ worthy
virtuous & pious Mother in Ifrael

wife to Mr Abel Janes Mrs Mary

Janes by Name when fhe had
Lieved Long a holy and Patient Life
Dyed April 24 1735 in yᵉ
80 year of Har age

Farwell my Loving Children
My Neigburs & my Friends
Sarve God in Truth while in Your Youth
& Til Your Life doth End

CHILDREN.

17 I. MARY, born 8 Oct., 1680; married (1) Benjamin
King, Northampton, 16 May, 1700, (2) Jonathan
Graves.

18 II. RUTH, born 5 June, 1682; married Ebenezer Chapin
of Springfield.

19 III. ELIZABETH, born 22 July, 1684!

20 IV. ELISHA,? born 1686;? married Mindwell; ...... supposed she afterwards married James Tisdale.

21 V. SARAH, born 1689;? married Waitsill Strong.

22 VI. WILLIAM, born 1692;? married Abigail Loomis, 5
June, 1712.

23 VII. ESTHER, born 1695; married Stephen Hunt of
Lebanon.

24 VIII. NOAH, born 30 Nov., 1697; unmarried.

25 IX. RACHEL, born 26 March, 1700.

26 X. BATHSHEBA, born 8 April, 1703.

6 (VI) RUTH, DAUGHTER OF WILLIAM.

Ruth m. John Searl, 3 July, 1667, at Northampton.
She was a victim of the Pasconiac massacre, severely
wounded, but afterwards recovered, being rescued from
the Indians, as they were fleeing before their white
pursuers.

Her young son, Elisha, was taken to Canada, while
three of his brethren were savagely murdered.[1]

---

[1] The savages learning they were being intercepted, commenced
killing the young lads they had kept for captives, and Elisha, fore-
seeing his fate, caught a pack and gave them to understand that he
could help them, and ran along ahead, and they spared his life believing he would serve them truly.

All they succeeded in taking to Canada, as prisoners, were Elisha
Searl, aged nine years, Esther, wife of Benoni Jones (an Ingersoll),
who died in Canada from persecution and hardships, and her niece,
Margaret Huggins, aged nineteen, who returned. When Elisha Searl
returned to see his friends, he could not speak to them intelligently
in his mother tongue, and had to make himself known by signs. He
discovered at home the identical stilts which he had used when a boy,
and taking them in hand, and walking with them, seemed to entirely

Elisha returned to Northampton, 1722, being from home among the Indians and French Catholics eighteen years, and was with reluctance constrained to remain, the government aiding by a military appointment.

Like some other New England children, he had been taught the Catholic religion, and was now strongly attached to this faith, and the Indian mode of life. As he was about to embark up the lakes on a trapping and fishing expedition with some Indians, he inquired of the priest what he should do on the way, as they would have no priest to confess to. The priest told him to confess to a tree, saying that would do just as well. He lost, by degrees, confidence in such a system, and in time embraced fully the protestant belief.

Three years later we find him a lieutenant, under Capt. Timothy Dwight, at Fort Dummer, a short distance south of the village of Brattleboro, Vt., who commanded on this northern frontier. He afterwards

---

convince them of his identity. When reluctant to remain away from Canada, his friends held out to him whatever inducement was in their power, and the government kindly interposed and appointed him lieutenant under Captain Timothy Dwight, who was sent up to build and command Fort Dummer, about a mile south of the now village of Brattleboro, Vermont.

Capt. Dwight's lieutenant was Elisha Searl of Northampton, who had been many years a captive among the Indians, and had seen the vast prairies of the west. Capt. Kellogg had been a captive, and had seen the Mississippi.

After this sudden slaughter of her three sons and her husband, and the capture of her youngest child, Ruth changed her widowhood for the relation of wife again, marrying Nathaniel Alexander of Northampton, then a widower.

settled down on the old homestead, and raised up a
family, many of whose descendants may be found
there and in the neighboring towns. His mother had
a silver hair pin or stay peculiar to the times, which
was preserved, and is still an heir-loom in the family of
some of her descendants.

CHILDREN.

27 I.   JAMES, born 12 Feb., 1675.
28 II. EBENEZER, born 9 Jan., 1679.
29 III. JOHN, born 6 August, 1690.
30 IV. ELISHA, born ......, 1695.

The three former were probably killed when the others were
knocked on the head and left for dead, some of whom recovered.

---

8 (VIII) WILLIAM, SON OF WILLIAM.

William Janes, son of William, settled in Stratford,
was a prominent man in the state, as a leader in the
first Episcopal society organized in Connecticut.

He chose to leave the Congregational order which
had nursed him and fed .his Christian faith, and join
in a new enterprise — the establishment of another
church not yet planted in the state.

History says of him " He took a leading part in or-
ganizing an Episcopal church in Stratford, as early as
1709. In 1710, he presented the case of the Episcopal
church of Stratford to the general assembly of the
colony, asking relief from taxation for the support of
the established church."

He was one of the church-wardens and vestry-men, and was an applicant to the society for the propagation of the gospel in foreign parts, for a missionary. George Pigot was the first missionary sent there, and his labors were acceptable among the people.

It is a subject of regret that we have so little knowledge of the family of this son of the first William. If a clear, full and well authenticated chain of evidence could have come down to us concerning his family, his descendants of after generations, it would have been gratifying. Notwithstanding, there is so little upon record, we feel confident we have the true line of those here called his descendants. But no one will wonder that there is some obscurity, when informed, that Michael, his only son on record, went south to Charleston, South Carolina, and remained some years, so that links in the chain of history might be wanting where we have diligently looked for them. What children sprang from his only son Michael, we know not, but are led to conclude that those in Richmond, in Petersburg and in different parts of Maryland, were his offspring.

William Janes m. Sarah Clark, dau. of James Clark of New Haven. Her mother was Deborah, who died 1705, dau. of John Pecoke, of Stratford. He died, November, 1726. She died, October, 1738.

Mrs. Clark's grave-stone is still seen in Stratford.

William Janes was married at thirty years of age, and probably his sister, who united with the Congregational church, 1697, kept his house till he married Sarah Clark.[1]

CHILDREN.

31 I.   MICHAEL, born 29 Sept., 1686.
32 II. HESTER, born 21 March, 1688; was married to Abram Beardslee, 17 April, 1723, by George Pigot, first Episcopal missionary.
33 III. MARY, born 1692; married Nathan Smith.
34 IV. SARAH, born 20 March, 1694; married Thomas Salmon.
35 V.   ELIZABETH, born 5 November, 1695; married John Outman, 30 Dec., 1725.
36 VI. DEBORAH, born 9 Sept., 1697; married Samuel Watkins, 1707.

---

13 (XIII) SAMUEL, SON OF WILLIAM.

Samuel Janes, son of William by (2) wife Hannah, born in Northampton, was a husbandman. He settled in ʼa part of the town called Pascomac, about a mile and a half from the centre of Northampton, with some four or five other families who felt in a measure secure from the incursions of the Indians. He married (1) Elizabeth Smead, in 1680. She died, so far as known, without issue. He married (2) Sarah Hinsdale, 1692. From this time some twelve years were passed in the social enjoyments of a Christian home, with his wife and children born to them, when most suddenly on an

---

[1] Town clerk of Stratford, writes, "I drink water from the same well that William Janes did when alive."

unfortunate morning, his household was assaulted and cloven down by the hand of a ruthless and savage foe.[1]

Himself, wife and three children were cut down at once, and soon after on the way, when the Indians were pursued by a small company from the town, the two older sons, Samuel and Jonathan, who, with some others were captives on their way to Canada, were struck, stunned, tomahawked, and left for dead. This occurred on the 13 May, 1704, old style, or 24 May, present reckoning, and is recorded upon the books of the town, at the time, which the compiler has seen, together with an account of the administration of the property of Samuel Janes, and some incidental notices of his brothers and family.

The two surviving sons, Samuel and Jonathan, grew up and settled, one in Pascomac, and the other, at Northfield. Concerning these Indians, it was afterward

---

[1] They were called a company of French and Indians, who fell upon a fortified house in Pascomuck, where no watch was kept. The people were alarmed in their beds by a noise of the enemy's rushing on the house, and before the inhabitants could arise the Indians had got their guns into the port-holes, and shot those that first appeared, and wounded others. The surprised people made what resistance they could, firing briskly on the enemy, but the house being set on fire, they were forced to yield. Fearing a pursuit, the enemy sent back a messenger to say that if they were pursued they would kill all the captives. (It is said this messenger was an old man, and stopped to rest and fell asleep). The whites pursued; three made an escape, eight were rescued, nineteen were slain, and three carried captive to Canada. Seven knocked on the head, recovered. Among the nineteen killed, were nine by the name of Janes. Two knocked on the head that recovered, were the boys, Samuel Janes, aged eleven, and Jonathan Janes, aged eight, whose father, mother, and other children were destroyed at the time.— *Wars of New England*, p. 15.

confessed by them, that they were so very hungry and nearly famished, that they thought seriously of giving themselves up to the white people, so they might obtain food for themselves, but inspired with hope of an easy victory, and reward from the French in Canada, for scalps and captives, and seeing from Mount Tom, the day previously, the situation of the houses, and the intervening flood that would protect them from the town's people, they venture to attack, in the gray of the morning, these isolated inhabitants before the people had waked from their slumbers, and surprise and kill and capture as many as were to be found, and with hasty eating and securing of provisions, push on towards Canada.

Benjamin Janes was spared to carry their provisions. He was ordered to empty his straw bed, nothing else being more convenient, and to put into it his pork, and carry it along with them. As he was encumbered with his load, he lagged a little behind, purposely, and near a small ravine leading down to the water where he knew a boat was tied, he dropped quite suddenly his burden, and escaping observation by the friendly covering of shade trees, and running down leaped into the boat, and pushed away toward the other side and hastily rowed himself over to relate to the villagers the horrid scenes that had just passed before his eyes. In the summer of 1865, the writer visited these grounds, and noticed particularly this identical *ravine* through which he escaped from savage hands, to give notice of the sad condition of his unfortunate neighbors and friends.

12

The few rescuers and defenders of the slaughtered or captured neighbors, hastily rushed around the flood, then spreading over thousands of acres in Northampton, and in what is now East Hampton, intercepting the Indians, who suddenly turned to kill and scalp as many as they could, and defended themselves till they could get a better start with their booty and a few captives which they chose to take with them.

In this hasty skirmish, the captain of the company more bold than prudent, was killed, and the Indians cowardly fled with scalps and some captives who could not break away from them with any hope of life.

The descendants of Samuel Janes, Jr., keep the tradition of his being stunned by a blow from a tomahawk, and also the descendants of his brother Jonathan, the Northfield branch, where Jonathan settled, equally well remember the story of their progenitors, that Jonathan experienced the same tragic stunning. No doubt both were struck and wounded at this juncture, for the Indians saw plainly that this attack of the whites would deprive them of their captives whom now they determined to kill, and scalp if possible. The writer, when a youth, had many conversations with, and cannot but well remember the tradition of his great aunt, Hannah (Oliver) Janes, daughter of this Jonathan, who had often heard from the lips of her own father the account, which, though occurring at so early an age, was vividly pictured on the tablet of his memory, so much of it being witnessed by himself. On what a slender thread is suspended the lives of the sons of men. It was indeed a slender thread on which the destinies of hundreds of families were hung, who have since multiplied and spread themselves over the country, and are here partially recorded.

SAMUEL AND HANNAH'S [1] CHILDREN.

37 I. SAMUEL, born 30 Sept., 1693 ; married Abigail ......
38 II. HEPZIBAH, born 4 Jan., 1695 ; died young.
39 III. JONATHAN, born 14 Jan., 1696 ; married Jemima Graves.
40 IV. OBADIAH, born 21 April, 1697 ; died young.
41 V. OBADIAH, born 3 April, 1699.
42 VI. EBENEZER, born 16 May, 1701.
43 VII. SARAH, born 9 May, 1703.

The three latter were killed at once by the Indians.

16 (XVI) BENJAMIN, SON OF WILLIAM.

Benjamin was born 1672; the year before his father, went to Northfield with the first pioneers of the new colony, to locate themselves in a new settlement.

He was thirty-two years of age when his wife and

[1] Hannah was daughter of Samuel Hinsdale of Hadley, who married Mehitable Johnson, perhaps daughter of Humphry Johnson of Roxbury. Sarah's mother, Mehitable, married (2) John Root, (3) Deacon John Colman. Samuel's father, Robert Hinsdale, moved to Deerfield. He married (1) Ann ...., (2) Elizabeth .... a widow. He, with his sons John and Samuel, were slain at the fearful massacre at Bloody Brook. His children are believed to be by his first wife, Ann. Most of our great-grandmother's near relations were thus early killed by the Indians.

children, his brother Samuel, and his family, and their
few neighbors were suddenly and violently assaulted,
and many of them murdered or taken captive by the
savages who roamed the forest and were easily excited
against the whites, but had recently turned into bitter
enmity through the influence of King Philip.

It was about the year 1700 that Samuel and Benjamin moved out from the village of Northampton to
this settlement (two miles out), called Pascomac.

Immediately after the massacre, the Indians, for fear
of the exasperated white inhabitants, hastened away
from these desolated cottages, and learning that troops
were coming from the town to intercept them on the
west, they commenced killing and scalping their prisoners that they might take, in their escape at least,
their scalps; some were only stunned by a blow,
others were killed and scalped. Samuel and Jonathan,
sons of Samuel, were thus stunned and escaped death.
The wife of Benjamin was found farther away from
this scene on the side of Pomeroy's mountain, scalped
and nearly dead.[1]

On their return from their pursuit, they found some
of them coming to consciousness who were supposed
dead. Hannah, the wife of Benjamin, was found on the

---

[1] Three were alive, knocked on the head, and one of them scalped.
They all recovered. The wife of Benjamin Janes, who was scalped,
was under the care of Dr. Gershom Buckley and others, at Wethersfield, several years. Her husband lived in Wethersfield with her,
and the governor and council kindly gave him a brief, May 8, 1707,
craving the charity of the people of Branford, Guilford, Killingworth
and Saybrook. She was finally cured, and they settled in Coventry.

side of this mountain sitting and leaning against a log,
and stroking the blood from her forehead and eyes. Her
infant was dashed against the door post, before they
started on their way to free the captive mother from
any incumbrance that would impede her travel, and
they left her scalped just where they came to the
conclusion that they could only take her scalp in
safety and avoid being overtaken by just avengers.

She was taken to the village on a litter, and by
much care and attention was so far revived as to give
hope of final recovery.

Afterward she was taken to Westfield, and under
the care of Dr. Gershom Buckley and other surgeons,
she finally rose from a long confinement and years of
suffering to the comforts of life.

About the year 1712 or 1713 they moved from
Wethersfield to Coventry, with other pioneers, for a
newer settlement, where land was cheap or free, and
the hope of a good living was promising. During
these latter years God gave them other children to
comfort their desolated hearts, whose descendants are
more numerous than that of any other member of the
family.

We wish we could trace the parentage of one whose
life so trembled in the balance or by some means
obtain the maiden name of this heroic sufferer, but all
effort seems vain and fruitless. How many years Benjamin continued in this newer colony, which was only
a few miles from his brother Abel's, we have not fully
ascertained, but about the year 1722 we find him and

some of his family in Northfield where his father had
obtained title to lands which no one of the other
children lived to occupy. Here he was an officer in
the church, and was chosen constable in 1725, and was
a useful citizen in this Christian settlement, where he
desired to contribute his part to advance purity and
true religion, as he had endeavored to promote the
best interest of the church and people while in Coventry. He always took an active part with the self-
denying men in promoting the fundamental principles
of Christianity and the blessings it carries in its train.
Wherever he sojourned, he was a pattern of noble goodness, zealous in the cause of education and true piety.

His sons remained in Coventry, and probably Benjamin settled with his nephew Jonathan and others at
Northfield, who purchased his estate, and he returned
in time to his old home in Coventry to spend his last
days among his early friends, and where his sons afterward married and raised up their families.

CHILDREN.

44 I.   HANNAH, born 14 May, 1696.
45 II.   MIRIAM, born 7 Jan., 1700.
46 III. NATHAN, born 18 Jan., 1703.
              Hannah was raised almost from the grave and bore
         other children as follows:
47 IV.   HEPZIBAH, born 14 Dec., 1706; died an infant.
48 V.   SILENCE, born 1708; married 1725, Henry Curtis;
         she died 2 Nov. 1745.
49 VI.   HANNAH (twin), born at Wethersfield, Ct., 16 June,
         1710; married John Brown, 28 Nov., 1725, at
         Northfield, Mass.

50 VII. HEPZIBAH (twin), born 16 June, 1710.
51 VIII. SETH, born 1713; married 2 Jan., 1739, Sarah Larabee.
52 IX. ELISHA, born 1715; married 23 April, 1740, Mrs. Mary Dimock.

The first three children killed at once by Indians, 13 May, 1704.

FOURTH GENERATION.

LINE OF ABEL.

17 (I) MARY, DAUGHTER OF ABEL.

Mary, oldest daughter of Abel, married (1) Benjamin King, son of John King, on the 16 May, 1700.

CHILD.

· 53 I. ELISHA, born 11 Nov., 1717; married 20 May, 1753, Jemima Graves, who had two daughters, Mary and Jemima.

Mary married, (2) Jonathan Graves of Hadley, Mass.

CHILDREN.

54 II. MARY, born 20 August, 1722 ; married Noah Loomis of Harwinton, Conn.
55 III. ELIJAH, born 20 Dec., 1725 ; died 1739.
56 IV. SARAH, born 9 Feb., 1726.

18 (II) RUTH, DAUGHTER OF ABEL.

Ruth, married 1 Dec., 1702, Ebenezer Chapin of Enfield, born 26 June, 1677, and who settled at Enfield,

Conn. He died 13 Dec., 1772. She died 18 Jan.,
1736, aged 54.

CHILDREN.

57 I.   RACHEL, born 27 August, 1703.
58 II.   EBENEZER, born 23 Sept., 1705; died 1757.
59 III.   NOAH, born 25 Oct., 1707; died 1787.
60 IV.   SETH, born 28 Feb., 1709.
61 V.   KATHARINE, born 4 Jan., 1710; married Mr. Ellsworth
        of East Windsor, Conn.
62 VI.   MOSES, born 24 August, 1712; died 3 Nov., 1793.
63 VII.   AARON, born 28 Sept., 1714; died 19 April 1808.
64 VIII.   ELIAS, born 22 Oct., 1716; died 6 April, 1791.
65 IX. . REUBEN, born 13 Sept., 1718; died 1788.
66 X.   CHARLES, born 6 Dec., 1720; died 1813.
67 XI.   DAVID, born 13 August, 1722; died 1762.
68 XII.   ELISHA, born 18 April, 1725; died an infant.
69 XIII. PHINEAS, born 26 June, 1726; died 1747.

Without entering into the history of all the children
of Ruth Janes, who married Ebenezer Chapin, we
will record the following facts which have come to
our knowledge:

Reuben and Charles had large families in Salisbury.
David had a family in New Hartford, Conn. Rev. Mr.
Backus of Somers, who delivered a sermon at the
funeral of Moses Chapin, who died 3d of November,
1793, said, "He died in the eighty-second year of his
age, and his father died in the ninety-seventh year of
his age."

He had thirteen children, eleven sons and two
daughters; three of the sons are yet living. That eight
out of thirteen in one family should exceed the age of

three-score and ten, is very remarkable, even for a
healthy climate, and has been rarely equaled since the
days of the patriarchs. A little more than six years
ago, five of the brothers were living in this town, their
farms joined, and there was no neighbor between them;
with sincere fraternal affection they lived together,
pursuing the agricultural employment for more than
forty years. Of Ebenezer's eleven sons, six, viz: Ebenezer, Noah, Moses, Seth, Elias and Aaron, settled on
Somers mountain, their farms joined; and, after a time,
Ebenezer went back to take charge of his father's, and
he died in Enfield. Ebenezer, of six generations, has
lived on and occupied the same farm in Enfield.
One of that name is still living on the same place; the
other five who went to Somers, lived and died there.
We well know that many other interesting facts might
be gathered and communicated concerning this remarkable family. They were intelligent, stable and
Christian.

20 (IV) ELISHA, SON OF ABEL.

Elisha,? married Mindwell ....

CHILDREN.

70 I. DINAH, born about 1720.
71 II. JONATHAN,? born 1724; married Abigail.

13

21 (V) SARAH, DAUGHTER OF ABEL.

Sarah, married Waitsill Strong of Northampton, 19 December, 1701.

CHILD.

72. i. Waitsill, born 18 Jan., 1703.
    Probably others.

---

22 (VI) WILLIAM, SON OF ABEL.

William Janes was the prominent son and leading member of the family of Abel Janes. He raised up a large and honored family of sons and daughters. He was the favorite son of the family, and was at home with father and mother till some time after the death of his father, Abel (1718), and in time moved with all, or nearly all his family, from his native place, Lebanon, Conn., to lands he purchased for himself and sons in Brimfield, Mass. From records of the town of Brimfield, its settlement was commenced in 1717, and William Janes, grandson of the first William, the emigrant, was among the first, or nearly so, in purchasing and preparing for the future abode of his family. He might have removed there with his young family as soon as a part of his five hundred acre purchase was cleared and partially improved, and convenient buildings erected for their occupancy. The dates are not at hand to determine the point. But his oldest son was not born till 1713, and his youngest son was born in 1734. Their births are all recorded in Lebanon, and his mother, Mary, died in Lebanon 1736. The distance being about forty miles from Lebanon to Brimfield, no doubt a part of the family remained till after the death of their grandmother, Mary, and perhaps all of them spent their winters there till Brimfield could be made to seem to them a real home. His oldest, Jonathan, married Irene Bradford, granddaughter of Governor Bradford, of whom we make record on another page.

William, son of Abel and Mary m. Abigail Loomis, 5th June, 1712.

CHILDREN.

74 I.   JONATHAN, born 12 March, 1713; married Irene Bradford, granddaughter of Governor William Bradford.

75 II.   ABIGAIL, born 8 December, 1714; married Joshua Allen, 12 Feb., 1736.

76 III.   TIMOTHY, born 10 June, 1716; married Mary Colton, Springfield; baptized 17 July, 1716.

77 IV.   MARY, born 6 October, 1720; married, and united with church, 27 December, 1753.

78 V.   ABEL, born 24 April, 1724; married ....

79 VI.   WILLIAM, born 30 October, 1726; married Hannah Cheney.

80 VII.   ELIJAH, born 6 May, 1729; married Lucy Crocker, 9 December, 1756.

81 VIII. SARAH, born 18 October, 1731; died 1783.

82 IX.   ISRAEL, born 26 January, 1734; married Abigail Fay, 2 May, 1776.

23 (VII) ESTHER, DAUGHTER OF ABEL.

Esther, daughter of Abel, ? married 18 June, 1730, Stephen Hunt of Lebanon, son of Ebenezer Hunt of Lebanon ; she died 17 February, 1779, aged 84.

CHILDREN.

83 I.   STEPHEN, born 6 July, 1731.
84 II. ESTHER, born 29 January, 1732.
85 III. ELIJAH, born 22 June, 1734.
86 IV. SAMUEL, 2 March, 1735.
87 V.   JOHN, born 3 March, 1738 ; married......
88 VI. RACHEL, born 2 July, 1740; married Jonathan Clark.
89 VII. EUNICE, born 11 February, 1742; married Mr. Carter.
90 VIII. LYDIA, born 1745 ; married Hinkman Bennett.
91 IX. ELIJAH, born September, 1749 ; married Abigail Reynolds, 18 Nov., 1773, who had three sons and five daughters : one daughter married Calvin Billings.

FOURTH GENERATION.

LINE OF WILLIAM.

31 (I) MICHAEL, SON OF WILLIAM.

Michael Janes's son, 2d William, went to Charleston, South Carolina, when about twenty-one years of age; probably married late in life, following the example of his father.

Michael married ....

After returning north, and to Stratford, about 1730, and spending some years with his mother and sisters, he may have gone to Maryland or Virginia with his young family, or taken a wife there and gone north again, though there is found no record. The history of his early sojourn south would be a theme of conversation in the family; and the minds of some of the sons would be naturally guided in that direction. Hence, William, if that was his name, settled in Maryland, and some of his sons in Richmond.

Michael may have continued and died south, or some of his sons, probably William, hearing of the soil, climate, etc., through his father, may have gone to Richmond, before or after marriage. Miss Paine was the maiden name of his son's wife. Two sons of William, Thomas and David, resided for sometime in Richmond. Thomas married and had a family; was a distinguished architect ; many of the buildings now standing in Richmond, were constructed by him ; and when he died, his brother David went north among his old friends in New England, where he might, if he needed, obtain consolation in his bereavement.

The fact that Michael purchased property in Stratford, and became a landholder adjoining his mother's land, gives color to the idea that he left Charleston permanently, and perhaps only some of his sons went to Virginia and Maryland.

CHILDREN.

92 I. WILLIAM, born 1733 ; married Miss Paine.
93 II. THOMAS, born 1738 ; married Rachel Lines, Wallingford, Connecticut.
Probably others.

32 (II) ESTHER, DAUGHTER OF WILLIAM.

Esther Janes married Abraham Beardsley, son of John and Abigail Wakelyn, and was born 6 March, 1696. John was the second son of Joseph Beardsley, and was born November, 1668. This Joseph, born 1634, was the second son of William and Mary Beardsley, who were among the first settlers of Stratford, Conn., which settlement was begun 1639.

He embarked from London in the ship Planter, April, 1635. He came to Boston, and was admitted a freeman in Massachusetts, 7 December, 1636; emigrating afterward to Stratford with other planters, and was an original proprietor of that ancient town.

William Beardsley is described in the Custom House records, London, as a mason. The proportion of masons among the early emigrants to New England was very small, less than one in a hundred. He was thirty years of age, and his family consisted of Mary, his wife, aged twenty-six, and daughter, Mary, aged four years; sons, John, two years, Joseph, six months. Samuel, Daniel, Sarah and Hannah were born in this country.

Joseph, the second son, in his youth, appears to have been fond of the water, and his father, in his will, offered him certain advantages, on condition that "he married and left the sea." His wife's name is not at hand. In 1682 he lived in Stratford, and died there in 1712, aged seventy-seven years. Joseph's sons, Joseph and John, were the administrators on his estate. The branch which shot off from the parent tree in this direction, has, for the most part, had a pleasing growth. John, the father of Abraham, who married Esther Janes, had five sons, viz: Caleb, Jehiel, Abraham, John, and Andrew. John, senior, died in 1732, and his wife, Abigail, and his son, John, were his executors.

Abraham, who married Esther Janes, was great-grandson of William Beardsley, the emigrant, and Esther was the granddaughter of William Janes, the emigrant. Abraham and Esther were married 17 April, 1723, by Rev. George Pigot, a missionary of the (London) society for the propagation of the gospel in foreign parts.

Their's was the first recorded marriage in the missionary's register. Their children were baptized by Dr. Johnson, afterward president of Columbia College; the first baptisms recorded in the missionary's register, and these dates will approximate near the date of birth, not far from eight or ten weeks after.

. CHILDREN.

94 I.   ABRAHAM, 6 November, 1725.
95 II.   MARTHA, 28 April, 1728.
96 III.   ABIGAIL, 3 May, 1730.
97 IV.   WILLIAM, 9 April,.1732.
98 V.   ISAAC, 4 March, 1734.
99 VI.   JOHN, 18 January, 1736.
100 VII. SARAH, 1 January, 1738.
101 VIII. MICHAEL, 14 September, 1740.

Abraham, junior, married Bethia Curtis, and had the following children, baptized as follows: Curtis, 1754; Ephraim, 21 September, 1755; Betsy, 2 January, 1757; Mary, 14 May, 1758; John, 20 April, 1760; Abijah, 22 January, 1766, by Rev. Mr. Winslow; Sarah, 6 September, 1767; Abel, 28 July, 1770; Jerusha, 1772; baptized by Dr. Johnson.

FOURTH GENERATION.

LINE OF SAMUEL.

37 (I) SAMUEL, SON OF SAMUEL.

Samuel Janes was eleven years old when his father, mother, friends and neighbors were slain by the merciless Indians on the memorable 13 of May, 1704.

Coming to manhood he found himself in possession of a large estate, having obtained title under his father and uncle, Joseph. He owned principally what is called Pascomac, and it became a byword among the inhabitants who knew his very narrow escape, that "if the Indians had struck him another blow he would have owned the whole of Pascomac."

Samuel and Jonathan, the two escaped brothers, had an undivided interest in the lands in Northampton and Northfield. They mutually agreed upon a division; Samuel was to retain those in Northampton, and Jonathan those in Northfield.

These lands were the estate of their grandfather William, the emigrant, their own father, and their deceased uncles. A quit claim was executed to Jonathan which is in our present possession, preserved as an interesting relic of nearly a century and a half old, exhibiting the beautiful penmanship, though in the style of that day, now antique.

It bears date " 4 March, anno Domini 1729 – 30, and in the third year of the reign of our Sovereign Lord King George the second." (See page 63).

How wonderful the divine hand that snatched him from the cruel death that removed his parents and friends so tragically from earth.

He stands at the head of a numerous family, and will be remembered as the providential link in the chain which held in existence those whom an unfriendly fate would have denied birth.

The ways of the Lord are mysterious and too obscure for finite comprehension. His providence is infinitely beyond our control.

Samuel married Abigail ....

CHILDREN.

94 i.   ABIGAIL, born 29 Jan., 1720; died young.

95 ii. SAMUEL, born 13 Sept., 1724; married Hannah Brown; died 1788.

96 iii. JONATHAN, born 1 April, 1726; married Hannah Parsons; died 1825.

97 iv. OBADIAH, born 29 April, 1730; married Beulah Lyman; died 1817.

98 v.   MARTHA, born 1 April, 1732; died 3 Jan., 1746.

99 vi. ELISHA, born 7 March, 1734; married Sarah Phelps; died 1808.

100 vii. RACHEL, born 26 Dec., 1736; married Philip Clark.

14

Their son, Obadiah, who married Beulah Lyman, had no children, though always happy in such society, and called by a large circle of their young friends, Uncle Diah, and Aunt Beulah, who enjoyed not a few happy hours, under a roof of known and large hospitality.

Elisha Parsons now lives on the same spot, almost too near the roaring spring flood of the Connecticut river, which he was hardly ever known to cross.

Obadiah Janes was a teacher of common schools, which at that time was some considerable honor, as there were not many in those early days of the town. He was chosen deacon of the church, which office he filled for almost a quarter of a century. His wife was the daughter of a substantial citizen, Abner Lyman of Northampton, and was known as a woman of strong mind, affectionate manners and fervid piety. They both died in their eighty-eighth year, and within a few weeks of each other, he dying first, and both leaving behind them a sweet godly influence, so that many shall rise up to call them blessed.

39 (III) JONATHAN, SON OF SAMUEL.

Jonathan, like his brother Samuel, was lifted from the power of the destroying angel, and thus made the representative of a large posterity, whose life, under God, was so to depend upon his.

In charge of his uncles, Joseph and Abel, he grew to manhood, under such educational influences and training, as the times allowed. He eventually went to occupy the lands which were left by his grandfather William, in Northfield. Without a definite record, we suppose he accompanied the persevering colonists in their third attempt to settle this frontier town, or that he went up there soon after. He was then about seventeen years of age. This third venture was made about the year 1715, when a bold company of pioneers go up to repair the wastes and ruins where the savages had held full sway for about twenty years preceding; where the repossessing of valuable lands, might in part make amends for former losses, if not former perils and reinstate lawful heirs to the possession of a former generation.

Jonathan Janes, though young, was a worthy representative of his name and of his grandfather's family, always esteemed for his uprightness and integrity of character, and kindness to those in distress. He was a large land holder, and filled many town offices. He stood among the first as to property, as to virtue and intelligence. He left but one son to represent him, and to preserve his name to other generations. His wife and faithful companion survived him some fourteen years, and died in a good old age, ripe in all the Christian virtues, and prepared for the rich fruitions of a better land.

Aprill ye 19*th* A. D. 1732

There was jyned together in marr dg Jonathan Janes & Jemimah Graves. By the Honorrable Colinell Samuell Patridg, Juſtic of Peace.

CHILDREN.

101 I.   HANNAH, born 31 August, 1734; married 3 August,
         1752, by Rev. John Hubbard, James Oliver; she
         died 4 Oct., 1831.
102 II. EBENEZER, born 31 July 1736; married (1) Sarah
         Field, (2) Mehitable Alexander; died 22 Jan., 1808.
103 III. SARAH, born 26 Dec., 1738; married Ora Harvey;
         died 12 Nov., 1764.
104 IV. JEMIMA, born 11 May, 1742; died 25 Oct., 1748.

James Oliver, son of William, was a protestant from the
north of Ireland.   William had four sons, John, James,
Robert and William.   They were men of fine carriage
and form, and bore an excellent character.   James had
no issue.   These brothers were early settlers in Athol,
Mass., where their influence was long felt for truth,
goodness, for virtue and pure religion.   It was this
kind of men, stern in principle, unwavering in their
faith, brave and public spirited in their acts, that
moulded the early society of New England, and eventually gathered up such fountains of morality and real
goodness, that glad streams flowed out from them to
bless the nation, if not to save the world.

Hannah, the wife of James Oliver, was a godly,
fervent woman, a pattern of the old type of praying,
holy Christians.   Spending her last days, by the request
of her younger brother, my grandfather, the present
writer had full opportunity, in early youth, to witness
the holiness of her life, and the yearning desire of her
heart for the salvation of all around her.   The loss of
a kind mother in boyhood was in part made good by

the especial attentions of this excellent kinswoman, to the author of this volume. She lived to the age of one hundred years, and would often relate anecdotes of her playing with the papooses when friendship marked their conduct; and when the Indian and French wars were waged, she knew the sorrows that filled many hearts in her own community, and in others, where her immediate friends and relations resided. There was too little cessation from Indian hostilities, and too little freedom from harrassing fears. Too many had fallen from the sudden and savage attacks of an especially revengeful foe. Fearfulness and trembling when retiring at nightfall, and hopeful deliverance were awaited during the sorrowful day, by the scattered New England settlers.

Her own father could relate, and did tell the story of the Pascomac massacre, as it still was painted before him on the canvas of his memory, as he was a suffering witness of their hurried and impartial slaughter of his parents and others, and the sudden stunning of himself by a blow upon the head with their ever present tomahawk, was ever recalled with a shudder. The remains of this sainted heroine, and her father's and mother's, with many others who bear the name, born in Northfield, rest in the burying ground near the hillside of the great meadow, and in a valley of picturesque beauty and richness. Often did those hands of gentle sweetness press this forehead in hope, and often did some kind wish find utterance, that this priceless soul might be born into a spiritual kingdom, and this heart beat in unison with the Saviour's.

If any soul was ever borne up to Heaven in the arms of true faith for the application of Christ's atoning blood : and if any prayer was ever offered for the spiritual uplifting of a sinner from sin, in her was that faith, and from her went up that prayer. Eternity alone can tell how much the writer and the other children are indebted to her for her godly life, her disinterested piety and her constant, spiritual labors. A happy reunion above may consummate the blessedness commenced on the earth.

FOURTH GENERATION.

LINE OF BENJAMIN.

49 (VI) HANNAH DAUGHTER OF BENJAMIN.

Hannah married John Brown at Northfield, Mass. He was probably of the Coventry Browns, though they lived in Northfield, as appears from the record of births of children.   They were married 28 November, 1725.

CHILDREN.

105 I   JOHN, born 5 April, 1726.
106 II.   BENJAMIN, born 14 October, 1727.
107 III.   SILAS, born 21 June, 1729.
108 IV.   EUNICE, born 17 December, 1730.
109 V.   HANNAH, born 2 November, 1732.
110 VI.   LOIS, born 14 August, 1734.
111 VII.   RUFUS, born 5 July, 1736.

50 (VII) HEPZIBAH, DAUGHTER OF BENJAMIN.

Hepzibah, twin with Hannah, married 11 March, 1729, 'George Hawkins of Coventry. From her has descended a large posterity of the name of Root. Hepzibah's daughter Phebe married Ebenezer Root. Ebenezer's daughter Elizabeth married Abner Fitch (a descendant of Rev. James and Priscilla Mason, daughter of Captain John Mason, conqueror of the Pequots). Her son Ebenezer R. married Sarah Dow, who had two sons and a daughter, Mariamne, wife of Hon. J. S. T. Stranahan of Brooklyn. Hepzibah and George Hawkins's children are as follows:

CHILDREN.

112 I. HANNAH, born 7 April, 1730.
113 II. HEPZIBAH, born 17 December, 1731.
114 III. PHEBE, born 4 January, 1734; married Ebenezer Root.
115 IV. OZIAS, born 1 August, 1736; married Anna Rose.
116 V. DARKIS, born 22 April, 1738.
117 VI. EUNICE, born 26 February, 1739–40.
118 VII. ANNA, born 23 September, 1741; married Elijah Janes.
119 VIII. DEBORAH, born 8 February, 1743–44.
120 IX. GEORGE, born 13 April, 1746; died an infant.

51 (VIII) SETH, SON OF BENJAMIN.

Seth Janes was well reported of as a good man, and we believe a deacon in the church at Coventry his native town, where he lived to exert his Christian influence, which followed a long line of worthy Puritans. We have not been able to obtain the history of Seth, or of all his children, as would have been agreeable. He married Sarah Larabe of Coventry, 2 June, 1739. She died 1801.

CHILDREN.

121 I. IRANY, born 11 February, 1740; died 12 March, 1744.

122 II. LUCY, born 19 June, 1742.

123 III. ELIJAH, born 17 April, 1744; married Anna Hawkins.

124 IV. EUNICE, born 10 March, 1748.

125 V. SAMUEL, born 9 March, 1750; married Abigail Brooks.

126 VI. ELIAS, born 17 March, 1752; married Susan Robinson.

127 VII. OLIVER, born 2 November, 1754, married Judith Rollo.

128 VIII. SETH, born 8 July, 1756; married Elizabeth Francis.

129 IX. SOLOMON, born 6 February, 1758; married Susanna Trapp.

130 X. TIMOTHY, born 9 March, 1760.

---

52 (IX) ELISHA, SON OF BENJAMIN.

Elisha Janes, the youngest son, married Mrs. Mary Dimock, on the 23 April, 1740. Elisha Janes, with his son Elisha, built a stone house, and was always industrious, if not penurious. He died there amidst his early associations, but some of his children moved away. After the death of Elisha the family moved to Canaan, N Y., where they lived till 1867. The family name is hardly known in Coventry at the present day, in this ancient town, where so many of the name were born and first breathed their vitality, and were thrilled with joyous hopes and flushed with high expectations. We have no particular outline of the character of Elisha or the major part of his children. We know of only three marriages among the nine children, and the records of Coventry do not shine much upon the subject so painfully obscure at this writing.

CHILDREN.

131 I   ELISHA, born 30 June, 1741; married Desire Thompson.
132 II.   BATHSHEBA, born 10 February, 1743; married John Tilden.
133 III. MARY, born 10 February, 1744.
134 { IV. SAMUEL, born 1746; died infant.
      { IV. DANIEL, born 1746; died infant.
135 V.   BENJAMIN, born 1 March, 1748; married Irene Sawyer.
136 VI.   DANIEL, born 17 March, 1750; died young.
137 VII. JERUSHA, born 17 July, 1752.
138 VIII. TIMOTHY, born 3 July, 1755.
139 IX.   TABBATHY, born 22 February, 1757.

15

FIFTH GENERATION.

LINE OF ABEL.

71 (II) JONATHAN, SON OF ELISHA.

This Jonathan, who married Abigail.........about 1753, has on record at Lebanon his children's births and nothing further, is known of this large family. Death may have early thinned their ranks, or the tide of western emigration may have swept them to some distant part of the country, where the changes are often so sudden that they are lost to sight or hearing and buried from remembrance. Thus many will remain unheralded and unrecorded in any genealogy.

CHILDREN.

140 I.   JONATHAN, born 11 May, 1754.
141 II. LOIS, born 5 May, 1757.
142 III. SAMUEL, born 3 December, 1759.
143 IV. AMOS, born 31 August, 1762.
144 V.   ESTHER, born 18 September, 1765.
145 VI. ENOCH, born 10 January, 1767.
146 VII. IRENICA, born 3 May, 1770.

47 (I) JONATHAN, SON OF WILLIAM.

Jonathan married Irene Bradford, granddaughter of William Bradford, well known in colonial history.

William Bradford was born in March, 1590, at Austerfield, Yorkshire, on the borders of England. He was a dissenter from the church of England, and in 1607, when only eighteen years of age, in company with others, made an unsuccessful attempt to go to Amsterdam, in Holland, and through the treachery of the master of the vessel, they were thrown into prison. Another attempt, afterward, was successful. He was active in preparing to come to America with Rev. John Robinson's church. He was foremost in finding a proper place for a settlement of the new colony. On the death of Governor Carver, he was elected as the second governor of the Plymouth colony. Bradford was governor, in all thirty-three years.

William Bradford's wife, Dorothy May, was drowned before she got ashore at Plymouth.

He married second, Mrs. Alice Southworth (Carpenter), widow of Edward Southworth. They lived near William Bradford when he was in England. She was about thirty-three years old. She waived her right of a personal visit, which would call the governor away from duties of vast importance, to their new colony, in the wilderness.

She brought with her considerable property. She was well educated, of extraordinary capacity and of great moral worth. She incessantly toiled for the literary improvement and refinement of Plymouth colony. If ever she felt honored by being married to Edward Southworth, descendant of Sir Gilbert Southworth, knight of Lancaster, she must have felt more happy in being the companion of him, who laid the foundation of civil and religious freedom in a new

world, and whose name would be held illustrious by
the generations to come after him to the end of time.

His son, Joseph Bradford, married October, 1698,
Miss Anne Fitch. They settled at Norwich, Conn.,
and removed to Lebanon, a short distance from
Norwich. He died 17 October, 1718. Her children
were Anne, Joseph and Priscilla. Priscilla married
Samuel Hyde. Alithea and Irene died infants. Sarah,
Hannah, Elizabeth; Alithea, and Irene born 18 September,
1715. Irene married Jonathan Janes of Lebanon,
18 March, 1736. •Alithea, twin, married David Hyde.
Jonathan and Irene lived a happy life, and raised up
an excellent family of children, who have honored
some of the highest positions in the country, though
we cannot accord the highest excellence to them all.

CHILDREN.

147 I.   DAVID, born 25 December, 1736; married Jemima
          Vorce.
148 II.   JONATHAN, born 28 January, 1739; baptized 7 days
          old, and died.
149 III. IRENE, born 5 April, 1741; died at two years.
150 IV.   ELIPHALET, born 23 February, 1743; married
          Elfleda Lyon.
151 V.   IRENE, born 30 July, 1745.
152 VI.   SOLOMON, born 20 June, 1748; married Beulah Fisk.
153 VII. DANIEL, born 17 March, 1751; married Annie
          Saunders.
154 VIII. MARY, born 28 April, 1753; married Rowland Powell.
155 IX.   JONATHAN, born 8 January, 1756; married Patty
          Plympton.
156 X.   ABIGAIL, born 24 January, 1759.
157 XI.   ANN, born 12 December, 1761.

76 (III) TIMOTHY, SON OF WILLIAM.

We have a very slight history of Timothy, who married Mary Colton, probably of Springfield, as there is found the record.   Cannot ascertain where he spent his last days.

CHILDREN.

158 I. TIMOTHY ?
159 II. ELIJAH ?
Probably others.

---

78 (V) ABEL, SON OF WILLIAM.

Abel Janes connected himself with the church of Christ, 27 September, 1741, in the seventeenth year of his age.   This is another family which cannot be fully hunted up, as many efforts have proved.   They may be numerous and prosperous for aught we can learn, or they may be few.

CHILDREN.

160 I. ABEL.
161 II. LOUISA.

---

79 (VI) WILLIAM, SON OF WILLIAM.

This third William Janes married Harriet Cheney, of Sturbridge.   We have comparatively few facts concerning the children of William.   So many years have elapsed since they were upon the stage in Brimfield, that we find little information except what is on record, and the records contain but little beyond the dates of births of children.

He married about 1757.

CHILDREN.

162 I.   WILLIAM, born 3 October, 1758; married Nabby Belknap.
163 II.   PELEG CHENEY, born 2 December, 1760; married Patty Coy.
164 III. CYNTHIA, born 23 June, 1763.
165 IV.   SILAS, born 24 June, 1765; died 24 June, 1765.
166 V.   HANNAH, born 6 September, 1766; died 1 June, 1767.
167 IV.   NATHAN, born 20 June, 1768.
168 VII. HANNAH, born 8 March, 1770.
169 VIII. ELIZABETH, born 29 August, 1772.
170 IX.   LAVINA, born 1 November, 1775.
171 X.   SIMON, born 22 October, 1781; married Chloe Shumway of Sturbridge.

---

80 (VII) ELIJAH, SON OF WILLIAM.

This is the first Elijah Janes mentioned among the number, and we find quite a full list who are called by this name, after this one. He inherited a part of his father's property, and by frugality and industry made himself a good home and maintained a respectable standing among his fellow townsmen. He died at the age of fifty-four years, being large and corpulent; we might say gross, as he weighed 340 lbs, which is 15 lbs more than any other one of the family that has come under our knowledge. He married Lucy Crooker, December, 1756, in Lebanon, Conn., She was remarkably strong, athletic, and full of vitality. Their house was on a hill-side, and descending from it on one side to a spring, it is at an angle of 50 degrees. She would leave her infant in the cradle and go down a half mile to the spring, fill two pails with water and return with them, without stopping till she came in sight of her child. Such native force, such self-sacrifice, may seem in proper keeping with the early settlement of New England; but few at the present day would look upon it as consistent, would feel equal to the task, would be willing to endure the hardship. He died 21 June, 1783.

CHILDREN.

172 I.   ELIJAH, born 8 July, 1758; married Phebe Gay, and died June, 1823.

173 II.   ISRAEL CHAMPION, born 26 August, 1760; married (1) Mary Ann Marsh, (2) Lucina.........died 1817.

174 III. ISAAC, born 26 December, 1762; died young.

175 IV. CYRUS, born 5 March, 1765; married Lavina Holbrook.

176 V.   LUCY, born 10 Nov., 1766; married Wait Wooster of Cornwall, Vt.

177 VI. PARTHENIA, born 30 June, 1768; married Asa Backus of Norwich, Conn.

178 VII. ABEL, born 18 July, 1770; died 1779.

179 VIII. POLLY, born 11 April, 1772; married Eli Stone.

180 IX. ELISHA, born 9 June, 1774; married Bethia Huntington; died 1828.

181 X.   LIBERTY, born 4 July, 1776; married Clarinda Fuller; died 1851.

182 XI. PROPERTY, born 4 April, 1778; married Charlotte Psalmist; died 1813.

82 (IX) ISRAEL, SON OF WILLIAM.

Israel Janes married Abigail Fay of Brimfield, 2 May, 1764, and raised up a family of nine children.

CHILDREN.

183 I.   ORSAMUS, born 1765; married Ruth Shepherd Warren, born 1773.

184 II.   THANKFUL, born 1767; married Mr.........Shepherd; she died 1845.

185 III.   NABBY, born 1769.

186 IV.   SALLY, born 1771.

187 V.   CHLOE, born 1772.

188 VI.   ISRAEL, born 1774.

189 VII.   LEVI, born 1775; married Mary Lombard of Brimfield.

190 VIII.   EZRA, born 1777.

191 IX.   BATHSHEBA, born 1779.

FIFTH GENERATION.

LINE OF WILLIAM.

92 (I) WILLIAM, SON OF MICHAEL.

William married Miss .... Paine, about 1745. They lived in the neighborhood of Richmond, Va., for some years.

CHILDREN.

192 I.   WILLIAM, born 1746?; married Margaret Sybert.

193 II.   JOHN, born 1748.

194 III.   SAMUEL, born 1750.

195 IV.   THOMAS, born 1752.

196 V.   DAVID, born 1755.

197 VI.   DAUGHTER, born 1757.

198 VII.   DAUGHTER, born 1759.

The second son, Captain John Janes, was connected
with the 7th Maryland Regiment, 1 June, 1778, which
was commanded by Colonel Greenby.

93 (II) THOMAS, SON OF MICHAEL.

Thomas Janes's birth place and particular history is
not fully known. We find him in the service of his
country, in the war of the revolution in a Connecticut
regiment of infantry, under Colonel Moses Thayer,
from 1 January, 1777, to January, 1782, five years.

He returned to his young family and engaged again
in the humble pursuits of agriculture, and within two
years, after escaping the dangers of the battle-field, was
killed by the overturning of a loaded cart. Such is the
wonderful providence of God, that permits our lives to
enjoy all needed shelter from bullets or sword, to the
brave soldier, and then by a singular accident calls the
weather beaten warrior to his reward.

Thus providentially were left a widow and a young
orphan family, the oldest but twelve years of age, to
struggle and battle with life, and learn how to depend
upon their own exertions for successful efforts in securing a competence, and in adorning life with the social
virtues, and the virtue of industry and integrity. This
brave patriot soldier was the worthy progenitor of
Benjamin Janes of Wallingford, the father of Bishop
Edmund Storer Janes. Thomas Janes was a spirited,

16

thorough, thoughtful man, ready to retort when crowded with sharp repartees. He was killed 1784. His wife lived to 1820.

CHILDREN.

199 I.   BENJAMIN, born 12 December, 1772; married Sally Wood.
200 II.   THOMAS MILES, born 8 May, 1775; married (2) Lucy Jones.
201 III.   MARY, born 26 December, 1778.
202 IV.   WILLIAM, born 27 August, 1781; killed by kick of a horse.
203 V.   SARAH, born 27 July, 1785; married Alexander Hine.

FIFTH GENERATION.

LINE OF SAMUEL.

95 (II) SAMUEL, SON OF SAMUEL.

Samuel Janes married Hannah Brown. They lived in Northampton, (Pascomac) now called Easthampton.

CHILDREN.

204 I.   MARTHA, born 9 January, 1752.
205 II.   NOAH, born 19 November, 1753; married Naomi Strong.
206 III.   SAMUEL, born 28 August, 1757; married ....
207 IV.   ASAHEL, born 7 February, 1760.
208 V.   HANNAH, born 31 December, 1761; married Uriel Clark.
209 VI.   ENOS, born.........1765; married Hannah Wright.
210 VII.   SETH, born.........1762; married Mary Ferry.
211 VIII. SARAH, born.........1775; married.........Caldwell.

96 (III) JONATHAN, SON OF SAMUEL.

Jonathan Janes born in 1726, lived till the year 1825, a ripe old age, full of rich and ripe experiences. He lived one-eighteenth part of the time since our Saviour and one sixtieth since the world was created. During his life some of the most important events in human history transpired; the rise and fall of many empires, the settling of some of the profoundest social questions of any century. He was a soldier in the French war while we were a colony of Great Britain. He was at the surrender of the French at Louisburgh. to the British and Colonial Forces, 26 July, 1758, Through life he was very social, full of good cheer, and full of anecdotes. He once had quite an adventure with an untamed, frantic beast, that plunged down from an eminence, on Mount Tom, to escape the determined pursuers, and he used to relate the circumstances without regard to his value, and ended by saying " he came near spoiling his hide."

Jonathan married (1) Esther......; (2) Hannah Parsons. Esther, first wife, died 24 May, 1761.

CHILDREN.

212 I. EBENEZER, born 10 January, 1765; married Submit Clark.

213 II. JONATHAN, born 1771; married (1) Rachel Clark, (2) Mary Kingsley.

214 III. OBADIAH, born 2 September, 1776; married (1) Esther Lyman, (2) Mary Chapman, (3) Elizabeth Davis.

215 IV. PARSONS, born 1778; married Dorcas Clark.
216 V. REBECCA, born 1780; married Daniel Wright.
217 VI. LOIS, born 1783; married Deacon Solomon Lyman.
218 VII. ESTHER, born 1785; unmarried.

99 (VI) ELISHA, SON OF SAMUEL.

Elisha, and his brother Obadiah, who married Beulah Lyman, lived in the same house, and the music of his children supplied the wants of both families, for, as before written, Obadiah had no children.

CHILDREN.

219 I. SARAH, married Asahel Parsons.
220 II. RACHEL, married Joel Parsons.
221 III. MERCY, married Thaddeus Parsons.

100 (VII) RACHEL, DAUGHTER OF SAMUEL.

Rachel Janes married Philip Clark, who was born 21 February, 1732.

CHILDREN.

222 I. PHILIP.
223 II. ELAM.
224 III. URIEL.

Rachel died, and Philip Clark married (2) Abigail Grant of East Hartford.

CHILDREN.

225 I. CALVIN.
226 II. RACHEL, born 23 November, 1770; married Jonathan Janes.

102 (II) EBENEZER, SON OF JONATHAN.

Ebenezer married (1) Sarah Field, March, 1755; (2) Mehitable Alexander, daughter of Simeon and sister of Rev. Caleb Alexander. Sarah died March, 1766. Ebenezer died 22 January, 1808.

Deacon Ebenezer Janes was a great-grandson of the first William, and the grandfather of the writer and compiler of this genealogy. He was born in Northfield, at the old homestead, and maintained from early life a character for probity and virtue which furnished him an easy passport to the highest posts of distinction among his fellow townsmen. He inherited the estate and, good name of his father, and was a large landholder in Northfield and the adjoining towns. He was a representative of the town at the general court at Boston, a town and church officer and town clerk for many years previous to his death.

He was a good, kind counsellor and a pattern of religious fidelity and godliness. He died some three months previous to the author's birth. He built the present house on the old homestead in the latter part of the life of Jonathan, his respected father, which, though occupied by some five generations of the family, is in a good condition, and is still regarded a friendly shelter for many friends, and a pleasant retreat. In times past, here, many innocent youthful sports have caused many a ring of merriment and jubilant exultation, and many dry jokes were cracked, as well as *butternuts*, and some of a still harder nature, and many fair maidens have here been led to the hymenial altar; and from this parental covering many robust sons have gone forth to unite their interests with other families to perpetuate their own names and to allure fortune, worldly joys and riches, to their own hearthstones. To this old homestead have they silently turned their eyes when battling with life, in ardent toil of duty, in new and untried enterprises, in whatever clime providence has cast their lot. Though Ebenezer had no brother, his offspring is about as numerous as those of his three Easthampton cousins, who started with him in the race of life. He had six sons who raised up families, and three daughters whose children are scattered far and wide through the country. They are located in many different states, and many of them are religious, industrious and frugal, and have acquired a name worthy to bequeath to their children.

Deacon Ebenezer Janes will long be remembered in the history of the people, and when the present generation has departed, the impress of his influence will prove permanently good. His counsel was not easily rejected, his word was not doubted, his example was influential. His wish was the law of the household and the guide of the neighborhood. He died at a good old age, respected and beloved as a kind neighbor, father and Christian friend, and an exemplary member and officer of the church of Christ.

Mehitable Alexander, his (2) wife, the writer's paternal grandmother, was a native of Northfield, in the 5th generation from George, a man of strong mind and stirring influence in his native Scotland, and obnoxious to the imperial party that sustained Charles II in his persecution and execution of the judges. He came to this country for a more quiet life and greater security, till the political parties should change their balance. He early settled in Windsor, Conn. From thence he came to Northampton, and with many others was interested in the negotiation of the lands with the Indians at Northfield, where his son John settled for life and raised up a large family. John had a son Ebenezer, and Ebenezer had a son Simeon, who was the father of my grandmother Mehitable Alexander. A large number of influential brothers were in this family, among whom was Caleb Alexander, the author of Alexander's *Grammar* and translator of Virgil, etc., and all of whom were considered indomitable in perseverance and noted for thrift.[1]

CHILDREN.

227 I. JONATHAN, born 25 February, 1756; married Caroline Mattoon, 1777.

228 II. JEMIMA, born 16 May, 1757; married 6 July, 1771, John Allen.

229 III. RUTH, born 16 May, 1757; married Calvin Bliss.

---

[1] As Mehitable's great-grandmother was Sarah Gaylord, it. may be well to record this item which follows: Joseph Loomis, born in England, near Bristol, sailed with his family (having four sons) from Plymouth, 20 March, 1630, in the ship Mary and John, Capt. Squidd, and arrived in America, May 30. Josiah Hull married his daughter Elizabeth, Samuel Gaylord married their daughter Elizabeth, and John Alexander married their daughter Sarah Gaylord. His father, George, married Susan Sage. John's son, Ebenezer, married Mehitable Buck. Ebenezer's son, Simeon, married Sarah Howe.

230 IV.   OBADIAH, born 9 July, 1759; married (1) Polly
Oliver, (2) Harmony Bingham.
231 V.   SALIMA, born 11 March, 1761; married Seth Munn.
232 VI.   HANNAH, born 5 January, 1763.
233 VII. SAMUEL, born 11 May, 1764; married Susan Merriman.
234 VIII. EBENEZER, born 1 Jan., 1765; died 6 November, 1766.

Ebenezer married (2) Mehitable Alexander.

CHILDREN.

235 IX.   EBENEZER, born 5 February, 1771.
236 X.   XENOPHON, born 3 September, 1772; married Sally
Patrie.
237 XI.   SARAH, born 11 October, 1774; died 1 September,
1775.
238 XII. SARAH, born 28 April, 1777; died 24 September,
1779.
239 XIII. EBENEZER, born 13 September, 1779; married
Lucretia Smith.
240 XIV. JAMES Oliver, born 6 July, 1782; married (1) Roxana Field, (2) Joanna Holton.
241 XV.   ALEXANDER, born 8 October, 1784; died 3 June,
1787.

103 (III) SARAH, DAUGHTER OF JONATHAN.

Sarah, sister of Ebenezer, married (1) Ora Harvey
of Chesterfield, N. H., about the year 1758. She
died early. He married (2) Lucy Wright. The following are Sarah's descendants.

CHILDREN.

242 I.   ELECTA, born 1760; married a Dr. Ellis.
243 II.   RUFUS, born 1762; married Rachel Partridge.
244 III. ORA, born 1764; died a youth.
245 IV.   SARAH, born 1768; married Amos Partridge.

FIFTH GENERATION.

LINE OF BENJAMIN.

$\int$ 12$ (III) ELIJAH, SON OF SETH.

Elijah Janes of Pittsfield, born in Coventry, Conn., of respected parents, was among the early settlers of the town. He married in 1763, Anna Hawkins, daughter of George and Hepzibah Hawkins of Coventry. She was two years older than Elijah. He had three brothers, Samuel, Elias and Seth, who came to Pittsfield after him. Seth remained and became a permanent inhabitant, but the others were not permanent, except Elijah, who was for many years an inhabitant previous to his going with his family to South Hero, Vermont (Grand Isle) who sold out there, and returned again to Pittsfield among old acquaintances, perhaps through the influence of his grown children or perhaps to occupy lands which had not yet passed from the family. When the tide of emigration swept over New England and set in so strongly for the state of Ohio, the parents, then in years, buckled on their emigrating outfit and traveled with their children to the great central agricultural state of the Union. Elijah Janes is mentioned on the records of Pittsfield as a juror 7 April, 1773. Again mentioned as being sent with twenty others under Captain William Francis and Lieutenant William Ford, to Williamstown, as minute

17

man, to respond to some sudden call, and then dismissed 21 September, 1776. Again he was similarly sent with sixteen others to New York, under Lieutenant William Barker, 30 September, 1776. They were dismissed 27 November, 1776.

Elijah Janes served with honor and bravery in the war of the revolution. He was among the minute men, and was frequently called out to very great inconvenience to himself and family.

He was afterward a lieutenant in a regiment of dragoons, under Colonel Elisha Sheldon, from 1 January, 1781, to August, 1781, and quartermaster from that time to 1 July, 1782. His record was that of a true, brave and loyal man. He died in Ohio in the year 1826. His wife, Anna, survived him about sixteen years, living to see one hundred years and eight months, a Christian heroine, having seen much of the good hand of God in her life, and having adorned a good profession for many long years. She joined the Congregational Church in 1793, in South Hero, Vermont, under the pastoral charge of Rev. Asa Lyon. She afterward joined the Methodists, so frequently done in the new states, and died in 1842, and was buried on the banks of the Alum creek, in Delaware county, Ohio, to wait, in hope of a glorious resurrection.

> " Her voyage of life's at an end,
>   The mortal affliction is past,
>   The age which in heaven she spends,
>   Forever and ever shall last."

CHILDREN.

246 I.   ANNA, born 1764; married Abraham Church Brown.
247 II.   HEMAN, born 9 June, 1765; married Abigail Burdick.
248 III.   LAVINA, born ......; married Selah Andrews.
249 IV.   HUMPHREY, born 19 December, 1769; married
Thankful Campbell.
250 V.   JOHN, born 12 August, 1771; married Hannah
Rockwell.
251 VI.   ELIJAH, born 1776; married Anna Baker.
252 VII.   OLIVER, born ......; married Jemima Hall.
253 VIII.   DAVID, born 1790; married Martha Smedtz.

125 (V) SAMUEL, SON OF SETH.

Samuel Janes of Coventry, moved to Pittsfield some
time before the war of the revolution. His intention
of marriage to Abigail Brooks of Killingly, Conn.,
was published at Pittsfield, 18 December, 1772,
and they were probably married the 1 January, 1773.
Abigail died 11 October, 1791. Whether he married
a second time in Pittsfield, or lived there after his
second marriage, we are not informed, or of the marriages of the children.

CHILDREN.

254 I.   EUNICE, born 17 Jan. 1774; married Daniel Robertson.
255 II.   PARTHENA, born 2 March, 1775.
256 III.   LUCY, born 22 May, 1777.
257 IV.   ABIGAIL, born 19 July, 1779.
258 V.   ROYAL, born 7 October, 1781.
259 VI.   JOSEPH, born 23 May, 1784; died 1801.
260 VII.   JAMES, born 3 July, 1786; married Elizabeth
Woodruff.

Samuel married (2) Rebecca House, 4 Dec., 1791.

CHILD.

262 IX. SARAH, born 17 September, 1792.

---

126 (VI) ELIAS, SON OF SETH.

Elias Janes also resided for a time in Pittsfield. He married (1) Susan Robertson, 13 February, 1774. She died of consumption in Pittsfield, 16 November, 1787, thirteen years from the time of their marriage.

CHILDREN.

263 I. ELIAS, born 1775; died 21 January, 1776.
264 II. AMELIA, born 1778.
265 III. NATHAN, born 1782; died 17 November, 1787.

Elias married (2) Hannah Thompson, 1788.

CHILDREN.

266 IV. OLIVER, born 29 April, 1789.
267 V. POLLY, born 2 September, 1790; married Chauncey Ellis.
268 VI. STERLING, born 24 December, 1792; married Huldah Loomis.
269 VII. CHAUNCEY, born 11 June, 1795; married Mrs. Susan (Thompson) Sweetland.
270 VIII. HARMONY, born 8 November, 1797; married Silas Giles.
271 IX. CLARISSA, born 9 June, 1801; married Francis Lathrop.

127 (VII) OLIVER, SON OF SETH.

Oliver married Judith Rollo, 22 February, 1775. It has been said they were the handsomest couple that ever went into the Coventry church to be married. A little more than a year and a half from their sweet bridal morning he died, a patriot soldier, in the service of his country, then connected with the army of the United States at East Chester near New York city. He probably died of camp fever, 7 October, 1776, aged only twenty-three.

CHILD.

272 I. SARAH, born 31 January, 1776.

---

128 (VIII) SETH, SON OF SETH.

Captain Seth Janes was a bold, athletic, fearless young man, born on the hills in Coventry, and probably was influenced to go to Pittsfield by his brother Elijah, who was twelve years his senior, and who had fixed himself there, in a comfortable home. He married Elizabeth Francis, daughter of William Francis. He went often to Vermont while engaged in raising an improved stock of horses, as he enjoyed there some better facilities. He is said to have imported the first blooded horses from England.

He imported the Florazella, the North Star and another horse. The first published paper of Pittsfield, contains advertisements of horses kept at his stables.

He lived about a mile from the village west, on the Albany road, on the place now occupied by Mrs. Chapman.   They tell an anecdote of him which may be true.   Once while taking some horses on his jour- ney, he came to very sudden grief, for a spunky, proud young man that knew something of the world.   He stopped to feed his horses in a stranger's field, where grass was plenty if not cheap, and the owner having come that way ordered him off.   He thought he would intimidate the man and not hurry away, and he said to him, "Begone yourself, or I will serve you as I did the man under the blackberry bushes yesterday."   The man left him, and reported the threat to the neigh- bors, who made thorough search and came upon the body of a man who had been killed some days.

Seth Janes was arrested, tried and proving a good character, and the man's body found, being too long -dead, he was cleared from any guilt in that matter on the trial.

By whom that man was killed was not known. Though Seth was now released, he thought of his foolish dodge and his imprudent remark, and never forgot the lesson of that occasion.   He was an ener- getic, nimble man, and when more than three-score years and ten, he could spring upon the saddle like a young man.   He was then a well known and respected citizen of Pittsfield.

Some of the old inhabitants still remember Mrs. Janes, the fine graceful form, habited in her satin pelisse, amiable, kind-hearted, always ready to welcome her friends, who enjoyed under her roof a gladsome visit.

When a young wife, and all Pittsfield was like a forest, she was one day alarmed by a sudden rush, at her cabin door, of the sheep. On opening it, and seeing a ravenous wolf ready for his prey, she took her husband's gun ready loaded, and shot the intruder dead. It was quite a feat, and beautifully accomplished for a refined, unwarlike matron.

CHILDREN.

273 I. WILLIAM, born 30 March, 1782; married Lovina Pepoon.
274 II. ETHAN, born 20 June, 1784; married Charlotte Williams.
275 III. SARAH, born 19 March, 1787 ; married Allen Luce.
276 IV. HENRY, born 28 December, 1792; married Clarissa Belden.

129 (IX) SOLOMON, SON OF SETH.

Solomon Janes married Susanna Trapp of Coventry, 20 July, 1793.

CHILDREN.

277 I. HENRY, born 11 October, 1796.
278 II. SALLY, born ....1788 ; married Mr. Learned.
279 III. WEALTHY, born.........1800 ; married Mr. Bissell.

131 (I) ELISHA, SON OF ELISHA.

Elisha Janes married (1) Elizabeth Davenport, 1763. She had one child.

CHILD.

280 I.   ELIZABETH, born 30 May, 1764; married Malachi Barker of New Lebanon, a traveling preacher.

Elisha married (2) Desire Thompson.

CHILDREN.

281 II.   ROGER, born 7 August, 1767; married Elizabeth Warner.

282 III.   ESTHER, born 17 January, 1769; married Oliver Sanford.

283 IV.   DANIEL, born 9 August, 1770; married Temperance Tinker.

284 V.   ELISHAMA, born 29 January, 1772; married Betsy Jeroloman.

285 VI.   POLLY, born 10 June, 1774; married Cyrus Davis.

286 VII.   NATHANIEL, born 23 September, 1777; married Achsa Barnes.

287 VIII.   JESSE, born 28 June, 1779; married Julia M. Wickham.

288 IX.   LAVINA, born 26 June, 1781; married Obadiah Latham.

289 X.   DAVID, born 27 January, 1783; liberally educated, fine address, but died 1809.

290 XI.   HANNAH, born 11 February, 1787; married Seth Birge.

When Hannah was of age the father looking upon the fine form of his noble looking sons and daughters, the oldest of whom had passed forty, he proposed to

have them weighed and the result was that the average
weight equaled 181 ℔s.   One of the family told the
writer, he was certain it was more than that figure, for
a number of the sons weighed over 250 ℔s.

132 (II) BATHSHEBA, DAUGHTER OF ELISHA.

Bathsheba Janes married John Tilden of Lebanon,
Conn., grandfather of the distinguished Samuel J.
Tilden of New York city.

CHILDREN.

291 I.   LOIS.
292 II. LUCINA.
293 III. ANN.
294 IV. JOHN.
295 V.   OLIVE.
296 VI. CYNTHIA.
297 VII. ELIA, born ....; married Polly Younglove Jones.

Their children were: John, Mary Elizabeth, Moses
Y., Samuel J., a leading democratic lawyer, Henry,
Henrietta, twins.

135 (V) BENJAMIN, SON OF ELISHA.

Benjamin Janes went from Coventry for a time to
Vermont, and returned to make his home among his
kindred.   He lived most of his days, near his native
town, Coventry.

He died, leaving one son.

CHILD.

298 I. BENJAMIN, born July, 1772; married Zebiah Hunt-
            ington.

18

SIXTH GENERATION.

LINE OF ABEL.

147 (I) DAVID, SON OF JONATHAN.

David Janes, born in Brimfield, Mass., emigrated to Vermont with some of his sisters and his brothers, Daniel, and Jonathan or Judge Janes. They settled in Richford, Franklin county, near Lake Champlain. Jonathan moved from Richford to the flourishing village of St. Albans while David continued there. While in Brimfield he married Jemima Vorce in the year 1765.

CHILDREN.

299 I. TIMOTHY, born..........; married Miss Pearce, of Ira, N. Y., and resided there some time.

300 II. BRADFORD, born .... It is said that Bradford and his father went west.

150 (IV) ELIPHALET, SON OF JONATHAN.

Eliphalet Janes was a man of some talent and wit. The customs of the times decoyed some from the paths of temperance, and affected their industrious habits. If he had any such fault, he was a kind hearted, friendly man, even balanced in temper and happy in seeing others happy.

Uncle Liff, as he was commonly called, was famous for extemporaneous and comic poetry. One time meeting a group of his neighbors, one Mr. Day, a Mr. Snow, a Mr. Knight, and a Mr. Winter, he was set upon to give them some verses, *apropos*, in consideration of a treat. He signified assent, and began by saying:

> There was a *Day* in the month of June
> When *Knight* came on before 'twas noon,
> Rough *Winter* at the time passed by,
> And *Snow* it was full six feet high.

At another time Mr. Deane, the miller, wished him to give him a suitable epitaph for his tombstone and so bantered him that he let off the following characteristic strain:

> Under this stone there lies a Deane,
> The biggest cheat that ever was seen,
> He tends his mill both still and whist,
> And for his toll takes half the grist.

He married a very worthy woman, Elfleda Lyon, of Eastford, Conn.

She was aunt to General Lyon, who was killed in Missouri in one of the fiercest struggles for freedom. She was born 27 May, 1749, and died 1 March, 1792. He died, aged ninety-three, in Sturbridge, at the house of his daughter, Mrs. Lucinda Gibbs.

CHILDREN.

301 I.   LUCINDA, born 11 March, 1769; married Zephaniah Gibbs.

302 II.   ROXYLENA, born 29 November, 1771; married Edwin Fox.

303 III.   MARSILVY, born 14 June, 1774; married Benjamin Eastman.

304 IV.   ALFRED, born 9 March, 1776; married Mary Warren.

305 V.   WALTER, born 27 February, 1779; married Cynthia Richards.

306 VI.   ALMARIN, born 11 July, 1781; married (1) Polly Fay, (2) Mrs. Wilcoxon.

307 VII.   BRADFORD, born 6 May, 1784; married Sabra Gibbs.

308 VIII.   SALLY, born 1 December, 1788; married Abijah Richards.

---

152 (VI) SOLOMON, SON OF JONATHAN.

Solomon Janes married Beulah Fisk, born 26 April, 1757.   He died 4 April, 1812, at Calais, Vt.   She died 28 February, 1848.   He was a farmer in Richford, and afterwards moved to Calais.

CHILDREN.

309 I.   NATHAN, born ......; married Celinda Dexter.

310 II.   PARDON, born ......; married at Calais, Vt.

311 III.   HENRY F., born 18 October, 1798; married Fanny Butler.

312 IV.   LORENZO, born 18 September, 1801; married Elvenah Cooper.

313 V.   LORINDA, born.......

314 VI.   BEULAH, born.......

315 VII.   POLLY, born.......

316 VIII.   LUCRETIA, born.......

153 (VII) DANIEL, SON OF JONATHAN.

Daniel Janes moved from Brimfield, Mass., with his brothers, and went to Richford, Vt., and married Annie Saunders, who was born in Charleston, January 24, 1757. They were married in June, 1776. He died in Richford, Vt., March 20, 1809. Mrs. Janes afterwards married Amos Page of Cambridge.

CHILDREN.

317 I.   RACHEL, born 2 May, 1777; married Oliver Skinner.
318 II.   CHARLES, born 5 June, 1779; died, aged 6 years.
319 III. ANNIE, born 10 October, 1782; married T. J. Shepherd.
320 IV.   JEREMIAH, born 2 January, 1785; married Sarah Allen.
321 V.   CHARLES, born 14 March, 1787; died, aged 14 years.
322 VI.   DANIEL, born 25 September, 1789; married (1) Hannah Lathrop, (2) Polly Powell.
323 VII. IRA, born 30 April, 1794; married (1) Precinda Wright, (2) Caroline Breese.
324 VIII. IRENE, born ......; married Mr. Allen.
325 IX.   LYDIA S., born February, 1799; married Mr. Cook.

154 (VIII) MARY, DAUGHTER OF JONATHAN.

Mary Janes married Rowland Powell, and resided in Richford, Vt. She died in October, 1813.

She was a godly woman, and much beloved by her friends and acquaintances.

CHILDREN.

326 I.   BRADFORD, born ......; married Clarissa Goff.
327 II.   JOHN, born ......; married Aurelia Fassett.
328 III. ANNA, born ......; married (1) Daniel Miller, (2) Daniel Cheney.
329 IV.   HORATIO, born ......; married Hannah Russel.
330 V.   LUCY, born ......; married Elisha Smith.
331 VI.   ELFLEDA, born ......; married Mr. ...... Rogers.
332 VII. MARY (Polly), born ......; married a cousin, Daniel Janes.
333 VIII. CHESTER, born ......; married and lived in Missouri.
334 IX.   HORACE, born ......; married Harriet Parker.
335 X.   CYNTHIA, born ......; married Russell Lathrop.
336 XI.   PROSPER, born 7 September, 1795; married Mary Goff.

---

155 (IX) JONATHAN, SON OF JONATHAN.

Jonathan Janes was born in Brimfield, and went from there to the city of Hartford; was engaged in some public business, probably the law, and resided there thirteen years, where he was active, trustworthy and influential. He was a member of the general court and legislature of Connecticut. He was appointed by a land company of Hartford to take charge of their lands in Northern Vermont.

He settled in Richford, and being appointed a judge of the county court, and afterward probate judge, he found it more convenient to reside in St. Albans. He was highly esteemed, and may well be called a candid, worthy, upright judge. His descendants are a numerous train of children, grandchildren and great-grandchildren, now scattered over the country. A fuller and more complete record of this distinguished man should have found page room, but no one was willing to give attention to the subject as it "would not pay" them.

He married Patty Plympton of Sturbridge, in 1780, and died 30 June, 1823.

CHILDREN.

337 I.   HORACE, born 18 September, 1781; married (1) Catharine Barnard, (2) M. Brown, (3) E. S. Partridge.
338 II. CYNTHIA, born 8 July, 1783; married Ebenezer Marvin.
339 III. RUBY, born 9 May, 1785; married (1) E. Hubbard, (2) Rev. Asaph Morgan.
340 IV. MARTHA, born 2 July, 1787; married (1) William Foote, (2) William H. Wilkins.
341 V.   JONATHAN, born 23 March, 1789, congregational clergyman.
342 VI. GERSHOM, born 3 October, 1790.
343 VII. HENRY NEWELL, born 1 June, 1792; married Betsy Allis.
344 VIII. JULIA A., born 15 October, 1794; married Jason C. Pierce.
345 IX. CHARLOTTE, born 22 May, 1796.
346 X.   LEWIS MARCY, born 6 February, 1798; married Abbey P. Allyn.
347 XI. DWIGHT P., born 31 July, 1801; married Jane W. Flynn.
348 XII. FRANCES R., born 24 June, 1802; married Luther Conklin.

SIXTH GENERATION.

LINE OF ABEL.

162 (I) WILLIAM, SON OF WILLIAM.

William Janes, of Brimfield, had a large family of daughters and sons. We know of but one of their sons getting married, and two of their daughters. A number of them died young and unmarried. He married Nabby Belknap, of Holland, Mass., and he died 31 December, 1841.

CHILDREN.

349 I. CAPHIRA, born 15 February, 1782; married Jacob Sherman; died 23 March, 1837.

350 II. ALBAN, born 16 September, 1783; married Mary Bliss.

351 III. SOPHIA, born 14 August, 1785; married Barzillia Sherman; died 29 August, 1841.

352 IV. DEXTER, born 13 November, 1787; died at the South, 2 October, 1813.

353 V. HANNAH, born 11 March, 1790; married Mr. Putnam.

354 VI. BETSEY, born 27 January, 1792; died February, 1816.

355 VII. ORIL, born 8 July, 1794; died 23 November, 1824.

356 VIII. NORMAN, born 29 April, 1796; died 13 October, 1798.

357 IX. EUDOCIA, born 25 September, 1798; unmarried.

358 X. HARRIET, born 13 December, 1800; unmarried; died November, 1865.

163 (II) PELEG C., SON OF WILLIAM.

Peleg C. Janes of Brimfield, married Patty Coy of Royalston, Vt., 24 January, 1782, and resided in Brimfield.

CHILDREN.

359 I.   AUGUSTUS, born 12 May, 1787; married Betsey Bingham, Royalston, Vt.

360 II.   CYNTHIA, born 19 February, 1788; married Mr. Gregg.

361 III.   TIMOTHY, born 28 April, 1791; married Lydia Tyler.

362 IV.   FLAVILLA, born 15 April, 1793; married Mr. Ward.

363 V.   ADOTIA, born 18 March, 1795; died 1817.

364 VI.   CLEMENTINA, born 24 July, 1802; married Edward Parsons.

365 VII.   WILLIAM C., born 5 July, 1805; married Adelphia Fuller.

---

171 (X) SIMON, SON OF WILLIAM.

Simon Janes married Chloe Shumway of Sturbridge, where they now reside.

CHILDREN.

366 I.   LEWIS, born......, 1775. (?)

367 II.   EDWARD, born......, 1777. (?)

368 III.   GEORGE, born......, 1780. (?)

173 (II) ISRAEL CHAMPION, SON OF ELIJAH.

Israel Champion Janes went from Brimfield, Mass., when a young man, to Cornwall, Vt. He *moved* on horseback according to the custom of that day, and manifested indomitable energy and perseverance in subduing the then virgin forest around the place, and in preparing the young town of Cornwall to shine brightly in the galaxy of towns in that part of the state, and in rendering it an abode of comfort for true civilization, for educational and religious refinement.

He was among the first settlers of the town, and one of the leading citizens of that now flourishing and wealthy township.

It is a good farming town, and is of late famous for trade in the finer grades of Spanish Merino sheep. Some bucks raised there have sold for a number of thousand dollars, and some fortunes have been made by the traffic; and some sheepy ones have had the wool too thickly pulled over their eyes by the crafty.

Most of the descendants of Israel C. Janes are deceased or moved away.

His excellent, only living, son resides on the old homestead, and is a worthy representative of the name. Israel C. was a good man — reliable, worthy, active and Christian. He lived to a good old age, adorned with Christian virtues, and endowed with substance.

He married (1) Mary Ann Marsh, 1787; and (2) Lucina Reeves, who was born 11 April, 1767.

CHILDREN.

369 I. HORACE, born 16 October, 1789; married Lucretia Bascom.

370 II. ELIJAH, born 27 January, 1791; died 28 June, 1791.

371 III. LUCY, born 14 March, 1792; married Asa Bond.

372 IV. ANNA, born 24 December, 1793; married Rufus Mead.

373 V. ELIJAH, born 3 September, 1795; died 16 August, 1796.

Israel C. married (2) Lucina Reeves.

CHILDREN.

374 VI. MARY, born 25 April, 1799; died an infant.

375 VII. LUCINA, born 25 August, 1801; married John Mayhew, of Parishville, N. Y.

376 VIII. POLLY, born 7 March, 1803; married Nathan Parker of Bethel, Vt.

377 IX. ELECTA, born 16 March, 1805.

378 X. BETSEY, born 15 November, 1807.

---

175 (IV) CYRUS, SON OF ELIJAH.

Cyrus Janes married (1) Lovinia Holbrook, of Sturbridge, who was born 1764; (2) Electa Williston of Springfield, who died 1836. He resided on the farm left by his father, and owned by the family from the settlement of the town.

CHILDREN.

379 I. ABEL, born 3 August, 1794; married Eurydice Greenwood, of Hebron, Me.

380 II. HORACE, born 9 June, 1796; married Almira Dole.

381 III. ALVAN, born 5 April, 1798; died 25 October, 1799.
382 IV. ALVAN, born 19 January, 1800; married Mary
          Homer.
383 V.   AUSTIN, born 18 September, 1801; unmarried. A
          physician.
384 VI. VELINA, born 24 July, 1803; married (1) Nathan
          Hitchcock, (2) William Tucker.
385 VII. HARVEY, born 15 January, 1806; married Screpta
          Harding.
386 VIII. SOPHIA, born 18 January, 1809; married.........
          Cutting.

Horace was for a time a wealthy Wall street broker,
inheriting his uncle Elijah's fortune. His style of life
and mind-wearing business did not tend to prolong
his days. He died 5 May, 1844, in New York city.
Dr. Austin went into practice in Macon, Ga., and
died 28 October, 1829.

176 (V) LUCY, DAUGHTER OF ELIJAH.

Lucy Janes married Wait Wooster, in Waterbury,
Conn., b. 28 October, 1764. They lived in Cornwall,
Vt., and raised a large and honored family. She died
1 May, 1825, and he died 16 November, 1829.

CHILDREN.

387 I.   DORASTUS J., born 6 October, 1799; married Hannah
          S. Gates.
388 II. ABEL J., born 27 November, 1802; married Harriet
          Gates.
389 III. MARY S., born 9 January, 1807; married John Foote.
390 IV. BENJAMIN P., born 6 July, 1814; married Hannah
          Warner.

177 (VI) PARTHENA, DAUGHTER OF ELIJAH.

Parthena Janes married Asa Backus of Franklin, Conn., where they lived in the enjoyment of connubial felicity in their younger days, and afterwards they moved to Norwich, and there spent the remaining days of their earthly life. They were married about 1790.

CHILDREN.

391 I.   SIMON, born 17 July, 1792 ; married Elizabeth Spicer.
392 II.   ELIJAH, born 15 July, 1796; married Joanna R. Ellis.
393 III.   MARY, born 21 September, 1799 ; married Lewis Hyde.
394 IV.   ASA, born 7 April, 1805 ; married Caroline Rooth.

Simon died 1823 : Asa died 1836.

SIMON had one son, Elijah Janes Backus.

ELIJAH J. had a son Rev. Joseph W. Backus, who married Martha Woodward of Watertown, Conn. He had beside Julia R., Eunice J.

ASA had two daughters and a son. Daughter Caroline married Rev. Joseph Bloomer, who died. She afterward married C. Lewis Dunlop, and she died 26 August, 1861, at Norwich.

Cynthia M. married Charles W. Dennison, 17 April, 1861.

Asa married Julia W. Bissell.

MARY, only daughter of Asa and Parthena Backus, married Lewis Hyde of Franklin, who moved to Norwich. They had Lewis A., George R., and Mary P. J.

Lewis married (1) Annie C. Webster ; (2) Mary E. Huntington ; they had Mary A., Lewis H., William Trumbull.

George R. married Clara S. Dickey.

Mary Parthena Janes Hyde married Thomas L., Stedman : she died 4 September, 1852; he died 9 April, 1853.

Mary Eunice Stedman was born 22 September, 1846 ; their only living child. Her only brother died at the age of two years.

———

179 (VIII) POLLY, DAUGHTER OF ELIJAH.

Polly Janes married Eli Stone, a teacher by profession. While in conversation he suddenly fell from his seat and expired. He had been laboring through the day, and some vital disturbance of the system at once caused death. Polly died 13 July, 1852.

CHILDREN.

395 I.   LUCY, born......, 1794 (?); married ......; died 1807.

396 II.   ISAAC, born......, 1706 (?); married Anna Howe.

397 III.   BETSEY, born......, 1798 (?); married Jesse Ellsworth of Cornwall, Vt.

398 IV.   MARY, born ......, 1800 (?); married Benjamin Williams of Goshen, Ill.

399 V.   SILAS, born ......, 1802 (?); married Susan Brown.

400 VI.   ELI, born ......, 1804 (?); married (1) Pamelia Hulbert, (2) Anna Landon.

401 VII.   HIRAM, born 1805 (?); married Irene Jones.

402 VIII.   LYMAN, born ......, 1807 (?); killed by falling of a tree in Ohio, æ. 33.

403 IX.   LUCY, born ......, 1809 (?); married Myron M. Blake of Cornwall, Vt.

404 X.   ELIJAH J., born ......, 1811 (?); married Laura Watkins, now of Michigan.

Isaac J. had one daughter who married a Mr. Cummings of Poland, Me. Silas had a daughter who married a Mr. Wiggins of Michigan.

Lucy Blake has one or two sons in the ministry, and of considerable promise, of the Congregational order.

———

180 (IX) ELISHA, SON OF ELIJAH.

Elisha Janes married Bethia Huntington, whose brother, Robert, was a lawyer in Lansingburgh. Mrs. B. H. Janes was a true and beloved woman in the circle of her friends. Her Christian fortitude sustained her in her many trials which intemperance brought to her abode. Her husband, Elisha, died 1828. She lived to 27 October, 1851, and then died.

CHILDREN.

405 I.   HARRIET, born 1 December, 1800.
406 II. ELIJAH, born ......, 1803.
407 III. LAURA, born ......, 1805.
408 IV. Mary Jane born ......, 1809.
409 V.   OLIVE, born ......, 1812.

Olive was a teacher at the south, and then afterwards went west.

———

181 (X) LIBERTY, SON OF ELIJAH.

Liberty Janes married Clarinda Fuller of Shoreham, Vt. They moved from there to Berkshire, in 1800, when the country was new, and the most hardy pioneers were required to subdue the virgin forests. He was a man of great industry and perseverance, and went through many hardships to open the way for social comforts and suitable prosperity in old age. For himself and children he prepared a good, quiet home. He died there in 1851, with the respect of all who knew him.

CHILDREN.

410 I. ISAAC, resides in Canada.
411 II. NELSON L., sold the homestead, and went west.

---

182 (XI) PROPERTY, SON OF ELIJAH.

Property Janes married Charlotte Psalmist, and lived and died in Shaftsbury Vt. Mrs. Janes was a sister of Mrs. Governor Galusha, who was in the chair of state about 1813.

CHILDREN.

412 I. ISAAC, born 18 January, 1809.
413 II. DELIA, born 22 September, 1810.

---

183 (I) ORSAMUS, SON OF ISRAEL.

Orsamus Janes married Ruth Shepherd, who was born 1793, in Warren, Mass.

CHILDREN.

414 I. RUTH C., born......, 1803; married Philomel Moon of Brimfield.
415 II. MARY ELIZA, born......, 1805; married Frederick H. Purington of Bristol Conn.
416 III. NANCY ELMIRA, born......, 1807; married John Ross of Kansas.
417 IV. EUNICE C., born......, 1809; married Jonathan Emerson.

189 (VII) LEVI, SON OF ISRAEL.

Levi Janes married Mary Lombard of Brimfield, about 1802.

CHILDREN.

418 I.   SUMNER, born......
419 II.   DEXTER, born......
420 III. CHLOE MATILDA, born......, 1801 ; married Mr. Osgood.
421 IV. TIRZA, born......; married Mr. Pierce.
422 V.   LYMAN, born......
423 VI. NANCY, born......
424 VII. MARIA, born......
425 VIII. NANCY, born......
426 IX. JOSEPH, born......

SIXTH GENERATION.

LINE OF WILLIAM.

192 (I) WILLIAM, SON OF WILLIAM.

William Janes married Margaret Sybert in Maryland, about the year 1770.

CHILDREN.

427 I.   HENRY, born......, 1771.
428 II.   ELEANOR, born......, 1773.
429 III. WILLIAM, born......, 1775.
430 IV. JOHN, born......, 1777.
431 V.   SAMUEL, born......, 1779.
432 VI. EDWARD, born......, 1783 ; died 1861.
433 VII. ELIZABETH, born......, 1785.   `
434 VIII. MARGARET, born......, 1787.

John was probably Captain John Janes, or the Janes mentioned as connected with the 7th Maryland Regiment, Colonel Greenby.

195 (IV) THOMAS, SON OF WILLIAM.

Thomas Janes lived and died in Richmond, Va. He was an architect of some distinction, and many of the buildings now standing were erected under his superintendence. He became comparatively wealthy, and died in the prime of manhood. He married Miss Reams.

CHILDREN.

435 I.   WILLIAM, born 9 December, 1771; married Selah Greshom.
436 II. SUSAN, born......; died young.
437 III. LOVICIA, born......; married Mr. Evans.

199 (I) BENJAMIN, SON OF THOMAS.

Benjamin Janes, son of Thomas and Rachel Lines Janes, was born in Wallingford, Conn., and moved to Sheffield, Mass., adjoining the line of Connecticut, and was a carpenter and joiner. He married Sally Wood, who was born in Chatham, 9th June, 1773. They were respectable and industrious people, and raised up to manhood and womanhood a large family of children, some of them well known to the world.

CHILDREN.

438 I. ESTHER MARIA, born 10 December, 1798; married
        Amasa Barden.
439 II. SARAH SOPHRONIA, born 1 August, 1800; married
        Ira Adams.
440 III. HAMILTON B., born 29 July, 1804; married Edith
        Wentworth.
441 IV. EDMUND STORER (twin), born 27 April, 1807;
        married Charlotte Thibeau.
442 V. EDWIN LINES (twin), born 27 April, 1807; married
        Elizabeth Ogden.
443 VI. HANNAH ELIZA, born 9 September, 1809; married
        John A. Elliott.
444 VII. JOHN WOOD, born 7 September, 1811; married A.
        S. Hatch, (2) H. M. L. Deming.
445 VIII. ALMOND T., born 29 May, 1813; married Lucia
        Wilcox.

200 (II) THOMAS M., SON OF THOMAS.

Thomas M. Janes was a soldier of the war of 1812,
and died at some fort on Lake Erie. He married some
years before the war: (1) Miss......., and went out west
where he had one son, and losing his wife he returned
to Wallingford, Conn., and married again.

CHILD.

446 I. THOMAS, remained west.

Thomas married (2) Lucy Janes.

CHILDREN.

447 II. RACHEL, born ......; married John Lane.
448 III. DAMARIS, born 30 May, 1807; married Albert Judd.
449 IV. ELIZA, born ......
450 V. LUCINDA, born ......; married Charles Blackman.

203 (V) SARAH, DAUGHTER OF THOMAS.

Sarah Janes married Alexander Hine. Living apart from their relatives, their families are not well known.

CHILDREN.

451 I. HIRAM, born ......; resides in Wallingford.
452 II. ALEXANDER, born ......; married James Peck.
453 III. PHILANDER, born ......; resides in Waterbury.

SIXTH GENERATION.

LINE OF SAMUEL.

205 (II) NOAH, SON OF SAMUEL.

Captain Noah Janes was an officer of the army of the government, to quash the Shays rebellion. Afterward, when others emigrated to Vermont, he went with the tide, to Vergennes, for settlement, and married 11 January, 1776, Naomi Strong, who was born at Sheldon, 18 July, 1757. He was a farmer and a good citizen.

CHILDREN.

454 I.   PATTY, born 16 September, 1776; married Solomon Strong.
455 II. NAOMI, born 1 August, 1778; married Sylvester Lyman.
456 III. SYLVANUS, born 6 September, 1780; married Laura McNamara.

457 IV. NOAII, born 29 April, 1783; married Sally Currier.
458 V. CIIESTER, born 8 September, 1785; married Anne Fish.
459 VI. ELECTA, born 12 November, 1789.
460 VII. SAMUEL, born 26 January, 1790.
461 VIII. LUCAS (twin), born 1793; married Sally Wood.
462 IX. JULIUS (twin), born 1793; married Nancy Eggleston.
463 X. LEWIS, born 27 August, 1795; married IIuldah Wilder.

. 206 (II) SAMUEL, SON OF SAMUEL.

Samuel Janes married ......, and lived at Watertown, Mass.

CHILDREN.

464 I. MARY, born ......; married Ebenezer Billings.
465 II. LUCRETIA, born ......; married Elijah Morgan.

208 (III) HANNAH, DAUGHTER OF SAMUEL.

Hannah Janes married Uriel Clark, 30 December, 1784.

CHILDREN.

466 I. URIEL, born 21 October, 1786.
467 II. SAMUEL, born 16 June, 1789.
468 III. PHILIP, born 25 April, 1791.
469 IV. SUSANNA, born 9 March, 1795.
470 V. ANNA, born 9 July, 1799; died young.
471 VI. ANNA, born 21 June, 1802.

209 (VI) ENOS, SON OF SAMUEL.

Enos Janes married Hannah Wright, about the year 1788, at Northampton.

CHILDREN.

472 I.   NANCY, born ......; married Zenas Sykes, West-
           borough.
473 II.   LOVISA, born ......; married David Montague.
474 III. MELZER, born ......
475 IV.   LUKE, born . ....; married Dorothy Wright.
476 V.   HELENA, born ......; married Dwight Lyman.
477 VI.   MELZER, born ......
478 VII. SAMUEL, born ......; married Sarah Parsons.

---

210 (VII) SETH, SON OF SAMUEL.

Seth Janes married Mary Ferry, about 1797.

CHILDREN.

479 I.   ASENAH, born 1799 (?); married Lowell Janes.
480 II. MARY, born 1801 (?); married Jason Janes.

---

211 (VIII) SARAH, DAUGHTER OF SAMUEL.

Sarah Janes married Matthew Caldwell.

CHILDREN.

481 I.   SARAH, born ......
482 II.   JANES, born ......
483 III. ARETAS, born ......
484 IV.   WINDSOR, born ......
485 V.   ADELIA, born ......
486 VI.   AN INFANT, born ......
487 VII. HANNAH, born ......

212 (I) EBENEZER, SON OF JONATHAN.

Ebenezer Janes settled in Otisco, state of New York, and married 13 May, 1790, Submit Clark, born 12 April, 1766.

CHILDREN.

488 I.   SUBMIT, born 22 March, 1791; married Thomas King, Otisco.

489 II.   MORRIS, born 22 May, 1792; married Betsey Hickox.

490 III. FIDELIA, born 22 Nov., 1793; married Apollos King.

491 IV.   HANNAH, born 11 September, 1795; married Timothy Boardman.

492 V.   EBENEZER, born 4 Aug., 1797; married Phebe Wells.

493 VI.   EDWARD, born 2 September, 1799; married Sally H. Hare, born in Pa., 1 November, 1800.

494 VII. OTIS, born 10 April, 1801; married Sophronia Beardsley.

495 VIII. HARVEY, born 4 Feb., 1803; married Virena Cowles.

496 IX.   CHAUNCEY, born 16 December, 1805.

497 X.   PHILENA, born 6 June, 1807; married Nelson Boardman.

213 (II) JONATHAN, SON OF JONATHAN.

Lieut. Jonathan lived at Northampton, and was the father of a large and influential family. He married (1) 1793, Rachel Clark.

CHILDREN.

498 I.   LOWELL, born 23 Feb., 1794; marrried Asenah Janes.

499 II.   JONATHAN, born 15 Oct., 1797.

500 III. RACHEL, born ......; 1798; married Ezekiel White, who died 1842.

501 IV.   ABIGAIL, born ......; died infant.

502 v.   JASON, ...; 1800; married Mary Janes.
503 vi.   ABIGAIL, born ......; died infant.
504 vii.   SPENCER, born 1807; married Jennette Avery, died
           1854.
505 viii. ABIGAIL, born ......

Jonathan married (2) Mary Kingsley.

---

214 (III) OBADIAH, SON OF JONATHAN.

Obadiah Janes was a merchant for some years in
East Hampton, and also town clerk for the town.
He was a pleasant, kind-hearted, agreeable gentleman,
a whole-souled companion and friend.   He married 29
November, 1799, (1) Esther Lyman, who was born 19
October, 1779, and died 28 September, 1813.

CHILDREN.

506 i.   THEODORE, born 13 August, 1800; married Caro-
           line Ward.
507 ii.   OBADIAH L., born 30 December, 1801; died 29
           January, 1810.
508 iii.   FRANCIS, born 18 May, 1803; married Emily A.
           Marsh.
509 iv.   ESTHER, born 14 Dec., 1804; married Coleman Clark.
510 v.   JUSTUS L., born 1 September, 1808; married
           Abigail Ely.
511 vi.   ALEXANDER II., born 6 January, 1810; married at
           Sheffield, Ill.
512 vii.   OLIVER E., born 1 Nov., 1811; died 15 August, 1814.
513 viii. LYDIA, born 11 January, 1813; died 13 July, 1838.

Obadiah married (2) Mary Chapman, who was born
20 July, 1778, and died 25 April, 1820.

CHILDREN.

514 IX. OLIVER E., born 25 August, 1815; married Elvira Hope.

515 X. OBADIAH, born 8 Feb. 1817; died 10 April, 1817.

516 XI. MARY CHARLOTTE, born 16 May, 1818; married Edward Sackett of Hartford, 30 October, 1839.

Obadiah married (3) Elizabeth Davis, 16 October, 1822. She was born 16 January, 1789.

CHILDREN.

517 XII. JULIA STRONG, born 27 July, 1824; married James C. Miller.

518 XIII. OBADIAH LYMAN, born 4 June, 1826; married Rhoda Ann Smith.

519 XIV. EBENEZER DAVIS, born 18 September. 1831; married Sarah C. Long, and resides at Des Moines, Iowa.

215 (IV) PARSONS, SON OF JONATHAN.

Parsons Janes was a respectable citizen of East Hampton, and married Dorcas Clark, 31 October, 1805.

CHILDREN.

519a I. DORCAS, born 1 March, 1807; married Joel Parsons.

520 II. TRYPHENA, born 27 Oct., 1808; married William Clapp.

521 III. ALFRED, born 9 April, 1810; died young.

522 IV. JULIA, born 11 Dec., 1811; married Charles E. Wait.

523 V. LOIS, born 27 Dec., 1812; married Horace Clark.

524 VI. MARIA, born 16 Dec., 1814; married Chester Wait.

525 VII. HARRIET, born 4 Oct., 1817; married Charles E. Wait.

526 VIII. ALFRED EDWIN, born 26 December, 1819; married Catharine Wright.

527 IX. EMILY, born 3 Oct., 1821; married William Clapp.
528 X.   GEORGE LEWIS, born 14 May, 1823; died young.
529 XI. ELVIRA, born 13 Oct., 1827; married Waldo Prouty.
530 XII. MARY ANN, born 31 Aug., 1829; died young.

---

216 (V) REBECCA married Daniel Wright.

CHILD.

531 I. REBECCA, born ......; married Elijah Morgan.

---

217 (VI) LOIS married Deacon Solomon Lyman.

CHILDREN.

532 I.   THEODOCIA, born ......; died young.
533 II. THEODOCIA, born ......; married Julius Edwards.
534 III. LOIS, born ......; married Asenah Parsons, (2) Philip
         Clark.
535 IV. SUSAN, born ......; married Elisha Lyman.
536 V.   SON, born ......; died an infant.
537 VI   SOLOMON, born 11 Jan., 1795; married Mary Curtis.
538 VII. MERCY, born 31 March, 1796.

---

219 (I) SARAH, DAUGHTER OF ELISHA.

Sarah Janes married Asahel Parsons, in April, 1798,
and lived in East Hampton.

CHILDREN.

539 I.   CHAUNCEY, born ......, 1799; married Anna Clark.
540 II. SARAH, born ......, 1801; married Thaddeus Parsons.
541 III. EDMOND, born ......; 1803; married Emeline Morgan.

220 (II) RACHEL, DAUGHTER OF ELISHA.

Rachel Janes married Joel Parsons, 27 April, 1797, of whom descended.

CHILDREN.

542 I.   RACHEL, born ...... ;
543 II.   RALPH, born ...... ;
544 III. JOEL, born ...... ;
545 IV.   HENRY, born ...... ;
546 V.   LUMAN, born ...... ;
547 VI.   DIXALANA, born ...... ;
548 VII. CLIMENA, born ...... ;
549 VIII. OBADIAH, born ...... ;

227 (I) JONATHAN, SON OF EBENEZER.

Jonathan Janes was a highly esteemed citizen of Northfield. The family lived a little east on a rise of. the mountain, and was at a convenient distance for many merry visits from their friends on the street.

Their relatives the Fields, Mattoons, and Janeses, made many a friendly call, and possibly a few selfish ones in the spring, when all were cheerful and merry around the golden maple sugar, the syrup or the wax which was cooled upon the white driven snow, and crackled in the mouth.

How great the change from our boyhood. The house and farm remain. The maples are cut down for fuel. The family are scattered; and the majority passed from earth.

Time works out its own changes, and hushes many a gleeful and innocent voice, and curtains with the somber shades of mourning.

Jonathan married 1777, Caroline Mattoon, daughter of Dr. Elihu Mattoon, she was born 6 December, 1757; she died 15 August, 1821.   He died 23 March, 1813.

CHILDREN.

550	I.	ELIHU, born 27 July, 1778; married Sarah Jarvis.
551	II.	ONDA, born 18 Nov., 1780; married Horace Wright.
552	III.	HENRY, born 29 July, 1782; drowned 17 April, 1805.
553	IV.	ROBERT, born 7 June, 1784; unmarried; died 2 July, 1819.
554	V.	CAROLINE, born 23 March, 1787; married Noah Perry.
555	VI.	SALLY, born 23 Jan., 1789; married Arnold Cook.
556	VII.	JONATHAN, born 29 Jan., 1791; married Harriet Cheney.
557	VIII.	ABIGAIL, born 29 May, 1792; married Richard Lyman.
558	IX.	PHILENA, born 5 April, 1794; married Jacob Newcomb.
559	X.	CYNTHIA, born 23 March, 1797; married Thomas Russel.
560	XI.	MARY T., born 14 June, 1799; unmarried; died 25 September, 1812.
561	XII.	WILLIAM, born 7 Sept., 1802; married Mrs. Clark, 14 December, 1829.

Mrs. Clark was the mother of Richard P. Clark, a thorough business man, a merchant in New York city. He is a thinker, a speaker, and clear minded Sabbath school teacher, and active in works of benevolence.

228 (II) JEMIMA, DAUGHTER OF EBENEZER.

Jemima Janes married 1772, John Allen.

CHILDREN.

562 I.   HANNAH, born 9 Oct., 1773; married Joseph Bell of Colrain.

563 II. SARAH, born Feb., 1775; married Wm. Henderson, (2) John Williams; she died 1842.

564 III. LUCY, born April, 1776; married Nathan Cary.

565 IV. JEMIMA, born 3 Dec., 1777; married John Bates.

566 V. RHODA, born 3 March, 1779; married Jeremiah Dean.

567 VI. JOHN, born 9 Oct., 1781; married Mary Kingman.

568 VII. ERASTUS, born 15 May, 1783; married Paulina Wilder.

569 VIII. MARY, born ......, 1785; married John Cary.

229 (III) RUTH, DAUGHTER OF EBENEZER.

Ruth Janes married Calvin Bliss, 1776.

CHILDREN.

570 I.   RUBY, born ......, 1777.

571 II. PHILENA, born ......

572 III. HULDAH, born ......; married Mr. Murdock.

573 IV. SOLOMON, born ......; married Miss Hibbard.

574 V. RUTH, born ......

575 VI. MEHITABLE, born ......

576 VII. CALVIN, born ......

577 VIII. BREWSTER, born ......

230 (IV) OBADIAH, SON OF EBENEZER.

Obadiah Janes was brought up to the work of the farm. He lived a few years on a farm bought for him by his father, Deacon Ebenezer, about three miles from the village of Northfield, known as the Perry place by later generations. He afterwards bought lands in Bridport, Vt., and sojourned there a number of years.

When Ohio opened her arms, to receive so joyfully the sons of New England, he sold out, and took his family to what is now called East Cleveland. Here he secured good homes for his children, and enjoyed the fruits of his labors to a good old age.

When nearly sixty years of age, he visited his eastern friends, going all the journey on foot, out and back, without any apparent difficulty. He was a short and thick set man, as were the majority of this line of the Janeses.

He married (1) Polly Oliver, daughter of John, of Athol; (2) Harmony Bingham. She died 2 August, 1823.

CHILDREN.

578 I.   POLLY, born 19 March, 1787; married Joel Doolittle; died 22 Feb., 1815.

579 II.   JABEZ, born 24 Jan., 1789; died 24 Sept., 1813.

580 III.   MALINDA, born 5 Sept., 1791; married (1) Otis Munn, (2) Samuel Chapin; died Nov., 1817.

581 IV.   OLIVER, born 24 Sept., 1793; married Hannah Clement.

582 V.   HARMONY, born 2 Sept., 1795; married Adolphus Hosley; died 15 Oct., 1854.

583 vi. NAOMI, born 4 Aug., 1797; married Wm. Mitchel.

584 vii. LAURA, born 27 Aug., 1799; died 6 March, 1833.

585 viii. ALONZO, born 21 Sept., 1802; married (1) Mary Ann Disbrow, (2) Harriet Convers.

586 ix. JOHN, born 24 Feb., 1804; died 25 Oct., 1817.

587 x. SOPHIA, born 11 June, 1806; married Asbury Sabine.

588 xi. LUCRETIA, born 13 April, 1808; married 1828, Solomon Dunton; died in Iowa, 1852.

589 xii. HARRIS, born 21 June, 1810; married 1834, Julia King; died 1843.

231 (V) SALIMA, DAUGHTER OF EBENEZER.

Salima Janes was a social, kind, Christian mother, full of goodness and hospitality. She was a warm and true friend, and beloved by her family.

CHILDREN.

590 i. OTIS, born 28 Sept., 1784; married Melinda Janes, a cousin, and moved to Ohio.

591 ii. SYLVIA, born 1 May, 1788; married Samuel Chapin.

592 iii. SETH, born 15 Aug., 1789; married Gratia Wright, (2) Melitta Griswold, (3) Elvira D. Philips.

593 iv. SOPHIA, born 15 April, 1792; died young.

594 v. ORA, born 17 Feb., 1794; married Orralina Hosley.

595 vi. RHODA, born 10 Aug., 1796; married Henry Bascom.

596 vii. OBADIAH, born 26 Oct., 1798; married Orrilla Adgate, moved to Ohio.

597 viii. LUTHER, born 25 Jan., 1800; married Mrs. Lucinda Mayo.

233 (VI) SAMUEL, SON OF EBENEZER.

Samuel Janes was a quiet, thoughtful, domestic citizen, attentive to his own duties, seldom out of town or away from the family circle. He was a broad, stout built, short man, strong and athletic. He could easily take two full bags of corn from the wagon, or cast and swing them on his shoulders, right and left, and carry them into his mill.

He joined the Methodist church in middle life, and was by far the most liberal contributor towards the church edifice, which is still standing, a monument of his beneficence. When the district needed a school-house, and the neighbors were unwilling to do their part, he gave the land, and paid principally, the expenses. He raised up a large family, and some of his sons were the most strong and athletic men in the state.

He married Susan Merriman, 1786.

CHILDREN.

598 I.   HARRIS, born 29 Nov., 1687; married Harriet W.
            . Mason; died 1864.
599 II.   MARY, born 8 Dec., 1789.
600 III.   POLLY, born 1793; married Alvah Ballard died
            1864.
601 IV.   SUSAN, born ......; died an infant.
602 V.   SALLY, born 25 July, 1794; married Eliphaz Chapin.
603 VI.   SUSAN, born 1 March, 1795.
604 VII.   HANNAH, born 1 Aug., 1800.
605 VIII.   SYLVANUS, born 8 March, 1804; married Eunice
            Moore; died 1865.

606 IX. SAMUEL, born 25 Dec., 1806; married Eveline
Ballard.

607 X. ALEXANDER, born August, 1810; married Martha
Moody.

236 (X) ZENOPHON, SON OF EBENEZER.

Deacon Zenophon Janes followed more nearly in
the path of his honored father than either of his
brothers, all of whom carried themselves honorably
through life. He was chosen town clerk, and held
the office through the balance of his natural life, as did .
his father. He was also an officer in the church, and
a representative in the general court, as was his father.
He maintained a good standing in whatever position
he was called to occupy.

He was universally regarded as a man of worth, of
sterling integrity, and unflinching justice. Social in
habit, he cultivated a large acquaintance, and from
the households of numerous relatives, there was a
constant contribution of company to the old fireside,
and sometimes to repletion. The numerous relatives and friends always found a warm welcome
around this domestic hearthstone. The hand of
kindness was always extended to the less fortunate,
and Christian love generally shone in this domestic
circle, during a period of many changes in the domestic realm, and the many dark shadowings of time.
When death threw his sable mantle over a mourning household, the mind that had counseled and

22

the heart that had loved, was indeed hushed in the
silent shadows of death. The nine children were all
then living, and some of them had large families. He
married Sarah (Sally) Patric of Windsor, Vt., 27
January, 1796. She was born November, 1775, and
died 3 May, 1814. He married (2), Tirza Childs 'of
Deerfield, 6 January, 1824. She died 5 April, 1858.
He died 21 October, 1829.

Sally Patric was the daughter of Samuel, born in Voluntown,
Conn. Her grandfather was from the north of Ireland, a
protestant, and had been for some time master and owner of a
vessel. Having been prosperous, he concluded that he would
make only one more voyage. But he left home never to return,
for his ship, it is believed, was foundered at sea. Sally Patric's
mother was a Miss Spicer. She died in middle life, and her
father married (2), Isabella Alexander. So that in her my
great aunt (she being sister to my grandmother, Mehitable
Alexander Janes), I had a step-grandmother. Thus, Sally
Patric had a number of brothers and sisters, and half-brothers
and sisters.

Isabella's son, Matthew, who is noticed below, if he had
lived, would have ranked senior officer of the army of the
United States, after the retirement of General Scott.

Note.—When some of the northern army were at Williamsport, Va., a place named after General Otho Holland Williams,
a distinguished hero and patriot in the armies of the United
States, who founded Williamsport in 1787, they noticed his
old tombstone; but the one which especially attracted their
attention, and interested a native Vermonter, and told its history
to a New Englander, and which has made many of the boys
look up the history of Maryland, is as follows : "In memory of
Capt. Matthew Alexander Patric, U. S. Army, born in Windsor, Vermont, April 13, 1794. Died in Williamsport, March

6, 1834. He was detached from Fort McHenry with his company for the security of this place, and died after a short illness, beloved and lamented."

CHILDREN.

608 I.   MEHITABLE, born 27 Oct., 1796; married Medad Alexander.

609 II.   AMY, born 21 May, 1798; unmarried.

610 III.   ISABEL, born 26 Dec., 1799; married John Howland.

611 IV.   PASCHAL, born 13 April, 1801; married Jane E. Hiller.

612 V.   SAMUEL, born 3 March, 1803; married Sarah Parsons.

613 VI.   SARAH, born 5 June, 1804; married Wait Cannon.

614 VII.   EBENEZER, born 4 March, 1806; married Martha Billings.

615 VIII.   FREDERIC, born 6 May, 1808; married (1) Paulina Burnell, (2) Rachel B. Trusdell.

616 IX.   MARY ANN, born 30 July, 1809; married Augustine Stebbins.

SHAYS'S REBELLION.—A slight rebellion broke out in Massachusetts soon after the close of the revolutionary war, excited by the popular discontent which so naturally grows up from a war, from depreciation of the value of the paper currency and from necessarily heavy taxes to pay public and private indebtedness. As is usual, government is held responsible for such distress. But demagogues, among whom Daniel Shays was prominent, were ready to embrace any opportunity to rise, at the sacrifice of others. They added fuel to the flame. Criminal courts were broken up by lawless mobs. They harangued conventions of the people, disclaimed all intentions of riotous proceedings, but spread the flames of burning hate to the established courts.

After breaking up some of the small courts, they undertook

to break up the supreme court at Springfield. But they were wisely defeated by law and order men, under General Shepherd. On the 25 January, 1787, they attempted to take the arsenal on Springfield hill. The general warned the rebels as they approached, to desist, but they paid no heed. He then ordered a discharge of his artillery at their right, and then at their left, then over their heads. It was too tame an attempt for them. Then he ordered a well directed shot, which, killing two of their men, alarmed the insurgents so that they fled. A small company went from Northfield to join General Shepherd, and Zenophon Janes, then fourteen years of age, being a fifer in the company, was permitted by his father, to attend them, the captain promising to take good care of him. He used to tell us boys, about the frightened soldiers who stood guard during the night, over the dead bodies.

The two guards were timid, and expected to see some ghosts. It happened that during the night, a white horse thrust his head through a stable window near their station, and they concluded this was the apparition that had come for them; so they threw down their muskets and ran for dear life.

---

239 (XIII) EBENEZER, SON OF EBENEZER.

Ebenezer Janes early pursued an education, and graduated at Dartmouth College, Hanover, N. H., and as his father thought all lawyers were corrupt, and that his son would be corrupted if he studied law to practice it, he could not consent for his son to be a lawyer; so he gave his attention to navigation.

He followed the sea for a number of years, as supercargo and master, and was taken prisoner during the Napoleonic war with the Danes, and lost his property by an unlawful confiscation of his cargo. He returned home in 1815, and the owners of the vessel or owner (we think it was Billy Gray), put him in charge of another vessel to engage in the South American trade. While at some port in that country, his ship was seized for the use of the government, which had then revolted from Spain. He returned home and spent several years in teaching at the north, but more years at the south, in Georgia and Alabama. In the spring of 1851, he came finally north, and his wife having died during his absence, soon went to Michigan to spend the short remainder of life, with his eldest son, Ebenezer, who was then residing there on his own farm.

He married Luerctia Smith, daughter of Joseph Smith, of Petersham, Mass., 7 March, 1811. Mrs. Lucretia Janes was a pious, godly, devoted mother. Her practical wisdom led many of her friends to seek her friendly counsel. The writer well remembers her clear and winning voice, her cultivated and refined manners, her sweet and profitable conversation, and her convincing way in presenting her views of truth and duty. He was present, also, and remembers the solemn scene when she parted from her dear children, and at the hour of death, when she made her earnest, dying appeal, exhorting them with pathetic tenderness to improve the privilege of living for Jesus, and the duty of striving to meet her in heaven. She was born 17 December, 1780, and died 30 October, 1831.

Her children grew up to habits of frugality and temperance, and are professedly Christian.

CHILDREN.

617 I. JULIANNA L., born 27 Feb., 1812; died young.
618 II. EBENEZER S., born 23 May, 1814; married Mary
         Odell.
619 III. JOSEPH, born 14 Nov., 1818; married (1) Hannah
          Holton, (2) Sarah Portlock.
620 IV. EDWARD H. born 3 Oct., 1820; married Jane E.
         Yates.
621 V. JULIANNA, born 20 Oct., 1822; married David San-
        ford.

---

240 (XIV) JAMES OLIVER, SON OF EBENEZER.

James Oliver Janes was named after his aunt Hannah, who married James Oliver. He was plain, unassuming, of good, sound sense, quite a reader, kind
hearted, and obliging to all. When a young man
he engaged with a company of men to go to Georgia
to cut yellow pine, for lumber for some northern
speculator.

He returned and spent his days in his native town.
He married (1) Roxanna, daughter of Walter Field, to
whom there were born two children. She died 5
November, 1810.

CHILDREN.

622 I. LUCRETIA F., born 17 Dec , 1808; married Daniel
        Callender.
623 II. ROXANNA, born 28 Sept., 1810; died 20 March, 1811.

James O. married (2) Joanna Holton.

624 III. ROXANNA (twin), born 17 Feb., 1824; died 23 Aug.,
          1830.
625 IV. JOANNA (twin), born 17 Feb., 1824; died an infant.

Daniel Callender was for some time engaged in mercantile business. He was town clerk for a few years; was always affable, polished, and a safe adviser; and was accounted, at the time of his death, the richest man that had ever died in the town.

ELIJAH JANES,[1] son of ELIJAH and LUCY CROCKER, was the oldest and most distinguished of the brothers in a social, military and commercial position. He was a lieutenant in the war of the revolution, and was basely wounded after the surrender of the American forces, to the British, by an English officer. Some of his fingers were severed, and he received a life pension. He went into mercantile business in Lansingburgh, and often went to New York to purchase goods. This very English officer was a third partner in the firm where he bought goods. Though familiar and very social with the other two, he looked upon the third as beneath notice, and though the offending party made repeated efforts to speak to him and become reconciled to him, yet Elijah chose to treat him as a cowardly miscreant and pass him in silent contempt.

He made quite a fortune by trade and speculation. He bought government paper when considerably depreciated, and by the rise in value, made thousands. He was the first president of the bank of Lansingburgh, a justice of some of the courts, and otherwise distinguished.

---

[1] This should have come in at top of page 146.

He married Phebe Gay of Farmington, a woman of great intellectual vigor and executive talent. As her sister, Almira, who married Mr. Dole of Troy, left a daughter, the sister, Mrs. Janes, adopted her and brought her up to womanhood, when she married Horace Janes, Elijah's nephew, son of Cyrus of Brimfield, and by this marriage, Horace had the whole of his uncle's property. By various speculations Horace spent the whole in the devil's quarters in New York city, and died in 1844. His uncle, Elijah, died in February, 1823, and Mrs. E. Janes survived him some years.

SIXTH GENERATION.

LINE OF BENJAMIN.

246 (I) ANNA, DAUGHTER OF ELIJAH.

Anna Janes was Elijah's oldest child. She married Abram Church Brown, 20 November, 1786, at Pittsfield, Mass. She died 1842, and he died 2 July, 1844.

CHILDREN.

626 I.   NANCY, born 11 June, 1787; married John Brooks.
627 II. SARAH, born 1 May, 1790; married John Weller.
628 III. HULDAH, born 2 Feb., 1792; married John Churchill.
629 IV. JOHN, born 10 Dec., 1793; died 26 April, 1797.
630 V.   JAMES, born 28 Sept., 1795; died 15 April, 1797.
631 VI. OLIVER, born 29 May, 1797; married Louisa Goodrich.
632 VII. TRYPHENA, born 31 Aug., 1799; died 21 Jan., 1801.
633 VIII. JOHN, born 17 May, 1801; married Laura Barker.

634 IX.   JAMES, born 10 January, 1803; married Mary
          Green, died 14 Oct., 1836.
635 X.   ABRAM C., born 10 June, 1808; married (1)
          Roxanna Smith, (2) Henrietta Janes.

247 (II) HEMAN, SON OF ELIJAH.

Heman Janes, oldest son of the family, married
Abigail Burdick, and lived in South Hero, Vt.

CHILDREN.

636 I.   HEMAN, born 10 July, 1789; married ......; and
          lived in Ingersoll, Canada.
637 II.   LAURA, born ......, 1791 ; married Rev. James Harris,
          in Canada.
638 III. ELIJAH, born ......, 1793; married Mary Clark.
639 IV.   JAMES, born 7 Aug., 1798; married Lucina Sage.

Heman married (2) ....

CHILDREN.

640 V.   DAVID, born ...... ;
641 VI.   LAVINA, born...... ;

248 (III) LAVINA, DAUGHTER OF ELIJAH.

Lavina Janes of Pittsfield married Selah Andrews
of Richmond, Mass., 21 December, 1796. He died
1853. She died in November, 1860.

CHILDREN.

642 I.   SON, born 27 Feb., 1798; died 3 March, 1799.
643 II.   NANCY, born 26 June, 1799; married Lewis Sher-
          rill.
644 III. CYRUS, born 11 Aug., 1801; died 22 Dec., 1802.

23

645 IV.   MARCIA, born 30 Oct., 1804; married Charles
          Kendall.
646 V.   AMY, born 23 March, 1807; died young.
647 VI.   TRUMAN, born 9 June, 1812.
648 VII. DAVID (twin), born 14 July, 1816.
649 VIII. DENNIS (twin), born 14 July, 1816; died 1860.
650 IX.   LUCIA CORNELIA, born 13 Nov., 1821; married
          Mr. Chittenden of Danbury, Conn.

---

249 (IV) HUMPHREY, SON OF ELIJAH.

Humphrey Janes was a farmer of good repute in
Grand Isle county, South Hero, Vt. He married 23
July, 1790, Miss Thankfull Campbell, of Scotch descent,
a family strong, hardy and athletic. They raised a
large and respectable family of sons and daughters, and
moved from South Hero to Northern Pennsylvania, Erie
county, but eventually moved from there to Johnstown,
Rock county, Wis., where many of the family now
reside, and where Humphrey, the father, died.

CHILDREN.

651 I.   HIRAM, born 21 Jan., 1791; married Hannah
          Andrews, (2) Sarah Bedient (Mrs. Fletcher).
652 II.   ANNA, born 17 March, 1792; married Martin Ruggles.
653 III. SALLY, born 5 Dec., 1793; married David Campbell.
654 IV.   HUMPHREY, born 1 Nov., 1795; married Remem-
          brance Andrews; no issue; died 16 Nov., 1845.
655 V.   SEYMOUR, born 14 Aug., 1797; married Polly East-
          man.
656 VI.   OLIVER, born 28 March, 1799; married Emily Lee.
657 VII. ORRIN, born 4 March, 1801; married Clarissa Whit-
          man of Canada.

658 VIII. SUSAN, born 4 March, 1803; married Cyrus Chambers.

659 IX.   ELI, born 5 March, 1805; married Sarah ....

660 X.   WILLIAM, born 13 March, 1807; married Catharine Brace.

661 XI.   ALBERT, born 14 Feb., 1809.

662 XII.   ELIJAH, born 17 April, 1811; married Matilda Burwell.

663 XIII. THANKFUL, born 3 April, 1813.

---

250 (V) JOHN, SON OF ELIJAH.

John Janes went from Pittsfield, Mass., his native place, to South Hero, Vt., with his father, Elijah, and was there a number of years; probably returned to Pittsfield in 1812, for in 1816 a Mrs. John Janes united with the Congregational church in Pittsfield. Not far from this period they all went to Ohio.

John was an eccentric genius; but more, he was a regular, rough, untamed backwoodsman, self-willed, dogmatic, looking upon refinement, courtesy and good breeding as irrelevant to practical life. But he is credited with various labors to do good to assist in religious services and to preach some peculiar views as he had opportunity. Jehu-like he drove around the country, having no idle days; and used to say, "When I live, I live, when I die, I die." He worked till the last day of his natural life, and died quite suddenly. He married (1) Hannah Rockwell, 1791, who died 2d September, 1832. He married (2) Fanny Cothran, 1833. She died 1842. He again married (3) Miss Rose.

・ CHILDREN.

664 I.   MARY, born 5 Sept., 1792, unm.; died 26 Sept., 1846.
665 II.   PHEBE, born 4 October, 1794; married Lemuel S. Rust.
666 III. PARMELIA, born 24 Aug. 1796; married Lemuel S. Rust.
667 IV.   LAVINA, born 22 March, 1798; married Hiram Nettlelon.
668 V.   HARRY, born 25 Dec., 1799; m. E. A. Dickerman.
669 VI.   JOHN, born 4 Jan., 1802; married Hannah Brown.
670 VII. MARIA, born 17 March, 1804; married A. Thompson.
671 VIII DANIEL, born 3 November, 1805; killed by falling off a tree in Ohio, 26 January, 1826.
672 IX.   HORACE, born 24 Dec., 1807; married M. Andrus.
673 X.   ALLURED A., born 8 April, 1809; married Caroline Caulkins.

John married (2) Fanny Cothran.

CHILDREN.

674 XI.   EMILY A., born 6 Sept., 1834; m. Perry Kenyon.
675 XII. FANNY E., born 24 July, 1840.

---

251 (VI) ELIJAH, SON OF ELIJAH.

Elijah Janes married Anna Baker, and resided in Georgia, Vt. He moved to Richford, a neighboring town, and died there 1846. His wife survived him ten years, died 1856.

CHILDREN.

676 I.   AMANDA, born 6 Oct., 1801; married S. Boyden.
677 II.   SETH, born 19 April, 1804; married Jerusha R. Fenton.

678 III.   CHESTER, born 1 April, 1806; married Eliza Dee.
679 IV.   LUCY, born 8 Aug., 1807 ; married Asa Minor.
680 V.   CYRUS, born 7 June, 1810; married Louisa Bliss.
681 VI.   MELVIN T., born 15 March, 1814; married Marcia Caulkins.
682 VII.   DANIEL M., born ......, 1816; married (1) Charlotte Himrod, (2) S. E. Law.
683 VIII.   ADELIA, born 4 July, 1820; married (1) ...... Williams, (2) Spaulding Spooner.

---

252 (VI) OLIVER, SON OF ELIJAH.

Oliver Janes married Jemina Hall, in South Hero, Vt., raised up his family and died there, so far as informed.

CHILDREN.

684 I.   CHARLES, born ......, 1804 ; killed by a fall, 1823.
685 II.   LORENZO, born 19 Feb., 1806 ; married Lucina M. Post.
686 III.   ORPHA, born ......, 1808; married D. Bull.
687 IV.   LUCY, born ......, 1810 ; married H. E. Dunton.

Oliver married (2) ......

CHILDREN.

688 V.   HARRIET, born ...... ;
689 VI.   HENRY, born ...... ;
690 VII.   HENRIETTA, born ...... ; married Abram C. Brown.

253 (VIII) DAVID, SON OF ELIJAH.

David Janes, the youngest child of the family, lived in Watertown, N. Y., and moved thence to Georgia, Vt., in 1820. He married Martha Smedtz of Williamstown, about 1806.

CHILDREN.

691 I. LUCINDA, born 22 June, 1807; married Thomas Dockum of Mo.

692 II. LESTER, born 9 Dec., 1812; married Sarah Smith.

693 III. OLIVER, born ......, 1814; lives in Mo.

694 IV. MARSHALL D., born ......, 1816.

695 V. CHARLOTTE, born ......, 1821; married Blake Barrows.

696 VI. HEMAN, born ...... 1828; married Martha Jones.

---

256 (III) LUCY, DAUGHTER OF SAMUEL.

Lucy Janes married Daniel Robertson of Coventry, Conn., and they had the following offspring :

CHILDREN.

697 I. GUY, born ......; married Mehitable ....

698 II DAUGHTER, born ......; married Mr. Youngs.

699 III. DANIEL, born ...... ; married Harmony Carpenter.

700 IV. SARAH, born ....

---

268 (VI) STERLING, SON OF ELIAS.

Sterling Janes married (1) Huldah Loomis, (2) Theodocia Lyman.

CHILD.

701 I. A SON, born ......; drowned when a youth.

269 (VII) CHAUNCEY, SON OF ELIAS.

Chauncey Janes was a good farmer, lived and died in Coventry, Conn. He married Mrs. Susan [Thompson] Sweetland. He died suddenly while unloading hay in the barn.

CHILDREN.

702 I. CHAUNCEY WOLCOTT, born 8 June, 1829; married Mrs. Mary Hall.

703 II. LEONARD T., born 25 Feb., 1831; married Sophronia E. Shaffer.

704 III. CHARLES, born 10 Dec., 1833.

705 IV. LAURA A., born 30 May, 1838; married John Gray.

706 V. ROYAL NELSON, born 19 June, 1841.

273 (I) WILLIAM, SON OF SETH.

William Janes of Pittsfield married Lavina Pepoon. They lived in Pittsford, N. Y., for some time. He went to Burlington, Iowa, and died there.

CHILDREN.

707 I. ELIZABETH, born ......, married L. Leonard.

708 II. WILLIAM EGBERT, born ......; was murdered when a young man.

709 III. CATHARINE, born, ... 1816; married Mr. Brown.

710 IV. LAVINA, born ......; married William Edgar, of St. Louis.

711 V. FREDERIC, born ......; resides in St. Louis.

274 (II) ETHAN, SON OF SETH.

Colonel Ethan Janes married (1) Charlotte Williams of Pittsfield, who died 2 May, 1821. He married (2) Elizabeth Ward of Pittsfield; lived some years in the enjoyment of a competence. He always found leisure to pursue his favorite sport, the hunting and shooting of foxes. He was noted for this sport through the whole region, and shot more game than any man known, in this line. He lived to a good old age, and died August, 1865.

CHILDREN.

712 I.　MARY E., born 4 Nov., 1818.
713 II.　SARAH ANN, born 6 Nov., 1820.

Ethan married (2) Elizabeth Ward, 1823.

CHILDREN.

714 III.　FRANCES, born 16 May, 1824; married William A. Russell.
715 IV.　CAROLINE, born 30 Sept., 1827; married Dr. William L. Jackson, who died August, 1856.
716 V.　SAMUEL WARD, born 20 May, 1830; died 1865.

276 (IV) HENRY, SON OF SETH.

Henry Janes married Clarissa Belden of Pittsfield, 1826. He was a pious, devoted Christian, and an officer in the church. He lived at Lima, N. Y.; and he died 1863.

CHILD.

717 I.　CLARISSA, born ......, 1827.

280 (I) ELIZABETH, DAUGHTER OF ELISHA.

Elizabeth Janes married Rev. Malachi Barker, a traveling Methodist preacher, who afterwards settled down at Hanover, Oneida county, N. Y. She died 1838.

CHILDREN.

718 I.   JASON, born ......;
719 II.   SOPHIA, born ......;
720 III. NANCY, born ......;
721 IV.   BETSEY, born ......;
722 V.   ESTHER, born ......;
723 VI.   HARRIET, born ......;
724 VII. HOPE, born ......;
725 VIII. EMILY, born ......;

---

281 (II) ROGER, SON OF ELISHA.

Roger Janes married Elizabeth Warner of Canaan, February, 1794, and was highly esteemed.

CHILDREN.

726 I.   CHANDLER, born 10 Nov., 1794.
727 II.   EMILY PITKINS, born 2 Oct., 1796; married David Parsons.
728 III. ELIZABETH, born 26 Oct., 1798.
729 IV.   WILLIAM WARNER, born 19 Sept., 1799; married Nancy Webb.
730 V.   ELISHA (twin) born 25 June, 1802; married Elizabeth Cryder.
731 VI.   ELIZA (twin), born 25 June, 1802; married cousin Richard Warner.
732 VII. JULIANNA, born 24 Oct., 1804; married Rev. E. Cole, (C).
733 VIII. ABIGAIL HAWLEY, born 15 Aug., 1806.

25

282 (III) ESTHER, DAUGHTER OF ELISHA.

Esther Janes married Oliver Sanford, 1800.   She died 17 January, 1844, in Oneida county, N. Y.

CHILDREN.

734 I   JANES (twin,) born 15 Oct., 1802; married (1) Mabel Green, 1828, (2) Amanda Wells, Oct., 1840, in Chambersburg, Pa.

735 II.   JOEL, (twin), born 15 Oct., 1802.

736 III.   ADALINE, born ......; married Joshua Palmer, 1833.

737 IV.   MINERVA, born 13 April, 1804; married Alden Brown, 4 Oct., 1830.

738 V.   CHARLES, born 8 March, 1806; married Miss Taylor, niece of General and President Taylor, 1835.

739 VI.   DAVID, born .....;

740 VII.   MARY, born 22 Feb., married (2) Hiram Hastings.

741 VIII.   AMELIA, born 6 April, 1810; married (1) Hiram Hastings.

---

283 (IV) DANIEL, SON OF ELISHA.

Daniel Janes married, 1792, Temperance Tinker, and he died 3 September, 1823.

CHILDREN.

742 I.   HARRIET, born ......, 1794; married Lewis Wilson, 1814.

743 II.   ALANSON, born ......, 1796; married Betsey Beman.

744 III.   CLARISSA, born ......, 1798; married Col. Samuel Stevens, 1830.

745 IV.   BRINDA, born ......, 1800; married Capt. Gehiel Munger, 1836.

746 V.   SOPHIA, born ......; married Mr. Gilbert.

747 VI.   MARTIN M., born ......, 1802; married Miss Kelleman 1866.

284 (V) ELISHAMA, SON OF ELISHA.

Elishama Janes married Betsey Jerolomon of Bethlehem, N. Y. She was born 1774, died 11 May, 1857, æ. 83.

CHILDREN.

748 I.   JANE, born ......, 1793;

749 II.   ELIZABETH, born ......; 1795; married Peter Springsteed.

750 III. ESTHER, born ......, 1798; married Gradus Becker.

751 IV. CHANCELLOR, born . ....; 1801; (?).

752 V.   DESIRE, born 28 April, 1804; married Darius Buck.

753 VI. WILLIAM, born 24 Oct., 1806; married Mary Ann Hawley.

754 VII. ADALINE, born 12 July, 1811; married Reuben B. Stiles.

755 VIII. MARIA, born ......, August, 1813; married John Pettitt.

756 IX. HANNAH, born ......, Feb., 1816; married Isaac Ten Eyck.

---

285 (VI) POLLY, DAUGHTER OF ELISHA.

Polly Janes married Cyrus Davis of Oneida county N. Y. He died 1853. She died 1862, æ. 91 years.

CHILDREN.

757 I. ELISHA, born ......, 1800; married Sarah Savage of Lenox.

758 II. MARY THOMPSON, born ......, 1805; married John L. Bigelow.

286 (VII) NATHANIEL, SON OF ELISHA.

Nathaniel Janes is a man of excellent character, erect in form, of strong constitution and ripe in years, being now (1867) 90 years of age. He married Achsa Barnes, who was a descendant of Richard Cromwell, brother of William, the protector of the commonwealth, a woman of remarkable memory, great activity of mind and well versed in the history of all her relatives. Perhaps the loss of her sight may have quickened her other faculties. They have raised up a large family of children.

CHILDREN.

759 I.   ELISHA BARNES, born 6 Nov., 1801; married Fanny B. Lord.

760 II.   LAURA WOLCOTT, born 6 June, 1803; married Sylvester Curtis.

761 III. LYDIA BARNES, born 5 Nov., 1805; died 3 Sept., 1826.

762 IV.   WALTER RALEIGH, born 3 August, 1808; married Anna Maria Adams.

763 V.   ELIZA WRIGHT, born 11 Aug., 1811; married Norman William.

764 VI.   HARRIET WILSON, born 3 Sept., 1813; married William Lawrence.

765 VII. ROBERT FRAZY, born ......; died an infant.

766 VIII. EMILY PITKINS, born 16 March, 1817.

767 IX.   ANN, born ......;

287 (VIII) JESSE, SON OF ELISHA.

Jesse married September, 1807, Julia M. Wickham of Long Island. He was very active and social. She was born 11 June, 1789; died 27 April, 1852. He died 2 April, 1828, in Pembroke, Genesee county, N. Y.

CHILDREN.

768 I.   HOWELL W., born 29 Dec., 1808; married Lucy Hall.

769 II.   DAVID, born 17 March, 1810; married Emily Hutchins.

770 III.   HARRIET G., born 8 Sept., 1813; married William N. Sanders.

771 IV.   CHARLES S., born 13 Nov., 1815; married Emily Peckham.

772 V.   JULIA W., born 9 Jan., 1818; married Joseph W. Corning.

773 VI.   JESSE R., born 10 April, 1820; married Mary Hammond.

774 VII.   ELLEN M., born 2 Dec., 1823.

775 VIII.   LAVINA P., born 13 Dec., 1826; married Jeremiah Mabie.

288 (IX) LAVINA, DAUGHTER OF ELISHA.

Lavina Janes married 4 August, 1804, Obadiah Latham, who was born in Groton, Conn., 29 February, 1780. He died 1 October, 1831. She died 21 January, 1859.

CHILDREN.

776 I.   ADELIA, born 27 March, 1806; married Charles Pixley.

777 II.   BENJAMIN F., born 1 July, 1807; married Harriet Crago.

778 iii.   Edward Smith, born 7 Oct., 1808; married Susan
           Foster.
779 iv.   Hannah, born 24 June, 1810; died 25 Jan., 1859.
780 v.   Esther S., born 16 Nov., 1811; died 15 Sept., 1824.
781 vi.   William H. Harrison, born 27 Aug., 1813;
           married Margaret Bushnell; died 29 Sept., 1865.
782 vii.   Oliver S., born 11 Jan., 1816; married Lucy M.
           Eastman.
783 viii. Mary E., 22 June, 1817; married William Webb.
784 ix.   Susan Lavina, born 12 May, 1819; married John
           A. Benham.
785 x.   Obadiah B., born 8 Sept., 1820; married Thank-
           ful Bushnell.
786 xi.   Nathaniel, born 28 Sept., 1822; married Maria
           Bishop.

---

290 (XI) HANNAH, DAUGHTER OF ELISHA.

Hannah Janes married Seth Birge of New Hartford,
N. Y., 13 October, 1812 (on the day of the battle
of Queenstown), in New Lebanon, Columbia county,
N. Y.

CHILDREN.

787 i.   Henry, born 30 Oct., 1814; died 30 March, 1815
788 ii.   Seth, born 1 March, 1816.
789 iii.   Joseph A., born 22 July, 1817.
790 iv.   John, born ....
791 v.   David, born ......, 26 July, 1825.
792 vi.   Reuben S., born ....
793 vii.   Hannah M., born ....

298 (I) BENJAMIN, SON OF BENJAMIN.

Benjamin Janes was the only child of Benjamin, son of Elisha, and son of Deacon Benjamin Janes, one of the first settlers of Coventry, Conn., 1710.

Benjamin, of the fifth generation, lived in or near Coventry, till the older members of the family got the western fever, and moved to the central part of the state of New York, or into Michigan. He married Zebiah Huntington, daughter of Captain Eleazer Huntington, who was at the battle of White Plains. Samuel Huntington, who signed the Declaration of Independence was his uncle. The copy of the *Windham Herald*, publishes this marriage, and her name is printed Zeruviah. They were married at Mansfield, Conn., February, 1797. He went to Michigan to spend his last days with his son, and died 1847.

CHILDREN.

794 I.. ERASTUS, born 9 Feb., 1798; married Lydia Woodruff·
795 II. ELEAZER, born 14 June, 1799; married Elizabeth Hempstead.
796 III. THOMAS, born 15 Nov., 1802; died young.
797 IV. DAVID, born 8 Feb., 1805; married Nancy Bacon, no issue.
798 V. IRENA, born 2 Oct., 1807; married Benjamin Bates.
799 VI. HUNTINGTON, born 27 April, 1810; married Chloe Woodruff.
800 VII. BENJAMIN F., born 25 Jan , 1821; died 1845.
801 VIII. MARY, born ......, 1823; died an infant.

Benjamin married (2) Lucy Flint.

CHILDREN.

802 IX. BENJAMIN F., born ......, married ......

SEVENTH GENERATION.

LINE OF ABEL.

301 (I) LUCINDA, DAUGHTER OF ELIPHALET.

Lucinda Janes married Zephaniah Gibbs, of Hopkinton, Mass., 20 December, 1787, by Rev. Mr. Reeves. He was born 26 September, 1761. They lived for a time in Holland, Mass. He died 30 April, 1826. She died 12 July, 1843, in Boston.

CHILDREN.

802 I. MARTHA, born 24 Dec., 1788; married W. Carpenter, 12 July, 1811; died 20 July, 1866.
803 II. ELFLEDA, born 15 Aug., 1792; married Samuel Chamberlain, 1833.
804 III. ALFRED, born 21 Feb., 1796.
805 IV. CYNTHIA, born 12 Aug., 1802; married Sewell Hiscock, 12 Aug., 1822.
806 V. LUCINDA, born 3 March, 1805; married Robert Mellen, 8 March, 1829.
807 VI. ARMEDA, born 28 June, 1807; unmarried; resides in East Boston.

302 (II) ROXYLENA, DAUGHTER OF ELIPHALET.

Roxylena Janes married Edmund Fox of Hartford, 1789, dates and names of all that married into the family, were not obtained in time.

CHILDREN.

808 I.   NANCY, born ......; married Oliver Dwight.
809 II.   GUERDON, born ......; married Sophia Kendall.
810 III.   HENRY, born ......; married Lydia Tracy.
811 IV.   HORATIO, born ......; married Martha Ostrander.
812 V.   ROYAL, born ......; married (1) ......; (2) ......
813 VI.   AMANDA, born ......; married Daniel Foster.
814 VII.   ELIZA, born ......; married Albert Risley.
815 VIII. ALVIN, born ......; unmarried.
816 IX.   JOHN, born ......; married Adaline Hosmer.
817 X.   SAMANTHA, born ......; married (1) ......; (2) Mr.
           Wheeler.
818 XI.   FIDELIA, born ......; married Gustavus A. Marsh.

------

303 (III) MARSYLVIA, DAUGHTER OF ELI-PHALET.

Marsylvia Janes married Benjamin Eastman. They had a number of children as follows:

CHILDREN.

819 I.   EUNICE, born ......;
820 II.   MARY, born ......;
821 III.   FIDELIA, born ......;
822 IV.   ROXYLENA, born ......;
823 V.   ROSWELL, born ......;
824 VI.   HIRAM, born ......;
825 VII.   EMILY, born ......;
826 VIII. ELIZABETH. born ......;
827 IX.   SUSAN, born ......;
828 X.   MASON, born ......;

304 (IV) ALFRED, SON OF ELIPHALET.

Alfred Janes was less permanent in residence and business, than some others of the family. He resided in Ashford, Conn., Sturbridge, Mass., Hartford, Conn., Auburn, and Seneca Falls, N. Y.

He was in the boot and shoe business, kept the City Hotel at Hartford, and after that went into the manufacturing of looking glasses, with his brother. On removing to New York, he engaged in the house painting business with his sons.

He possessed considerable inventive genius and experimented more than was profitable for the pocket book. He was fond of reading, had quite a taste for drawing. His conversational powers were fine; entering into conversation with more or less historical knowledge, and a large fund of anecdotes.

He married (1) Mary, daughter of Elizur Warren, and Elizabeth Skinner of Hartford, January, 1794. She was born 29 October, 1777, and died 5 April, 1799. He married (2) Alice Cross (in 1800), who was born 9 June, 1774, and died 1837.

CHILDREN.

829 I.   ELIZA, born 2 March, 1796; married Joseph Church.
830 II.   ADRIAN, born 4 Feb., 1798; married Adaline Root.

Alfred married (2) Alice Cross.

CHILDREN.

831 III. BENJAMIN, born 5 April, 1801; married (1) Nancy Mulks, (2) Hopey Cook.

832 IV. ALVIN, born 19 May, 1807; married Irene Watkins.
833 V. ALFRED, born 14 Feb., 1813; married (1) Susan
       Stottle, (2) Sarah Dermun.
834 VI. ADALINE, born 17 July, 1816; married Lewis Graves.

305 (V) WALTER, SON OF ELIPHALET.

Walter Janes was called a genius. He was a
scholar, a composer of music, and a very good per-
former; and at the laying of the corner stone of Bunker
Hill monument, the music of the occasion was led by
him. He stood high among the Freemasons, and was
appointed by them a lecturer in Connecticut and in
Massachusetts. He was an inventor, and a number of
patents were taken out by him which were thought
to be useful, but he never realized much profit from
them.

He composed a music book called the *Harmonic
Minstrelsy*, which we found in the New York State
Library, the title page running thus: " The *Harmonic
Minstrelsy*, containing a new collection of sacred music
in three parts, comprising variety of style, tune, time and
measure, and well proportioned to all the different
metres and keys commonly used in churches, together
with a number of set pieces, choruses and anthems
appropriate to Ordinations, Dedications, Thanksgivings,
etc., chiefly original : to which is prefixed the necessary
rules for learners. The whole being calculated and
designed for the use of schools and public worship. By
Walter Janes.

" Music hath magic powers and potent spells,
   To sooth the raging passions into peace,
   At dulcet tones, and modulated strains,
   Revenge assumes soft pity's placid mien.
   The lips of slander are in silence sealed,
   The eye of hate tears of compassion shed,
   The listening ear is charmed, the heart improved,
   A warm devotion fills the ravished soul.
                    " Printed by H. Mann, Dedham, Mass., 1807."

The book is thin and lean compared with our present large and extensive music books.   Forty of the tunes have the name of Janes attached as the author.

A quotation from his poetic address delivered at Mansfield, 1819, will show his masonic views and the style of his poetry :

*   *   *   *   *   *

And though our thoughts and actions be concealed
From mortal optics, yet they stand revealed,
To that *all-seeing eye*, which heav'n surveys,
Whom *sun*, and *moon*, and every *star* obeys;
Whose *care* directs the *comet's* devious course,
Guides every *wave*, and gives to *winds* their force,
Views the recesses of each *human heart*,
And, as they merit, *his* rewards impart.

These emblems of the *ark* and *hope* combine,
To form an emblem of that *ark divine*,
Which safely wafts us o'er life's troubled sea
To the vast realms of blest *eternity !*
And *anchors* us on that delightful *shore*
Where evils cease and troubles come no more.

He married Cynthia Richards of Eastford, Conn., in 1802, and lived in Ashford. He died 24 July, 1827.

CHILDREN.

835 I. MARIA T., born 3 June, 1803; married Calvin Whitney.
836 II. ALPHONZO, born 31 Dec., 1804; married Sophia Taft.
837 III. ARETHUSA, born 16 March, 1807; married Elisha Lord.
838 IV. LUCIUS L., born 2 April, 1809; died 1849.
839 V. PARTHENA P., born 21 June, 1812; unmarried.
840 VI. EDWIN E., born 14 Feb., 1815; died 9 June, 1854.
841 VII. GEORGE W., born 7 Dec., 1816.

---

306 (VII) ALMARIN, SON OF ELIPHALET.

Almarin Janes was a soldier of the war of 1820, and was appointed for a time to arrest deserters. From one of his last visits home, as he was traveling on duty, he returned to camp, and early in the morning, a part of the army marched into the deserted fort to take possession, and Almarin Janes was among the hundred that were blown to atoms, by the cunning of British treachery, 5 May, 1813.

He married Polly Fay, 1 December, 1803. She was born 23 July, 1784. After his disastrous death, she married (2) Samuel O. Wilcoxon.

CHILDREN.

842 I. ELFLEDA, born 25 Oct., 1804; married Peter Wormwood.
843 II. EMELINE, born 10 April, 1806; married Ward Munroe.

844 III. MARY, born 26 Sept., 1808; married Henry Philips.
845 IV. DIANTHA, born 30 July, 1810; married William
          Jackson.
846 V. LOUISA, born 15 Feb., 1816; died young.

---

307 (VII) BRADFORD, SON OF ELIPHALET.

Bradford Janes lived at Eastford, Conn., and at
Belchertown, Mass., spent more or less time in Vermont.
Past middle life, he went with his family to Illinois.
He was intelligent, active, and something of a poet for
a mechanic. He died about 1863. His wife died 1849.

CHILDREN.

847 I. IRVING E., born 3 Feb., 1810; married Nancy M.
          Day.
848 II. ELBRIDGE G., born 6 April, 1811; married Martha
          Gleason.
849 III. NANCY J., born 7 April, 1812; married J. W.
          Childs.
850 IV. ALMARIN, born 6 Sept., 1813; died Nov., 1832.
851 V. ERON, born 10 Oct., 1816; married Diantha Farns-
          worth.
852 VI. SARAH ANN (twin), born ......, 1819; married
          Luther A. Billings, and died 3 April, 1863.
853 VII. MARY ANN (twin), born ......, 1819; married
          Stanislaus Belanskie.
854 VIII. EDWARD, born 1 June, 1821; married Anna A.
          Smith.
855 IX. EDGAR, born ......; 1826; married Sarah Moore.

308 (VIII) SALLY, DAUGHTER OF ELIPHALET.

Sally Janes married Abijah Richards, and died in Hartford, 16 June, 1863. He died 10 June, 1860.

CHILDREN.

856 I. ANN, born ......; married Stephen Parker of Hartford, Conn.
857 II. ELIZA, born ......; died 1863.

---

309 (I) NATHAN, SON OF SOLOMON.

Nathan Janes married Celinda Dexter, and resides in Neenah, Winnebago county, Wis. He was born in Calais, Vt., where a part of the family now reside.

CHILDREN.

858 I. ORESTES, born ......; died unmarried.
859 II. LAURA, born ......; married William F. Cole.
860 III. HENRY CLINTON, born ......; married Almira Bullock.

---

311 (III) HENRY F., SON OF SOLOMON.

Henry F. Janes was a prominent statesman, and member of congress, from the state of Vermont. He was scholarly, and free from ostentation. He married Fanny Butler, daughter of Ezra Butler of Waterbury, Vt. He is a man of talent, and closely tied to his profession.

CHILDREN.

861 I. HELEN MARIA, born ......, 1828; died 30 May, 1842.
862 II. HENRY born 24 Jan., 1832. He was a surgeon in the army, in war for the union.

312 (IV) LORENZO, SON OF SOLOMON.

Lorenzo Janes is a practicing lawyer of Racine, Wis., where he has been in a prosperous and successful business for some time. He married Elvenah Cooper of Albany, 17 April, 1833. She was a daughter of Andrew and Louisa Cooper.

CHILDREN.

863 I.   EMELINE COOPER, born 1 June, 1834; married Charles C Crail of Cleveland, 10 Nov., 1857.
864 II.   MARY LOUISA, born 6 Jan., 1837.
865 III. HENRY LORENZO, born 14 Dec., 1839; died 25 June, 1860.
866 IV.   ELVENAH CROSBY, born 18 July, 1842; married John H. Kinzie, 25 April, 1861.
867 V.   ALMIRA KNAPP, born 16 April, 1845; died 14 June, 1849.
868 VI.   GEORGE SEELY, born 9 Oct., 1847.
869 VII. CORINNA, born 30 May, 1850.
870 VIII. DAVID GRIFFIN, born 2 April, 1852.
871 IX.   EDGAR, born 23 Dec., 1853.
872 X.   ELLIE, born 4 April, 1857.

317 (I) RACHEL, DAUGHTER OF DANIEL.

Rachel Janes born at Brimfield, Mass., married Oliver Skinner in East Windsor, 8 Oct., 1795. He was born in East Windsor, 25 Sept., 1772. He died 13 July, 1844. She died 14 September, 1849.

CHILDREN.

873 I.   ANNIE, born 31 Aug., 1797; married Hiram Strong.
874 II.   MARY R., born 4 March 1800; married Joseph L. Sadd.

875 III.　HIRAM, born 30 Aug., 1802; married Sarah M. Stiles.

876 IV.　CHARLES, born 24 Sept., 1805.

877 V.　MERILLA M., born 23 Feb., 1808; married James H. Stiles.

878 VI.　HORACE, born 6 Oct., 1810; married Harriet Sadd.

879 VII.　DANIEL J., born 3 April, 1813; married Aurelia Ellsworth.

880 VIII.　ROXEY, born 25 June, 1815; married Samuel Stiles.

881 IX.　ANNIE, born 13 Sept., 1818; married Emily Grant.

882 X.　ABIGAIL, born 9 Sept., 1820.

Hiram Skinner's son, Charles B., was fife major of the 16 Regiment, Conn. Volunteers. He came home from Virginia, and died in about 5 weeks.

319 (III) ANNIE E., DAUGHTER OF DANIEL.

Annie E. Janes born at Munson, Mass., married Thomas J. Shepherd (who was born in Holderness, N. H., 16 March, 1773), in Richford, Vt., 2 January, 1804. He died 27 December, 1822.

CHILDREN.

883 I.　SUSAN, born 26 July, 1806.

884 II.　RACHEL M., born 18 Sept., 1809.

885 III.　JOHN, born 19 Aug., 1811.

886 IV.　LYDIA S., born 3 Aug., 1818

887 V.　THOMAS, born 23 Sept., 1821.

320 (IV) JEREMIAH, SON OF DANIEL.

Jeremiah Janes married Sarah Allen, 8 February, 1807, and lived in Montgomery, Vt.

26

CHILDREN.

888 i.   ALICE, born 1 April, 1808.
889 ii. LEVI, born 5 June, 1810.
890 iii. IRA, born 17 June, 1812.
891 iv. ANNIE, born 17 Feb., 1815.
892 v.   HENRY, born 25 March, 1818.

---

322 (VI) DANIEL, SON OF DANIEL.

Daniel Janes Jr. married Hannah Lathrop, 26 February, 1811.   He died in the spring of 1868.

CHILDREN.

893 i. ELKANAH, born 13 Nov., 1811.
894 ii. HANNAH, born 23 Feb., 1813.

Daniel, Jr. married (2) Polly Powell, 1814.

CHILDREN.

895 iii. CHESTER, born 12 March, 1815.
896 iv. ALBERT, born 16 Oct., 1816.
897 v.   CHARLES, born 9 July, 1818.
898 vi. FANNY, born 18 Oct., 1820 ; died 5 Aug., 1822.
899 vii. MARY, born 1 April, 1822.

---

323 (VII) IRA, SON OF DANIEL.

Ira Janes married Precinda Wright, 4 July, 1815, and lived in Richford, Vt.   She was born 1793.   She died 18 November, 1822.

CHILDREN.

900 i.   CORDELIA P., born 28 March, 1816.
901 ii. URSULA, born 14 Nov., 1817.
902 iii. DANIEL W., born 18 Oct., 1819.

Ira married (2) Caroline Breese of Richford.

CHILDREN.

903 IV. OLIVER S., born ......;
904 V. PRECINDA, born ......;

Some of the younger children of Daniel married, but we have not the full record. There are quite a number of very respectable families in East Windsor and vicinity, descendants of Daniel Janes. They possess a good name and are endowed with substance.

337 (I) HORACE, SON OF JONATHAN.

Horace Janes was born in Brimfield, Mass. He moved in early life to Vermont, and lived for a time in Greenfield, Mass., but afterwards returned to St. Albans, Vt., and was postmaster, and published a paper which had considerable circulation at the time. He was industrious, public spirited and highly esteemed.

He married (1) Catharine Barnard, born 28 April, 1784, daughter of Samuel and Abigail Barnard of Hatfield, afterwards of Montgomery, Vt. They were married by Rev. Jonathan Janes, 20 September, 1802.

CHILDREN.

905 I.   FRANCES B., born 25 March, 1804; died at Montgomery, 1808.
906 II.   SARAH C., born 1 Aug., 1805; died at Greenfield, 1822.
907 III. CHARLES B., born 30 Dec., 1806; died 6 Oct., 1856.
908 IV.   JONATHAN, born 1 Oct., 1808; died at Hammond, N. Y., 1808.

Horace married (2) Mary Brown, born at Sandisfield, Mass., 11 April, 1782; married 10 November, 1813, by Rev. Jonas Coe. She died 18 June, 1822.

CHILDREN.

909 v.   FRANCES EMELINE, born 6 Oct., 1814; died 15
          Dec., 1847.
910 vi.   HENRY B., born 11 Oct., 1816.

Horace married (3) Eunice L. Partridge, born 16 June, 1800, in Hatfield, married by Joseph Lyman, D.D., 19 June, 1823.

CHILDREN.

911 vii. HORACE P., born 16 May, 1824; married Julia Hall.
912 viii. JOSEPH L., born 28 May, 1826.
913 ix.   CATHARINE M., born 27 March, 1828.
914 x.   LEWIS DWIGHT, born 27 April, 1830; died at St.
          Albans.
915 xi.   ABBY MARIA, born 10 May, 1832.

---

338 (II) CYNTHIA, DAUGHTER OF JONATHAN.

Cynthia Janes married Ebenezer Marvin, attorney at law, in Franklin, Vt. She died 16 August, 1854.

CHILDREN.

916 i.   EBENEZER, born ......, at Sheldon, Vt.; married Ann
          Gelston, at Montreal, and moved to Hayneville, Ala.
917 ii.   GEORGE COOK, born ......; married Jane Morrison,
          N. C.
918 iii. JULIA C., born ...... ; married B. H. Smalley, of St.
          Albans.
919 iv.   JONATHAN, born ......, at Hammond, St. Lawrence
          Co. N. Y.; he moved to Illinois, and married there.

339 (III) RUBY, DAUGHTER OF JONATHAN.

Ruby Janes married (1) Ethan Hubbard of Franklin, Vt.

CHILDREN.

921 I. GEORGE COOK, born ......;
922 II. CHARLOTTE, born ......;
923 III. MARTHA J., born ......;

Ruby married (2) Asaph Morgan, C. minister of Essex, N. Y.

CHILDREN.

924 IV. JONATHAN F., born ......; married Mary Ann Eastman, moved to Memphis, Tenn.
925 V. FRANCES E., born ......; married Irad Day ; of Musca-
tine.
926 VI. CHARLES D., born ......; married Mrs ......, and lived
out west.

340 (IV) MARTHA, DAUGHTER OF JONATHAN.

Martha P. married (1) William Foote of St. Albans. He died 28 July, 1834.

CHILDREN.

927 I. WILLIAM F., born ......;
928 II. MARY CURTIS, born ......; married Frederic Smith
of Burlington, Vt.

Martha married (2) William H. Wilkins.

CHILDREN.

929 III. ELIZABETH S., born ......; married William Ander-
son of Burlington, Vt.
930 IV. MARTHA R., born ..... ; married J. W. Taylor.
931 V. JONATHAN A., born ......; unmarried ; lives at Mata-
gordas, Texas.

343 (VII) HENRY N., SON OF JONATHAN.

Henry Newell Janes married Betsey Allis, and resided in Montgomery, Franklin county, Vt.

CHILDREN.

932 I.   JONATHAN, born 14 June, 1817; married Abigail H. Webb.

933 II.   WILLIAM W., born 14 Feb., 1819; died at Stockton, Cal.

934 III. HENRY N., born 22 Nov., 1820; died in London, England.

935 IV.   JULIA A., born 15 Aug., 1822; married W. H. Payne.

936 V.   GEORGE COOK, born 5 Sept., 1824; married Ann Parks.

937 VI.   MARTHA L., born 19 Sept., 1826; married T. J. Holmes.

938 VII. JULIA E., born 19 Nov., 1830.

939 VIII. FRANCES C., born 20 March, 1833; married George F. Brown.

344 (VIII) JULIA ANN, DAUGHTER OF JONATHAN.

Julia Ann Janes married Jason C. Pierce, and lived at St. Albans, Vt., 1813.

CHILDREN.

940 I.   CHARLES STUART, born ......, 1814, at St. Albans.

941 II.   FRANCES CAROLINE, born ......, at Troy.

942 III. CYNTHIA, born ......, at Montreal; married Dr. Wright of Scotland.

943 IV. MARGARET A., born ......; married William Hawley; they went to California. She died at Maysville.

944 V. EDWARD, born ......;

945 VI. JASON, born ......;

946 VII. MARY, born ......;

947 VIII. ESTHER, born ......;

948 IX. JULIA C., born ......;

---

346 (X) LEWIS MARCY, SON OF JONATHAN.

Lewis Marcy Janes married Abby P. Allyn, at Cayuga, near Auburn, N. Y., 25 July, 1821, Rev. Medad Pomeroy officiating. She was born at New London, Conn., 8 October, 1797, and died 23 October, 1847. He was lost on the steamer Pewabic, 9 August, 1865, on Lake Huron.

Mrs. Abby P. Janes was a neice of Thomas Mumford, president of the Auburn Bank, and they complimented him by giving his name to their first child.

CHILDREN.

949 I. THOMAS M., born 23 Sept., 1822; married Cornelia R. Livingston, Cleveland, Ohio.

950 II. MARTHA C., born 7 Nov., 1824; died at Akron, Ohio, 28 May, 1845.

951 III. F. HENRIETTA, born 12 April, 1827; died at Boston, Ohio, 11 June, 1842.

952 IV. MARY M., born 25 Nov., 1829.

953 V. L. FREDERIC, born 3 March, 1832.

954 VI. ELIZABETH L., born 25 Dec., 1833; died 19 April, 1852.

955 VII. EDWARD J., born 20 April, 1836.

348 (XII) FRANCES R., DAUGHTER OF JONATHAN.

Frances Rebecca Janes married Luther S. Conklin, and resides in Mexico, N. Y. She is the youngest child of the family, and to her honor, she manifests more interest in the genealogy, then all their family combined.

CHILDREN.

956 I.   LUTHER, born 15 June, 1823; married Sarah Sweeting Chandler.
957 II. JONATHAN J., born 16 August, ...;
958 III. GEORGE P., born 17 October, ...;
959 IV. DWIGHT P., born ......;
960 V.   J. FRANCES, born ......;
961 VI. FRANCES MAY, born ......;
962 VII. LEWIS MARVIN, born ......;

349 CAPHIRA, DAUGHTER OF WILLIAM.

Caphira Janes married (1) Jacob Sherman, (2) John Bond, and raised a large family. She died 23 March, 1857.

CHILDREN.

963 I.   MERRICK, born ......, June, 1802; lost at sea.
964 II. WILLIAM JANES, born 23 Jan., 1804.
965 III. CHENEY J., born 19 Nov., 1806; married (1) Marion Caldwell, (2) Sarah Caldwell.
966 IV. ORILLA, born 21 May, 1808; married Samuel Rockwell.
967 V.   ELIZA, born 15 Jan., 1811; married Capt. William Sigourney. She died 28 June, 1866.

Caphira married (2) John Bond of Leicester, Mass.

968 VI. DEXTER, born 6 Sept., ...; married Mary ....
969 VII. CAPHIRA B., born 26 Dec., ...; married (1) William Perry, (2) Mr. Cutting.
970 VIII. HARRIET J., born ......, November, ...;
971 IX. JULIA, born ......;
972 X. HENRY DWIGHT, born ......; (1) ......, (2) ....

---

350 (II) ALBAN, SON OF WILLIAM.

Alban Janes married Mary Bliss, about 1813.

CHILDREN.

973 I. ABIGAIL, born 28 Feb., 1814; died 8 July, 1839.
974 II. ELVIRA, born 10 March, 1815; died 27 April, 1841.
975 III. MARY ANN, born 13 Sept., 1818; died 14 June, 1838.
976 IV. SARAH, born 19 Nov., 1820: died April, 1847.
977 V. WILLIAM S., born 8 March, 1826; married Harriet Bixby.
978 VI. ELIZABETH, born 9 Dec., 1829; died 7 April, 1830.
979 VII. HARRIET, born 22 Dec., ...; married Judge Phillips of the Supreme Court, in Connecticut.
980 VIII. CAROLINE, born 10 Feb., ...; married Charles Brown of Brimfield.

---

359 (I) AUGUSTUS, SON OF PELEG C.

Augustus Janes married Betsey Bingham of Royalston, Vt., 19 February, 1818, and lived in Brimfield, Mass.

27

CHILDREN.

981 I. THOMAS B., born 3 Jan., 1819; married Laura Tarbel,
(2) Mrs. Hester.

982 II. LUCY ANN, born 16 Sept., 1821.

983 III. HENRY B., born 1 June, 1823; married Harriet N.
Souther.

984 IV. ADALINE A., born 7 Nov., 1824; married David
Hitchcock of Worcester.

985 V. EDWIN A., born 9 Dec., 1826; married Mrs. Wallace
of Holland.

986 VI. TIMOTHY C., born 25 Aug., 1830; married Maria
C. Holbrook.

----

360 (II) CYNTHIA, DAUGHTER OF PELEG C.

Cynthia Janes married Orlando Greggs of Brimfield,
about 1813.

CHILDREN.

987 I. WILLIAM, born ......; married Julia Phetteplace.

988 II. MARTHA, born ......; married Vernon Corcy.

989 III. MARY, born ......; married Mr. Munson.

990 IV. TIMOTHY, born ......; married ......

991 V. JOSEPH, born ......; married ......

992 VI. CYNTHIA, born ......; married ......

361 (III) TIMOTHY, SON OF PELEG C.

Timothy Janes married Lydia Tyler, of Warren, 1818.

CHILDREN.

993 I. CLEMENTINE, born ......; married Jeremiah Bean, Cincinnatus, N. Y.
994 II. WILLIAM C., born ......; married (1) Julia Tyler of Warren, (2) Martha Bliss of Springfield.
995 III. R. SUMNER, born ......; married Sylvia Webster, Bethel, Vt.
996 IV. LOUISA, born ......, May, 1840.
997 V. MARY, born ....., 1842; married A. M. Hale.

362 (IV) FLAVILLA, DAUGHTER OF PELEG C.

Flavilla Janes married Julius Ward, who was born 4 May, 1788. He died 14 November, 1828, æ. 41.

CHILDREN.

998 I. SARAH M.,[1] born ......, 1818; married Charles B. Lyman.
999 II. CALVIN M., born 25 Feb., 1820; married Sarah A. Brown.
1000 III. AUGUSTA A., born 28 March, 1822; married S. B. Ward.
1001 IV. JANE ELIZABETH, born 22 March, 1824; married Ebenezer Jackson.
1002 V. LUCY M., born 3 June, 1827.
1003 VI. MARY E., born 25 Feb., 1829.

[1] In the Genealogy of the Ward family, published, Emily is in place of Sarah M., and born 1814, unmarried.

364 (VI) CLEMENTINA, DAUGHTER OF PELEG C.

Clementina Janes married 1 January, 1828, Edward Parsons of Northampton. They now reside in Brimfield, Portage county, Ohio, where they moved in 1831, from Northampton.

CHILDREN.

1004 I.   EDWARD A., born 25 Jan., 1829; married Mary F. Underwood.

1005 II. TIMOTHY G., born 17 Sept., 1832; married Eleanor M. Sawyer.

1006 III. HARRIET J., born 24 June, 1835; married Sherman M. Blake.

1007 IV. MARTHA K., born 1 April, 1838; married George Crouse of Akron, Ohio.

1008 V.   WILLIAM C., born 19 Feb., 1841.

1009 VI. CLEMENTINA, born 30 Sept., 1843.

365 (VII) WILLIAM C., SON OF PELEG C.

William C. Janes married June, 1834, Adelphia Fuller of Union. He has made himself a comfortable home in New Haven, being engaged in the carriage manufacturing. He has two enterprising sons, in business, one in Boston, and the other in New York city.

CHILDREN.

1010 I. GEORGE, born 23 Feb., 1838.

1011 II. CHARLES, born 13 Nov., 1845; married Ella F. Janes.

369 (I) HORACE, SON OF ISRAEL C.

Dea. Horace Janes was an excellent man, and a great loss to his friends, the community and the church when he died. He married (1) Lucretia Bascom, 29 December, 1813.

CHILD.

1012 I.   HARRIET S., born 25 December, 1814; died December, 1818.

Horace married (2) Betsey Parker, who was born 3 June, 1794; and was married 18 January, 1816; she died 29 May, 1856.

CHILDREN.

1013 II.   ANNA C., born 27 March, 1818; married Henry Kingsley of Middlebury.

1014 III.   LUCRETIA, born 26 March, 1820.

1015 IV.   SARAH, born 4 March, 1822; married L. R. Bolton of Middlebury.

1016 V.   CHAMPION M., born 7 April, 1824; married Fidelia A. Holcomb.

1017 VI.   BETSEY, born 16 October, 1826; married Josiah W. Parker of New Haven.

1018 VII.   HENRIETTA (twin), born 28 April, 1831; died, infant.

1019 VIII.   HARRIET (twin), born 28 April, 1831.

1020 IX.   MARTHA E., born 3 January, 1834; died 20 April, 1856.

371 (III) LUCY, DAUGHTER OF ISRAEL C.

Lucy Janes married Asa Bond in Cornwall, Vt., 1811.

CHILDREN.

1021 I.   HORACE J., born ......, 1812; married Phebe Parkhurst.

1022 II.   HARTWELL, born ......, 1814; married Philura Harlow.

1023 III.   CHARLES H., born 5 October, 1817; married Lucia W. Brown.

1024 IV.   FRANKLIN, born ......, 1819; married Martha Southmayd.

1025 V.   CAROLINE, born ......, 1821; married James Douglas.

1026 VI.   LUCINA A., born ......, 1823; married Rollin E. Warner.

1027 VII.   WILLARD, born ......, 1825; married Mary Langworthy.

1028 VIII.   EMMA, born ......, 1826.

---

372 (IV) ANNA, DAUGHTER OF ISRAEL C.

Anna Janes married Rufus Mead, who was born in Cornwall, Vt., 4 April, 1793. He died 18 June, 1857. He was the son of Rufus Mead of Rutland, formerly of Connecticut.

CHILDREN.

1029 I.   MARY ANN, born 21 November, 1818; unmarried.

1030 II.   TRIPHENA, born ......; died, infant.

1031 III.   ISRAEL C., born 21 January, 1821.

1032 IV.   LYDIA, born 12 June, 1823; married Charles Smedly.

1033 v.   RUFUS, born 30 March, 1825; married Kate E. Tilden.

1034 vi.   HIRAM, born 10 May, 1827 ; married Elizabeth S. Billings.

1035 vii. HORACE J., born 22 April, 1830; married (1) Mary H. Matthews, (2) Mary A. Wooster.

1036 viii. LORING C., born 12 March, 1832; married (1) Roxana E. Peet, (2) Elizabeth Sheldon.

1037 ix.   MARTIN L., born 23 January, 1834 ; married (1) Hannah W. Treadwell, (2) Myra M. Jenkins of Conway, Mass.

1038 x.   CHARLES M., born 28 January, 1836 ; married Caroline Thayer.

The sons of Mrs. Anna Janes Mead, Hiram, Martin and Charles have obtained a liberal education, graduating at Middlebury College. Hiram entered the ministry, was settled at South Hadley, and receiving a call from a church in Nashua, N. H., he left the former field for one he considered more congenial to his taste and usefulness. He was installed in December, 1867.

Martin practices medicine at Albany, N. Y., where he is engaged in a good business, and has obtained a large circle of friends, and is efficient and active in the church of the Congregational order, where he is a worthy member.

Charles, since his travels in Europe, with his brother Hiram, has been elected professor of Hebrew language and Literature, in the Andover Theological Seminary. He pursued studies in Germany, and received the degree of Ph. D., from the University of Gottingen.

Rufus edited the *Middlebury Register* for several years, and afterward was appointed United States consul at Jan Juan del Sur, Nicaragua.

---

379 (I) ABEL, SON OF CYRUS.

Abel Janes married Eurydice Greenwood of Hebron, Me.

CHILDREN.

1039 I.   SOPHIA, born......; died October, 1864.
1040 II. ADELE, born......;
1041 III. MARY, born......;

---

381 (III) ALVAN, SON OF GYRUS.

Alvan Janes married Mary Homer of Brimfield, Mass.

CHILDREN.

1042 I.   DAVID W., born 1 February, 1827.
1043 II. CATHARINE P., born 5 October, 1829; married Charles A. Clark, of Worcester.
1044 III. CHARLES A., born 21 June, 1833.

---

384 (VI) VELINA, DAUGHTER OF CYRUS.

Velina Janes married in 1832, Nathan Hitchcock.

CHILDREN.

1045 I. JULIA S., born......;
1046 II. LAURA S., born......;

Velina married (2) William Tucker, and resides in Springfield.

385 (VII) HARVEY, SON OF CYRUS.

Harvey Janes resides on the old homestead, is an industrious, intelligent husbandman, and has the credit of doing, not a little, to furnish material for this genealogy, from Brimfield. He married Sarepta Harding of Southbridge.

CHILD.

1047 I. HORACE E., born 18 June, 1845.

406 (II) ELIJAH, SON OF ELISHA.

Elijah Janes married........., and lived for a time in Lansingburgh.

CHILDREN.

1048 I.   ELISHA (?), born......;
1049 II. OLIVE (?), born......;
1050 III. MARY (?), born......;
1051 IV. ELIJAH (?), born...... ;

411 (II) N. LORENZO, SON OF LIBERTY.

Nelson Lorenzo Janes, was raised on the mountains of Vermont, taking the old homestead so industriously cultivated by his father's earnest and laborious toil; and concluding that western enterprise was more inviting than rough farming, sold out, and became a western agent for Fairbanks's scales. He left Berkshire for a home in Racine, Wis.

CHILDREN.

1052 i.   LORENZO (?), born ...... ;
1053 ii.   ELIJAH, (?) born ......;
1054 iii. CLARINDA (?), born ...... ;
1055 iv.   SARAH (?), born ...... ;

---

414 (I) RUTH C., DAUGHTER OF ORSAMUS.

Ruth C. Janes married Philomel Moon of Brimfield, about 1840.

CHILDREN.

1056 i.   SON, born ...... ;
1057 ii.   EDWARD, born ...... ;

---

415 (II) MARY ELIZA, DAUGHTER OF ORSAMUS.

Mary Eliza Janes married Frederic H. Purington of Bristol, Conn., in 1827.

CHILDREN.

1058 i.   FREDERIC, born ...... ;
1059 ii.   ELIZABETH, born...... ; married ...... ; and has one daughter.

---

416 (VIII) NANCY E., DAUGHTER OF ORSAMUS.

Nancy E. Janes married November, 1829, John Ross of West Brookfield, Mass., who went in the fall of 1855, with others to Kansas; settled in Lawrence,

built one of the first houses there. It was burned in
the Quantrell raid and rebuilt the same year. He
now resides there. He was born in West Brookfield,
14 May, 1803. His father was Dea. John Ross.

CHILDREN.

1060 I.   NANCY M., born 25 July, 1832; married George F.
Needham of Baltimore.
1061 II. HENRIETTA, born 5 Nov., 1835; married Hon. Sidney Clark.
1062 III. JOHN PASCHAL, born 4 April, 1839; married Rosa-
line Spicer of New York, 1865.
1063 IV. FRANCES S., born ......;
1064 V.   JOSEPH, born ......;

———

417 (IV) EUNICE C., DAUGHTER OF ORSAMUS.

Eunice C. Janes married Jonathan Emerson.

CHILDREN.

1065 I.   FITZROY, born 1836 (?)
1066 II. JOSEPHINE, born 1838 (?)
1067 III. HELEN, born 1840 (?)
1068 IV. MARY, born 1842 (?)

SEVENTH GENERATION.

LINE OF WILLIAM.

432 (II) EDWARD, SON OF WILLIAM.

Edward Janes of Virginia married, perhaps, after he went west. Elizabeth Fleisher, daughter of Henry Fleisher, from Germany.

CHILDREN.

1069 I.   WILLIAM, born 6 July, 1802; died young.
1070 II.   HENRY F., born 12 Feb., 1804; married Keziah Ann Talbot.
1071 III. ANN, born March, 1806.
1072 IV.   MARGARET, born ......, 1808.
1073 V.   JOHN S., born ......, 1810.
1074 VI.   EDWARD P., born June, 1813; resides in California.
1075 VII. JOSEPH T., born 18 Nov., 1818; resides in Kansas.
1076 VIII. ELIZABETH, born ......, 1822; married S. McMullen; resides in Ill.
1077 IX.   ELLEN, born ......, 1825.

435 (I) WILLIAM, SON OF THOMAS.

William Janes, son of Thomas, of the southern branch, was born near Petersburgh, Va., and early moved to Wilkes county, Ga., in the year 1791, and was a planter and merchant. He became wealthy and possessed of influence. He was highly esteemed for his many natural and Christian graces, and his uniform benevolence.

He married Selah Gresham, 31 January, 1793, and died 9 July, 1827.

CHILDREN.

1078 I. THOMAS G., born 11 July, 1794; married (1) Miss West, (2) Miss West, (3) Miss Sanford. He died 1843.

1079 II. ABSALOM, born 8 Jan., 1796; married Cordelia Calloway. He died 1847.

1080 III. SUSAN, born 21 Dec., 1798; married Jesse Calloway. He died 1859.

1081 IV. ELIZABETH, born 18 July, 1800; married Robert Gibson.

1082 V. EDWARD, born 12 July, 1802; married (1) Miss Calloway, (2) Miss Bull, (3) Miss Ragan.

1083 VI. ARCHIBALD, born 7 Oct., 1804; married Miss Johnstone. He died 1859.

1084 VII. WILLIAM, born 27 Feb., 1807; married Rebecca Mercer. He died 28 Aug., 1854.

1085 VIII. SIMEON R., born 10 March, 1809; married Elizabeth Gresham. He died 1834.

1086 IX. LOVICIA, born 12 March, 1811; married Dr. L. B. Mercer. She died 1840.

1087 X. SELAH, born 21 Nov., 1812; married Rev. W. D. Cowdry.

1088 XI. DANIEL H., born 14 March, 1815; married Frances Lamar.

1089 XII. MARY F., born 18 July, 1818; married Dr. E. H. Richardson.

438 (1) ESTHER M., DAUGHTER OF BENJAMIN.

Esther Maria Janes married Amasa Barden. She died 4 February, 1837.

CHILDREN.

1090 I.   WEALTHY W., born 31 Aug., 1820 ; married Lucius G. Seeley, and resides in Bridgeport, Conn.

1091 II.   HORATIO, born 17 Sept., 1822; married Maria Hill.

1092 III. JESSE A., born 26 March, 1824; married Adaline Blake.

1093 IV.   SARAH M., born 23 Oct., 1826; married Nathan Price.

1094 V.   MARY E., born 3 April, 1829; married Ebenezer Hill.

1095 VI.   ALMA J., born 23 Sept., 1831; married Enoch B. Randall, and lives in Ill.

1096 VII. EDWIN J., born 29 Jan., 1835; married Sarah Jones.

---

439 (II) SARAH S., DAUGHTER OF BENJAMIN.

Sarah S. Janes married Ira Adams, 27 April, 1823. She died 7 January, 1855. He died 2 May, 1856.

CHILDREN.

1097 I.   ORVILLE, born 9 Nov., 1825; married Amanda Hill.

1098 II.   CARLOS W., born 6 May, 1829; married Mary Wentworth.

1099 III. HUBERT, born 6 March, 1831; died July, 1832.

1100 IV.   EDMUND J., born 8 Feb., 1834; married Phebe N. Williams.

440 (III) HAMILTON B., SON OF BENJAMIN.

Hamilton B. Janes married Edith Wentworth. She died October, 1853. He died 22 April, 1860.

CHILDREN.

1101 I. GEORGE L., born ......; married Clarissa Bonney.
1102 II. CAROLINE, born ......, 1843; married John Smith, a patriot soldier.
1103 III. ELIZABETH, born 15 April, 1845.
1104 IV. ALMOND T., born ......; resides with sister Caroline.

---

441 (IV) EDMUND STORER, SON OF BENJAMIN.

Edmund Storer Janes, D. D., senior bishop but one of the Methodist Episcopal church, is an extraordinary man and minister.

In assuming the delicate and responsible task of writing a condensed biographical sketch of this distinguished person for this genealogy, we hope to perform an act of justice, and truthfully to add to the record some facts not heretofore given to the public and but little known beyond a limited circle. It is well to gather up and place in consecutive order the scattered material concerning one who occupies so prominent a place in the eye of the world, and especially in his own communion.

He was born in Sheffield, Berkshire county, Mass., 27 April, 1807, twin with Rev. Edwin Lines Janes, now of Flushing, a discreet, true, and faithful member and minister of the M. E. church. Page

154 speaks of his father, page 121 his grandfather, page 100 his great-grandfather, page 85 his great-great-grandfather, and from 31 to 79 page, is the sketch of his great-great-great-grandfather the honored emigrant, William Janes or Jeanes, who died in Northampton, Mass., 1690, aged ninety years.

He was the *son of a carpenter*, and when four years of age, his father moved to Salisbury, Conn., an adjoining town, where he attended to farming as well as to his trade. Edmund Storer was principally engaged in labor upon the farm during the summer months till he was seventeen years of age.

From 1824 to 1830 he was for the most part engaged in teaching, and pursuing those practical branches, which would better qualify him for public life, whether for teaching or some other profession. He made rapid progress in his youth in the solid branches, in the literary classics and in some of the sciences. For some time he read books on law, with the intention of entering the legal profession. He was more especially brought under the influences of religion when about twenty years of age, at a time little previous to his expected entering upon the practice of the law, when God's solemn providence struck down suddenly his intended partner in business. This note of conscious warning turned his attention particularly from secular to spiritual things, and determined his other future plans for life which have brought him so eminently and so conspicuously before the world. Not long after this event he connected himself with the church of Christ, and his mind naturally revolved the inquiry concerning a clearer path in which to walk, and a more satisfactory way of doing some work for God and his church.

At the age of twenty-two he was licensed by the Quarterly conference of Belleville circuit, New Jersey, to preach the gospel. In April, 1830, he joined the Philadelphia conference of the Methodist Episcopal church. He was stationed for that, and the succeeding year, in Elizabeth, N. J. The following year he was appointed to Orange, N. J., and at the conference of 1833, was returned to that church; but in a few days, Bishop Emory appointed him an agent for Dickinson College to give a new impulse to her financial welfare. At the conference of 1834 and 1835, he was reappointed to the same laudable agency, employing in the whole, three years, to the arduous service of this institution.

Now commenced a new and important period in the life of this active, faithful man. He took a genial and heavenly-minded partner for his future life's voyage. He married Charlotte Thibou of New York city, whose parents and herself were honored members of the Episcopal church, and her mother was a sister of Bishop Croes of the diocese of New Jersey, who preceded Bishop Doane of the same diocese. But she devoted herself most actively to the interest of her adopted communion: a new and more appropriate field to call forth her rare womanly gifts, and evincing to her friends how well chosen was her new walk, and how certainly she would prove herself a happy and

valuable companion of so ardent a servant of Christ.
She was all to her husband that he had fondly anticipated, highly educated and disciplined to diligent
service in the church, cultivated for the most refined
society, capable of filling any required position in the
circle of female friends, and of stimulating by example
and precept those who came within the sweep of her
influence. Her grandfather was a descendant of the
Huguenots, and came from France to this land of
free religion, to enjoy more unfalteringly the faith of
his fathers. Mrs. Charlotte Janes was a true and affectionate help-mate to the man of God, the future bishop,
who in April, 1836, was appointed pastor of the Fifth
street church, Philadelphia, and it would not be *pre-
suming* to say, that she has done her part as an excellent wife, to bring out the talents of the man, and
assist him on, to a higher niche of fame and usefulness,
than under other circumstances he could have attained.
She is indeed the true woman, the polished, the modest,
the discreet, the fearless, the talented, the extraordinary
woman, mother, Christian, wife. During the latter part
of the first year in Philadelphia, Dr. Janes suffered
severely from an acute inflammation of the throat,
and at the conference of 1837, at his own request, he
was removed from the Fifth street church, being unable to speak in so large an audience room, and appointed to Nazareth church, Philadelphia, which had
a smaller audience room and one much more appropriate for him, as one who had an apparently injured
voice. He was reappointed to this church in 1838.

During these three years of pastoral work in Philadelphia, he read medicine with Dr. Hallowell, and attended medical lectures in the University of the State of Pennsylvania, and soon after received the degree of doctor of medicine from the Vermont University, and from that point a number of other degrees from Dickinson College. `

At the conference of 1839 he was transferred to the New York conference, and appointed pastor of the Mulberry street church. Near the close of that conference year, he was elected financial secretary of the American Bible Society. The congregation were so unwilling he should leave them, that he consented to be reappointed to the charge at the conference of 1840, and also filled the secretaryship; doing double duty all the year. The conference years of 1841, 1842 and 1843, were wholly and earnestly devoted to the interests of that noble institution, the American Bible Society. During these three years, he traveled in nearly all the states of the Union, and gave an impulse to the financial prosperity of that society, which is felt to this day.

He left the secretaryship when elected and ordained one of the bishops of the Methodist Episcopal church of America. He was ordained deacon in 1832 and elder in 1834. In 1842, he received the degree of, M. D. from the Vermont University, and in the same year, that of A. M. from the Dickinson College, and in 1844 that of D. D. from the same institution.

In fulfilling the duties of his high office as bishop,

he has had to perform extensive tours of travel throughout the length and breadth of the country.

He has twice visited California and Oregon, going and returning the way of the isthmus once, and once in returning from the Pacific coast (the year 1863) he crossed the mountains of Nevada and journeyed down the valleys and over the intervening sections of the country, which he desired to visit. On this this journey he stopped a considerable time at Salt Lake city, and preached the first time that any Methodist minister ever preached in that modern Sodom. He has also a number of times crossed the Atlantic ocean on business for the general conference, and twice visited the Methodist missions in France, Switzerland, Germany, Denmark, Norway and Sweden. During this visit to Europe he presided over one of the German conferences. In 1864, the general conference appointed him their representative to the British conference in England. He visited that conference in this representative capacity.

Bishop Janes had the responsibility of holding a conference in the town of Bonham, Texas, in February, 1859, which still adhered to the Methodist Episcopal church at a time when the blood of southern chivalry was up to a fever heat, when for one less bold and courageous and of less diplomatic tact, it would have been all his life was worth to be at work in any good cause among such hot-headed, fiery-tempered upstarts of that peculiar region and critical day. He faced the conscious offenders and bore himself with his usual dignity, grace and urbanity, as he rose to the importance of the occasion. He spoke calmly and with Christian forbearance to their impertinent leaders, who were lawyers and judges. His commanding presence, gentleness and extraordinary self-possession, triumphed over mob wrath, over the fury of these disturbers of good order, despisers of law, and of the rights of American citizens.

It may be said with truth he has been greatly prospered, in his various and important fields of labor. Wherever God has called him to efforts, in different pastoral charges, he has signally blessed his ministry, in the conversion of many souls to God, and the interest of the truth. He continues to preach the gospel as frequently as ever, in different towns and cities, and in various places throughout the United States. Where-ever he is making a flying visit on business for the conferences, he is captured and expected to preach. He must preach at camp meeting, he must preach at conferences, he must preach at the dedication of churches, he must preach in every city or town where he spends the Lord's day, and never entertain the thought of discharge in this war.

He has probably traveled more extensively on ministerial service, ordained more ministers, and consecrated more churches, than any man in America.

At a recent conference he spoke at some length on the solemn and impressive questions ordered by the Methodist church on the admission of deacons. "The first thing," he said, "that concerned a man was the salvation of his own soul. He must never decline in fervor, but let the love of Christ impel him to the proper discharge of his religious duties. Meditation and prayer are essential to spiritual advancement. None can increase in knowledge except by reading and meditation, and none can obtain the divine light except by prayer. The truly Christian minister must have the light of the Holy Ghost shed upon him. The Bible is the constant companion of the minister, but human nature and human character are as essential to study. The sermons preached ten years ago would not touch the hearts of people now. Those who would make their ministry successful must note carefully the constant changes in human society."

When we saw the bishop for the first time, a few years ago, he appeared quite small in stature, but of late he has rounded up and run to *waist*, not a little. His mental labors do not counteract the influence of good living incidental to his position and society.

The peculiar shrill notes of his voice will always attract attention and be remembered. If he has given it the rigid discipline and long training which Demosthenes did, he will hardly expect to acquire great compass of voice. Bishop Janes appears to be the embodiment of will. He is called the greatest ecclesiastical administrator of the age. His executive ability is superior; it towers high above most of his coadjutors, and is perhaps equal to any living man. He enforces the strictest discipline as best comporting with the highest interest of their system, and he readily convinces all his disciples of the utility and advantage of whatever relates to their ecclesastical order. He has genius, foresight, financial talent, clearness of intellectual perception, tact and fervor, which make him a decided leader, and crown with success his various efforts to advance the welfare of the Methodist Episcopal church in America, and elsewhere.

He has gray hair, a venerable, and a quiet though impressive dignity. His serious expression is not so severe, cold and searching as may be imagined, for all who know his heart, know he is a man of generous sympathies. He is a true thinker, and an earnest worker. His mind is always grappling, always solving, always illuminating the problems of the Christian's faith, and his energies are ever toiling, ever achieving and ever pressing onward in the line of his responsible duties. For him, rest and weariness of the mental and physical are almost strangers.

From the commencement of his teaching school up through his self-denying and various duties as pastor, as financial agent, or as bishop, his entire life has been made up of thought and effort. His countenance betokens the yearnings of his soul for intellectual, moral and spiritual advancement, and it shows that his decision and sternness of purpose are not likely to fail him, in carrying out his plans and in securing success. An acquaintance with the bishop will confirm such judgment. Though gentlemanly and courteous, he is slightly reserved; but most uniform and consistent in his opinions, open, frank, exhibiting sterling traits of character, large intelligence, and fervent piety. He stands before you. the highly educated gentleman, the devout Christian who teaches by a lofty aim, under no circumstances whatever to weary of expanding and adorning the mind, and of redeeming and purifying the soul.

Bishop Janes is a calm, unassuming preacher, speaking in large churches with some labor, but at intervals decidedly animated. He has not the bravo of the boisterous, or the declamatory style of crude, unfinished speakers; his whole delivery is forceful, keen, pungent, but subdued. All his sermons, which are generally extempore, wear the same aspect of deep thought, much premeditation, critical reasoning, and devout, religious fervor.

This brief sketch will here close, with the addition of some extracts, from an anniversary address, before the Bible Society in 1838, and some extracts from his few published sermons.

Extracts of an Address delivered May, 1838, at the City of New York before the American Bible Society at its Anniversary.

*   *   *   *   *   *   *

Yes, sir, the Bible cause furnishes a channel sufficiently wide and deep to receive and bear to a perishing world the confluent sympathies of the entire church. To fully meet the drafts upon its treasury would require the munificence of the Bible-enriched nations: and to perform all its mental and physical labors would employ all the mental and physical powers that have ever been consecrated to God and philanthropy.

The Bible in the moral world, like the sun in the solar system, attracts our vision, as a common centre, and then by

its effulgent irradiations discloses with perfect distinctness
every other subject within the whole circle of divine truth.

*   *   *   *   *   *   *   *

It is not the mere existence of so many colors, but their happy
combination that constitutes the rainbow, that latest specimen
of the divine penciling. In that pleasant symbol of mercy,
that bright and enduring seal of promise, the lustre of each color
contributes to the radiance and perfection of the whole beaute-
ous form and the loveliness of the entire figure affords a rich
revenue of glory to each separate color; and the brighter
any of these constituents shall shine, the richer will be the
glow, and the more enchanting the appearance of the whole;
and the more splendid the combination is rendered, the more
interesting becomes each integral part — so that all are indebted to each, and each are dependent upon all — the glory
of each is the glory of all, and the glory of all is the glory
of each. Thus, sir, with the church. It is the combined
excellencies of all the denominations that gives to her her
winning beauty and her powerful charms; and the more tran-
scendant the excellencies of any one denomination becomes,
the more resplendent the whole church is rendered, and the
more fascinating and attractive her graces appear; while the
more lustrous the whole church is constituted, the more vivid
and striking will be the phasis of each denomination. Sir,
it is not the simple existence of so many shining constellations,
but their existing together, side by side, in the same heavens,
shining *with* each other, and *upon* each other, that gives to
midnight her gorgeous canopy, her firmamental glory, her
overwhelming magnificence. And it is the existing together
of so many Christian denominations, bestudding and illuminating the same spiritual firmament, that presents to the world
the moral grandeur, the stupendous glory of the church,
which is destined to command the homage and the admiration
of all men; and even now renders her to her enemies, *terrible as an army with banners.* With these views I would say
to all denominations, "Arise and shine." "Put on thy

beautiful garments"—burnish anew your celestial armor—
multiply the trophies of your victories—and augment the
glory of your moral achievements.   *   *   *   *

The work of translating the Bible into all the languages and
dialects of the world, and affording a full supply of the scriptures thus translated, to all people, is a work so gigantic and
requiring so great an amount of means and efforts, that it appears to me all denominations ought to become incorporate for
the accomplishment of so magnificent and glorious a purpose.
The different denominations, acting independently, cannot
accomplish it without great delay, and needless expenditure
for duplicate stereotype plates, separate establishments, and
consequently increased incidental expenses. The condition
of the world requires of all Christians *prompt action* in this
cause, upon the most advantageous and economical plan. The
opportunity to do which is evidently afforded by this associa-
tion. The condition of the world! I must not occupy your
time with a description of it; but perhaps I shall be permitted to attempt a figurative representation thereof: in doing
which I would stretch my canvass from eternity to eternity.
I would then unroll so much of it as the short space called
time would permit. As we unrolled it, the first object dis-
cerned would be "the garden planted eastward in Eden," over
which the blighting curse of sin had passed, withering its
perrennial flowers and blasting its delectable fruits; leaving
nothing to relieve the saddened prospect but the lone star of
promise, that threw its few but cheering rays upon the uni-
versal gloom. The next object of prominence which we behold,
is Mount Sinai, covered with smoke, and cloud, and fire, trembling beneath the awfulness of the Godhead. Still further down
upon the canvass, we see Mount Calvary, reddened with
the blood of atonement. On its summit rests the bright cloud
of mercy, and around it, to a considerable distance, shines
strong and clear the light of heaven. The remaining object
which we particularize, is the river of Death, which forms the
boundary between earth and heaven, and rolls its dark and

rapid current on to the ocean of eternity. Over this river there is but one bridge, and that is formed by the blood-stained cross of Christ, resting one end upon the shore of time, and the other upon that of immortality, on which the enlightened few are passing safely, to enjoy "the rest that remains to the people of God." All the remaining part of the canvass is crowded with a benighted, polluted, and sensual multitude of human beings, amounting to more than six hundred millions, groping in darkness, famishing with want, and increasing in wickedness; and this entire mass of human population, under the same resistless influence, are moving with hurried steps, and confused and frantic views, directly towards the river of Death; not knowing whither they are going until its cold flood overwhelms them, and the gloom of that hopeless eternity to which they are borne, reveals to them the desperateness of their condition. Oh, sir, shall we not relieve this scene of its horrors? Shall we not cast upon this whole prospect the radiance of inspiration? Shall we not, by the agency of the Bible, pour all along this dark engulfing stream the blazing light of salvation; revealing to these perishing millions, in blessed relief, the cross of Christ, offering to them the safe and available means of access to that heaven for which they were created, and in which they alone can find fullness of enjoyment for their imperishable souls. What we do, sir, we must do *quickly*.

Extract of a Sermon preached before the Superintendents and Teachers of the Philadelphia Conference Sunday School Union, in 1837.

They afford an opportunity of doing good to the community. All the wickedness and unlawful and riotous conduct existing in society, arise either from the ignorance or depravity of the persons guilty of them. If, then, by sabbath and other schools, we instruct and educate all the rising generation, we wholly remove one of the prolific sources of public insecurity and calamity. And if, by the agency of these institutions, we bring the youthful population under moral and religious influences, and not only make them enlightened, but pious, when they come forward in life, we shall then have dried up entirely sources of public immoralities, disturbances, and tumults ; and, having removed the cause, the effect must cease. And, to whatever extent we can accomplish these purposes, in exactly the same proportion do we establish public morals and the general weal. I will here take occasion to observe that knowledge and religion are the only conservative powers upon which society can safely depend for quiet and happiness. Peace can look no where else for a mandate directed to the stormy passions of depraved men, saying " be still," which command shall hush them in undisturbed tranquillity.   And liberty, abused and endangered liberty, can turn her beseeching eye to no other power adequate to give stability to her empire and enlargement to her dominions. It was in view of these facts, that, after the French revolution had spent most of its terrific violence in blasphemy, anarchy, and bloodshed, the politic but irreligious Napoleon, having seized the helm of the government, declared, " We must restore the sanctions of religion." The same political sagacity, combined with genuine patriotism, induced the sage Franklin, when Paine's *Age of Reason* was submitted to him in manuscript, to say to the infidel author: " I would advise you not to attempt unchaining the tiger, but to burn this piece before it is seen by any other person. If men are so wicked with religion, what would they be without it ? "   However novel and startling the declaration may be to some, and however unwilling others may be to admit the truth, I nevertheless affirm the fact, that the unpretending, and too often unnoticed, but devoted, holy. and praying body of sabbath school laborers of the present day, are doing more for the promotion of public virtue and the establishment and perpetuity of free institutions, than all the legislation and political arrangements of the world.   They are the " standing army " of freedom. They are the Spartan band that have placed themselves in the

Thermopylæ of the moral world, and hold in check, until the the gospel shall subdue them, the more than Xerxean host of the vicious.

Extract of a Sermon preached at Camp-meeting at Morristown, Sunday morning, 18 August, 1867.

*   *   *   The gospel, nevertheless, is a law; it has its precepts; it has its requirements; it has its sanction; and in every respect is it a law. But, inasmuch as owing to our lapsed estate, we are incapable of rendering to God that perfect obedience which Adam could have rendered, God now permits us to fulfill this law by loving him with our might and mind and strength. And when we love him with all our heart, there will be found in that love an inspiration to all duty and to all devotion. It will incline us to every principle and precept which is laid down in the word of God. We shall be ready for all service, for all sacrifice, for all duty, for all obedience. If, then, under the gospel dispensation — our dispensation under this covenant of grace in which we are placed — we fail, through our Lord Jesus Christ, and the assistance of God's truth and Spirit, to love him with all our power, and consequently to serve him with all our ability, then our whole character and conduct are criminal before him. We need not specify men's transgression; we need not to-day accuse you of profaning the name of God; of violating his holy sabbath; of breaking his commandments. The great fact that makes us criminal before him is the one I have referred to, that we have failed to avail ourselves of the provisions of his grace, to obtain a character that shall itself incline us to a life of conformity to his will and word.

Our impenitence, our neglect of God, our failing to accept, Christ, our not receiving the gift of the Holy Ghost, our not becoming good, our not living right — here is the great offense, here is the sum of all sin, as it is the root of all evil, in our hearts and lives. We might have been saved from them. It is our crime that we remain in them. As the apostle says in our text : " If we say we have no sin, we deceive ourselves, and the truth is not in us." Our outward morality, our formal services, are not meeting our obligations to God. It is the love, inspired obedience and devotion, and consecration to him of hearts and service that meet our obligations and conform us to principles and precepts of the gospel of our Lord Jesus Christ.

Let me ask your attention for a moment to the extent of this law, to its spirituality. As we have just intimated, it does not merely refer to the outward conduct. It takes cognizance of our moral state; our motives; our spirit; our thoughts; our words; our negligences; our want of conformity, as well as our transgressions; and now when we look at our hearts and see our vain thoughts and sinful motives — at least our mixed and imperfect motives — our negligences; how we have failed of our obligations to our God, and even to our own soul; how we have misspent probationary time; failed to attain the image of God and the mind of Christ, and preparedness for his fellowship here and his fruition hereafter — oh how our sinfulness comes up before our mind! how great our criminality before God! And when we consider the character of him against whom we have sinned; the rightfulness of his authority; the wonderfulness of his love; the greatness of his forbearance; the tenderness of his entreaties, and remember we have sinned despite all his goodness and grace — how aggravated are our sins! how terrible the turpitude of our guilt in his sight!   *   *   *   *   *

But when we seek forgiveness, there must be a moment when God says, " Thy sins are forgiven thee." And when the pardon is written both in his book and on the heart, oh how quick it comes, and how consciously are we apprised of the fact! And I believe we may be a long time seeking our sanctification, and growing better all the while too. The work may be gradual according to the context, that " if we walk in the light as he is in the light, we have fellowship one with another, and the blood of Jesus Christ his Son cleanses us from all sin." This walking with God of itself is a sanctifying power, and the meditating upon God, reading the word of God, observing the sacraments and ordinances of God, are all transforming; and no man can be in a justified state, and walk in the light, without growing better. And if he continues to walk with God, there will come in his experience a moment when he will rejoice in the consciousness that the promise of the text has been fulfilled, that he is cleansed from all unrighteousness — every affection holy, every aspiration of his spirit pure, every motive right; he can say with the Psalmist, "Thou restorest my soul." He has received the spirit of power, and of love, and of a sound mind. The soul is restored — restored to the image and nature of God; he is "cleansed from all sin." 　　*　　*　　*　　*

CHILDREN.

1104 I. LEWIS THIBOU, born 7 May, 1836; married Mary Baird.

1105 II. CHARLOTTE THIBOU, born 19 July 1838; married Rev. Charles Harris.

1106 III. SARAH ELIZABETH, born 16 April, 1841.

1107 IV. MATILDA PALMER, born 15 Dec, 1847; died 7 March, 1864.

Rev. Edwin Lines Janes, son of Benjamin, and twin with Edmund Storer, taking his second name from his grandmother, Rachel Lines, married Elizabeth Ogden, who died a few years since leaving no issue.

He is a faithful preacher of the Methodist Episcopal church, unassuming, mild, active and efficient. He has labored for some years in New York and vicinity. He has taken much pains to aid the writer in various ways in arriving at the truth of facts, and can. be highly commended for his many noble qualities of mind and heart.

444   (VII) JOHN W., SON OF BENJAMIN.

John Wood Janes married (1) Abigail S. Hatch, (2) Harriet M. Deming. Abigail died 14 August, 1840.

CHILDREN.

1108 I.   CHARLOTTE ELIZABETH, born 17 February, 1844; died 23 December, 1858.

1109 II.   JOHN WESLEY, born 9 November, 1846; died 13 April, 1863.

1110 III. HARRIET ELIZA, born 19 June, 1853.

1111 IV.   FRANCES ELLIOTT, born 31 March, 1856.

1112 V.   CHARLOTTE ELSIE, born 14 June, 1858.

----

445 (VIII) ALMOND T., SON OF BENJAMIN.

Almond Thomas Janes bears the name of his grandfather, Thomas Janes, who was killed suddenly at Wallingford. He married Lucia Wilcox of Salisbury, Conn.

CHILDREN.

1113 I.   HENRY EDMUND, born 10 January, 1840.

1114 II.   EGBERT ALMOND, born 10 April, 1842; married Mary V. Howe.

1115 III. MARIA LORILLA, born 25 February, 1845 ; married Edgar Doughty.

1116 IV.   EDWIN CARLOS, born 11 May, 1848.

1117 V.   HELEN ELIZA, born 10 December, 1851.

1118 VI.   HUBERT DWIGHT, born 1 July, 1853.

1119 VII. MINNA IDELLA, born 5 August, 1855.

447 (II) RACHEL, DAUGHTER OF THOMAS M.

Rachel Janes married (1) John Lane, and lived in North Madison, Conn.

CHILD.

1120 I.   JOHN, born ......; a patriot soldier, was a member of
the 15th Conn. Infantry; and was killed in 1863.

Rachel married (2) Jesse Tooley.

CHILDREN.

1121 I.   MINERVA, born ......;
1122 III. OSCAR, born ......;
1123 IV. MARTHA, born ...... All reside in North Madison,
Conn.

---

448 (III) DAMARIS, DAUGHTER OF THOMAS M.

Damaris Janes married Albert Judd of Cheshire, Conn., who was born 20 October, 1805.

CHILDREN.

1124 I.   MARY, born 27 Oct., 1836; married Joseph Wurtz,
14 June, 1866.
1125 II. ISAAC W., born 17 Sept., 1839; died 13 Dec., 1843.
1126 III. MARTHA, born 30 July, 1842.
1127 IV. ISAAC, born 16 July, 1845.
1128 V.   MARIA E., born 5 July, 1848; died 27 March, 1849.

450 (V) LURINDA, DAUGHTER OF THOMAS M.

Lurinda Janes married Charles A. Blackman of Woodbury, Conn., where they now reside.

CHILDREN.

1129 I.   MARY ELIZA, born 24 April, 1835; married Jacob Tanner.

1130 II.   GEORGE BEECHER, born 11 October, 1837.

1131 III. JANE E., born 22 February, 1841; married Edward P. Cheeney.

1132 IV.   CHARLES FREDERICK, born 10 April, 1843.

1133 V.   SARAH ANN, born 30 July, 1847; married Henry Broas.

1134 VI.   FLORA ELLA, born 10 May, 1849.

1135 VII. JOHN WATSON, born 22 June, 1851; died 2 October, 1852.

1136 VIII. LUCY LURINDA, born 11 July, 1853.

1137 IX.   HATTIE ESTELLA, born 28 March, 1856.

Hon. Horace Greeley married Edward P. Cheeney's sister.

SEVENTH GENERATION.

454 (I) PATTY, DAUGHTER OF NOAH.

Patty (Martha) Janes married Solomon Strong, 3 January, 1799.   She died 4 April, 1810.

CHILDREN.

1138 I.   JOSHUA S., born ......; lived in Readsburgh, Wis.; died Oct., 1862.
1139 II. FOSTER CHURCHILL, born ......, 1809;
1140 III. A SON, born ......;
1141 IV. A DAUGHTER, born ......;

455 (II) NAOMI, DAUGHTER OF NOAH.

Naomi Janes married Deacon Sylvester Lyman, 6 November, 1800.   He was born May, 1773.

CHILDREN.

1142 I.   SON, born ......; 1802.
1143 II.   SAMUEL MOSELY, born 23 Dec., 1803.
1144 III. URSULA, born 13 May, 1806.
1145 IV.   NAOMI, born 26 Aug., 1808.
1146 V.   SYLVESTER, born ......; 1813.
1147 VI.   JOSEPH EMERSON, born 2 April, 1817.
1148 VII. ELIZABETH, born 25 May, 1820.
1149 VIII. TIRZAH, born 21 Nov., 1821.

456 (III) SYLVANUS, SON OF NOAH.

Sylvanus Janes of Vergennes, Vt., married Laura McNamara.

CHILDREN.

1150 I.   PATTY, born ......;
1151 II.   SALLY, born ......;
1152 III. GRISWOLD, born ......;
1153 IV.   ALBERT SYLVESTER, born......;
1154 V.   RUTH, born ......;
1155 VI.   CLARISSA, born ......;
1156 VII. HARRIET, born ......;

— —

458 (V) CHESTER, SON OF NOAH.

Chester Janes married Anna Fish of Sheldon, Vt.

CHILD.

1157 I. DANIEL FISH, born ......;

———

462 (IX) JULIUS, SON OF NOAH.

Julius Janes, was twin with Lucas (who married Sally Wood, having no issue), and married Nancy Eggleston.

CHILDREN.

1158 I.   JULIUS, born ......;
1159 II.   HARRIET, born ......;
1160 III. JUSTUS, born ......;
1161 IV.   ALBERT, born ......;
1162 V.   DAUGHTER, born ......;
1163 VI.   DAUGHTER, born ......;
1164 VII. JOHN, born ......;

463 (X) LEWIS, SON OF NOAH.

Dr. Lewis Janes married Huldah M. Wilder, and resides in Swanton Centre. He has felt quite an interest in the history of his fathers. He is a successful practitioner.

CHILDREN.

1165 I. EMILY M., born ......;
1166 II. ELLERY W., born ......;
1167 III. EDNA, born ......;

---

464 (I) MARY, DAUGHTER OF SAMUEL.

Mary Janes married Ebenezer Billings. We have heard they live near Boston.

CHILDREN.

1168 I. MARY, born ......;
1169 II. CHARLES H. HAMMETT, born ......;
1170 III. JOSEPH, born ......;
1171 IV. JANES, born ......;
1172 V. REBECCA, born ......;
1173 VI. GEORGE, born ......;
1174 VII. HANNAH, born ......;
1175 VIII. HENRY, born ......;

---

472 (I) NANCY, DAUGHTER OF ENOS.

Nancy Janes married Zenas Sykes of Westboro, Mass.

CHILDREN.

1176 I. ORENDO, born ......; married Miss Montague.
1177 II. LORING, born ......; married John Barney of Michigan.

1178 III. LUCINA, born ...... ;
1179 IV. PLINY, born ...... ;
1180 V. SAMUEL. born ... .. ;
1181 VI. ZENAS, born ...... ;
1182 VII. CHARLES, born ...... ;
1183 VIII. JOHN, born ...... ;

473 (II) LOVISA, DAUGHTER OF ENOS.

Lovisa Janes married David Montague, 20 January, 1810.

CHILDREN.

1184 I. MARY ANN, born ...... ; married Theodore ......
1185 II. SYLVA, born ...... ;
1186 III. MELZER, born ...... ; C. clergyman, and married Mary Hale.
1187 IV. ENOS J., born ...... ; married Faith Hooker.
1188 V. DAVID, born ...... ; married Lucinda Clark.
1189 VI. ALFRED, born ...... ; married Sophia Clapp.
1190 VII. HENRY, born ...... ;
1191 VIII. LOVISA, born ...... ;
1192 IX. LUCINDA, born ...... ;

475 (IV) LUKE, SON OF ENOS.

Luke Janes married Dorothy Wright, 15 November, 1827, resides at Pascomac near the long remembered locality of the massacre of 1704. He is a quiet farmer, but much afflicted by the loss of wife and most of his children. She died 1866.

CHILDREN.

1193 I. FRANKLIN WRIGHT, born ......;
1194 II. ANN ELIZA, born ......;
1195 III. HARRIET AMELIA, born ......;

---

476 (V) HELENA, DAUGHTER OF ENOS.

Helena Janes married Dwight Lyman, 24 December, 1822.

CHILDREN.

1196 I. MIRANDA, born ......; married Sheldon Clark, and died Aug., 1865.
1197 II. SAMUEL D., born .....; died young.
1198 III. LEWIS, born ......;
1199 IV. FRANCES, born ......;
1200 V. JANE AMELIA, born ......;

---

478 (VII) SAMUEL, SON OF ENOS.

Samuel Janes married Sarah Parsons.

CHILDREN.

1201 I. ESTHER PHILENA, born ......;
1202 II. EDWARD, born ......;
1203 III. SAMUEL P., born ......;
1204 IV. ELIZA, born ......;
1205 V. AUGUSTINE, born ......;

481 (I) SUBMIT, DAUGHTER OF EBENEZER.

Submit Janes of the Easthampton branch, married Thomas F. King of Otisco, N. Y., 6 December, 1810. He was born 13 April, 1785.

CHILDREN.

1206 I.   SERENO F., born 6 December, 1811 ; married Eliza Cowles.

1207 II.   HANSON C., born 24 March, 1813 ; married Sarah Robinson.

1208 III.   ADALINE, born 7 September, 1815 ; died 29 April, 1859.

1209 IV.   SEYMOUR, born 9 July, 1817 ; married Adaline Smith.

1210 V.   CHAUNCEY J., born 13 October, 1820 ; married ...... Miller.

1211 VI.   SOPHRONIA, born 10 June, 1822 ; died 17 October, 1847.

1212 VII.   EVANDER W., born 25 June, 1827 ; married Davis Howe.

---

489 (II) MORRIS, SON OF EBENEZER.

Morris Janes married Betsey Hickox.

CHILD.

1213 I. LORANIA, born ...... ;

490 (III) FIDELIA, DAUGHTER OF EBENEZER.

Fidelia Janes married Apollos King.

CHILDREN.

1214 I. MORRIS, born ...... ;
1215 II. ALANSON, born ...... ;
1216 III. HARVEY, born ...... ;
1217 IV. SON, born ...... ;
1218 V. SON, born ...... ;
1219 VI. SON, born ...... ;

---

491 (IV) HANNAH, DAUGHTER OF EBENEZER.

Hannah Janes married Timothy Boardman.

CHILDREN.

1220 I. HANNAH, born ...... ;
1221 II. FIDELIA, born ...... ;
1222 III. CHAUNCEY, born ...... ;

---

493 (VI) EDWARD, SON OF EBENEZER.

Edward Janes married Sarah H. Hare, 17 February, 1822.

CHILDREN.

1223 I.   PHILENA, born 25 Nov., 1822; married M. M. Cordey.
1224 II.   JOANNA, born 11 Sept., ...; married D. M. Smith.
1225 III. HARVEY, born 10 Jan., ...; married M. J. Robinson.

32

1226 IV. EDWARD, born 18 Feb., ...; married Barbara
Merry of Va., lost on Sultana, 26 April, 1865.

1227 V. WILLIAM ULYSSES, born 26 March, ...; died
10 May, 1833.

1228 VI. ELEANOR, born 3 Sept., ...; died 16 Sept., 1841.

1229 VII. LODEMA, born 17 June, ...; died 25 July, 1827.

1230 VIII. ELI M., born 7 June, ...; married Cora Virginia Tindall of Ill., 14 Oct., 1860.

1231 IX. BENJAMIN M., born 6 Dec. ......; married Louisa
D. Brown of Ohio, 2 May, 1866.

1232 X. JOHN WESLEY, born 7 Jan., ...;

---

494 (VII) OTIS, SON OF EBENEZER.

Otis Janes married Sophronia Beardsley.

CHILD.

1233 I. ELLEN, born ......; died young.

---

495 (VIII) HARVEY, SON OF EBENEZER.

Harvey Janes married (1) Virena Cowles, 6 September, 1827, Rev. R. S. Corning, officiating; (2) Dianna
Beardsley, 10 September, 1831, Rev. S. Cowles, officiating.

CHILD.

1234 I. DIANTHA, born ......; died young.

Harvey married (2), Dianna Beardsley.

CHILDREN.

1235 II. VIRENA D. born 8 April, 1837; married George M.
Fitch, 3 Oct., 1859.

1236 III. EDWIN F., born 21 Oct., 1838;. married Ida Hall.

1237 iv. OTIS A., born 9 April, 1840.

1238 v. ELLEN H., born 8 Dec., 1845.

1239 vi. EDMUND E., born 10 April, 1848.

1240 vii. SARAH E., born 1 Nov., 1851.

497 (X) PHILENA, DAUGHTER OF EBENEZER.

Philena Janes married Nelson Boardman.

CHILDREN.

1241 i.　EBENEZER ALONZO, born ......; married Oliver Harvey of Napoli.

1242 ii.　MARGARET VIRENA, born ......; married William Keniston.

1243 iii.　ELEANOR SOPHRONIA, born ......; married·Henry Boardman.

1243a iv. JONATHAN ALPHONZO, born ......; married Martha Boardman.

498 (I) LOWELL, SON OF LIEUT. JONATHAN.

Lowell Janes married his second cousin, Asenah Janes, daughter of Seth.

CHILD.

1244 i. JONATHAN EDWARDS, born 7 November, 1827.

500 (III) RACHEL, DAUGHTER OF LIEUT. JONATHAN.

Rachel Janes married Ezekiel White of Easthampton, their native place. He was an antiquarian and genealogist. He made some researches of value, and

is quoted as authority.   After his decease, his way-ward
son took some of his papers and traveled around the
country among the Janeses, and called himself and
signed himself John W. Janes, by which he received
entertainment and some information, and often said he
was assisting me; reported I had lost papers and needed
additional ones, and many other crude, unreliable state-
ments.   His conduct confused the minds of some, and
has prevented my obtaining all the information necessary from certain sources.   They say his demeanor
is suspicious, and his mind a little unbalanced from a
fall in youth.   We hope this son, Jonathan J. White,
has not materially disgraced the name of his much
honored father.   If he has ignorantly imposed upon
a number of the family it is not the fault of the
compiler.

Rachel married Ezekiel White, about 1827.

CHILDREN.

1245 i. JONATHAN J., born ... September, 1828.
1246 ii. MARY KINGSLEY, born ...... 1831; died young.

---

502 (V) JASON, SON OF LIEUT. JONATHAN.

Jason Janes followed the example of his brother
Lowell, and married Mary, a sister of Asenah, his
second cousin, 23 August, 1826.

CHILDREN.

1247 i. SAMUEL, born ...... ;
1248 ii. MARIETTA, born ...... ;
1249 iii. JULIA ANN, born ...... ;

1250 IV. SARAH, born ......;
1251 V. HELENA, born ......;
1252 VI. ABBY, born ......;

504 (VII) SPENCER, SON OF LIEUT. JONATHAN.

Spencer Janes married Jennette Avery, 20 October, 1831.

CHILDREN.

1253 I. EDWIN SPENCER, born 29 November, 1832; married Sarah Strong.
1254 II. JONATHAN WORCESTER, born 23 December, 1834; died young.

506 (I) THEODORE, SON OF OBADIAH.

Theodore Janes married Caroline Ward McFarland, about the year 1830.

CHILD.

1255 I. JOSEPH THEODORE, born 11 September, 1831; married Helen Whiting.

508 (III) FRANCIS, SON OF OBADIAH.

Rev. Francis Janes (C) was a native of Easthampton, and an ardent love of souls led him to desire a preparation for the ministerial office, though it cost the arduous struggle which poverty and a limited acquaintance demanded. His unfortunate embarrassments may have sharpened his trust in the Saviour, and have

moulded him for a higher position as a self-denying
laborer in the Lord's vineyard.

During his course of education, he was kind and
winning, and secured the esteem of all his Christian
associates, and many others. He was eminently a
pious man, and labored with great diligence and fervor
in the gospel ministry, while spared to labor. He
graduated at Williams College in 1828, then studying
for the ministry, he soon found a field of labor. He
preached at Chenango Forks and some other places in
central New York, where he will be long remembered
as a good, plain, Christian embassador of heaven.

His last field of labor was at Colchester, Delaware
county, N. Y., where he died in the midst of usefulness after twenty-two years of full ministerial service.
During these years he led many souls to the Saviour, and
sweetly closed his eyes upon earthly scenes to " go up
higher," and behold the crowns of his rejoicing in a
blissful sphere of light and glory.

The same indomitable energy that sustained him
through his collegiate course, in poverty, and embarrass-
ment; the same perseverance and Christian zeal that
carried him triumphantly through the whole course of
education, manifested itself in all the years of his
ministry. Who can say what loss the church would
have sustained if such a gospel torch had been extin-
guished in the lighting? The *Independent* in speaking of
him at the time, said :

        "   *   *   In every church where he has labored
God has blessed his instrumentality with precious re-

vivals, and as the fruit of these revivals, about three
hundred souls have been gathered into churches under
his care." He was noted for his ardent piety, implicit
faith, and a heart full of Christian sympathy and
Christian knowledge. He was a man full of faith and
the Holy Spirit. During his whole ministry he lost not
a sabbath or a day from sickness.

He married at Centre Lisle, 2 October, 1832, Emily
A. Marsh.

CHILDREN.

1256 I. LEON RICHMOND, born 15 May, 1833; married
     Frances Smith.
1257 II. GEORGE MARSH, born 14 Oct., 1843.
1258 III. CHARLES FRANCIS, born 7 Aug., 1847.

509 (IV) ESTHER, DAUGHTER OF OBADIAH.

Esther Janes married Colman Clark, 12 May, 1825.
She died 23 March, 1831.

CHILDREN.

1259 I. FANNIE P., born ......;
1260 II. MATTIE E., born ......;
1261 III. CHARLES C., born ......;
1262 IV. THEODORE C., born ......;

510 (V) JUSTUS L., SON OF OBADIAH.

Rev. Justus L. Janes, son of Obadiah, graduated at
Amherst College, about 1834, and pursued a three
years theological course, then entered the gospel
ministry (C) in full vigor.

He was settled in' Guilford, N. Y., and in Chester, Ohio, where he now labors. He has evidently a practical adaptation to his work, and presents divine truth to the mind with simple and forcible illustration. He has a patient and cheerful temper, and is a favorite among the young.

He married in 1839, Abigail Ely, daughter of John Ely, of West Springfield, Mass.

CHILDREN.

1263 I. JOHN ELY, born 1841.
1264 II. AMELIA LOUISA, born 1843.

---

511 (VI) ALEXANDER, SON OF OBADIAH.

Alexander Hamilton Janes married and resides at Sheffield, Ill., where he has a large family.

CHILDREN.

1265 I.   THEODORE (?), born ......;
1266 II.   MARY (?), born ......;
1267 III. OBADIAH (?), born ......;
1268 IV.   EBENEZER (?), born ......;
1269 V.   HAMILTON (?), born ......;
1270 VI.   ABIGAIL (?), born ......;
1271 VII. JULIA (?), born ......;
1272 VIII. ESTHER (?), born ......;
1273 IX.   JONATHAN (?), born ......;

512 (VII) OLIVER E., SON OF OBADIAH.

Oliver Ellsworth Janes married Eliza Hope.

CHILDREN.

1274 I.   MARTHA, born ...... ;
1275 II. CHARLES, born ...... ;
1276 III. GEORGE, born ...... ;
1277 IV. FRANCIS, born ...... ;
1278 V.   ELIZA, born ...... ;
1279 VI. THEODORE, born ...... ;

———

516 (XI) MARY C., DAUGHTER OF OBADIAH.

Mary Charlotte Janes married Edward Sackett, 30 October, 1839, and resides in Hartford, Conn.

Mr. Sackett is a prosperous merchant, and they both seem to enjoy the social and Christian blessings of refined society. They are training up an interesting and hopeful family.

CHILDREN.

1280 I.   EDWARD F., born 29 March, 1841.
1281 II. FREDERIC A., born 18 February, 1843.
1282 III. OSCAR JANES, born 19 September, 1846.
1283 IV. MARY ELIZABETH, born 16 November, 1848.
1284 V.   EDWARD ARTHUR, born 15 April, 1854.
1285 VI. EMILY CHARLOTTE, born 27 May, 1858; died
          11 May, 1860.
1286 VII. EMILY JULIA, born 10 May, 1862.

517 (XII) JULIA S., DAUGHTER OF OBADIAH.

Julia Strong Janes married James C. Miller.

CHILDREN.

1287 I. OBADIAH J. (?), born ......;
1288 II. JULIA S. (?), born ...... ;

---

518 (XIII) OBADIAH L., SON OF OBADIAH.

Obadiah Lyman Janes married Rhoda Ann Smith,
daughter of Lyman and Cynthia Smith of Lime,
N. H., 31 July, 1850.

CHILDREN.

1289 I.   FRANCES E., born 3 May, 1851.
1290 II. EDWARD L., born 23 November, 1852.
1291 III. WILLIAM P., born 19 May, 1855.
1292 IV. CHARLES H., born 1 September, 1857.
1293 V.   WILLIAM J., born 5 August, 1862.

---

519 (XIV) EBENEZER D., SON OF OBADIAH.

Ebenezer Davis Janes married 11 December, 1856,
Sarah C. Long.

CHILDREN.

1294 I.   SUSAN E., born 21 May, 1858.
1295 II. MEDORA, born 20 May, 1860.
1296 III. IDA LYDIA, born 30 December, 1864.

519a (I) DORCAS, DAUGHTER OF PARSONS.

Dorcas Janes married Joel Parsons, in the year 1835.

CHILDREN.

1297 I. ANGELINA, born ......; died infant.
1298 II. ANGELINA, born ......; died young.
1299 III. ELLEN, born ......; died æ. 18.
1300 IV. EMMA, born ......; died æ. 17.
1300 a V. JOEL, born ...... 1850.

---

520 (II) TRYPHENA, DAUGHTER OF PARSONS.

Tryphena Janes married William N. Clapp, December, 1833.

CHILDREN.

1300 b I. INFANT, born ......;
1300 c II. SARAH, born ......;
1300 d III. SOLOMON P., born ......;
1300 e IV. EDGAR WILLIAM, born ......;
1300 f V. ELIZA T., born ......;

Emily Janes married (2) William N. Clapp.

CHILDREN.

1301 I. EMILY MARIA, born ......;
1302 II. HARRIET ELLEN, born 13 October, 1851.

522 (IV) JULIA, DAUGHTER OF PARSONS.

Julia Janes married Charles E. Wait, 26 February, 1805.

CHILDREN.

1303 I.   JULIAMETTA, born ...... ;
1304 II. SUSAN, born ...... ;
1305 III. EDSON, born ...... ;

Julia married (2) Mr. Haynes.

CHILD.

1306 IV. JULIUS HARRIS, born ...... ;

---

523 (V) LOIS, DAUGHTER OF PARSONS.

Lois Janes married Horace Clark.

CHILDREN.

1307 I.   EMILY JANES, born ...... ;
1308 II. GEORGE WARREN, born ...... ;
1309 III. FLORA LOETTA, born ...... ;

---

524 (VI) MARIA, DAUGHTER OF PARSONS.

Maria Janes married Chester Wait, 23 September, 1839.

CHILDREN.

1310 I.   LEWIS, born ...... ;
1311 II. CHARLES, born ...... ;
1312 III. EDWIN P., born ...... ;
1313 IV. ELLEN MARIA, born ...... ;
1314 V.   JOHN CHESTER, born ...... ;

526 (VIII) ALFRED E., SON OF PARSONS.

Alfred E. Janes married Catherine Wright, 9 October, 1834. He died 26 March, 1848.

CHILDREN.

1315 I. EDWIN ELY, born 4 Nov., 1844; a patriot soldier.
1316 II. WILLIAM PARSONS, born ......, 1847.
1317 III. ALFRED ELIAKIM, born ......, 1849.

---

550 (I) ELIHU, SON OF JONATHAN.

Elihu Janes married on the 25 of May, 1806, Sally Jarvis, who was born 20 June, 1786. He was a kind, genial, benevolent, social and true friend. He went to Charlestown, Mass., where he went into business as a butcher, when comparatively a young man, and always maintained a respectable standing in the community, and was beloved and esteemed by a large family circle.

CHILDREN.

1318 I. ALBERT H., born ...... 1807; unmarried.
1319 II. CHARLES, born 19 September, 1809; married Sarah Cook.
1320 III. ELIHU, born 2 August, 1812; died infant.
1321 IV. ELIHU, born 12 September, 1813; married Emily Foster.
1322 V. F. MORTIMER, born 16 November, 1816; married Lucinda Flint.
1323 VI. F. PRESCOTT, born 12 March, 1819; married Lucilla Chickering.
1324 VII. BENJAMIN, born 4 February, 1822; died 1839.

1325 VIII. CALEB JARVIS, born 4 November, 1824; married
             Mary Hannegan.
1326 IX. SARAH E., born 19 March, 1827; married Seth
             C. Walker.

---

551 (II) ONDA, DAUGHTER OF JONATHAN.

Onda Janes married Horace Wright of Northfield,
1803.   She endured too much from an intemperate
husband.

CHILDREN.

1327 I.   ELIPHAS, born ......, 1804; died infant.
1328 II. HENRY JANES, born ......, 1806; died æ. 2 years.
1329 III. EMELINE A., born ......, 1808; married Warren
             Mattoon.
1330 IV. JONES TODD, born ......, 1810; not heard from
             since 21 years of age.
1331 V.   MARY JANES, born ......, 1813.
1332 VI. SAMUEL DEXTER, born ......, 1816; died æ. 6 years.
1333 VII. CAROLINE MATTOON, born ......, 1820.

---

554 (V) CAROLINE, DAUGHTER OF JONATHAN.

Caroline Janes married Noah Perry, 1815. (?)

CHILDREN.

1334 I.   HENRY A., born 21 March, 1816; married Ann
             Wells, (2) Harriet Shedd.
1335 II. CHARLES W. B., born 17 June, 1817.
1336 III. SAMUEL C. A., born 13 November, 1819; married
             Maria Wallings, 1840.
1337 IV. LOIS, born 26 January, 1821.
1338 V.   GEORGE, born 9 May, 1823; married Rebecca J.
             Freeman, 18 June, 1845.

555 (VI) SALLY, DAUGHTER OF JONATHAN.

Sally Janes married Arnold Cook, 28 June, 1812. She died 7 February, 1856, a highly esteemed mother, sister and friend.

CHILDREN.

1339 I. HENRY, born 8 March, 1813.
1340 II. SARAH, born 10 October, 1814.
1341 III. MARY, born 8 March, 1817.
1342 IV. WILLIAM SEABURY, born 23 June, 1818.
1343 V. EDWARD H., born 26 March, 1820.
1344 VI. THOMAS R., born 8 March, 1822.
1345 VII. MARY GRAY, born 4 May, 1826; died infant.
1346 VIII. ALBERT, born ......; died infant.
1347 IX. MARY GRAY, born 15 December, 1829.
1348 X. MARTHA TUFTS, born December, 1831.

556 (VII) JONATHAN, SON OF JONATHAN.

Jonathan Janes married Harriet Chency, 1818.

CHILDREN.

1349 I. MARY HARRIET, born 16 April, 1819; married (1) Robert Creighton, (2) George Bolton.
1350 II. WILLIAM, born 1 November, 1821; married Ann Creighton.
1351 III. HENRY, born ......, 1827.
1352 IV. JOSHUA, born 2 February, 1830.
1353 V. CAROLINE, born ......, 1833.

557 (VIII) ABIGAIL, DAUGHTER OF JONA-THAN.

Nabbe or Abigail Janes married Richard Lyman, 10 September, 1815. Mr. Lyman died 7 October, 1864. Mrs. Lyman is an excellent mother, a kind, amiable friend, and exemplary Christian woman; none more hospitable; none more happy to see her friends.

CHILDREN.

1354 I.   JAMES, born 14 June, 1814; married Mary Stratton.

1355 II.   JONATHAN, born 21 Dec., 1815; married (1) Harriet Woodward, (2) Charlotte Holton.

1356 III.   MARY, born 5 Nov., 1818; married James Brazer.

1357 IV.   GAD CORNELIUS, born 5 Dec., 1819; married (1) Fannie Wright, (2) Mrs. Rosena Mack.

1358 V.   WILLIAM, born 26 March, 1822.

1359 VI.   AARON LYMAN, born 15 Nov., 1826.

1360 VII.   ALBERT RICHARD, born 5 Oct., 1828; married Frances Brooks.

1361 VIII.   EDWIN L., born 20 Nov., 1830; married Rhoda Bridge.

1362 IX.   WARREN FAY, born 22 April, 1833.

---

559 (X) CYNTHIA, DAUGHTER OF JONA-THAN.

Cynthia Janes married Thomas Russell, 27 July, 1828, who died 18 March, 1857. He was an active and industrious man, engaged in the cabinet trade

Cynthia was for a time engaged in teaching before her marriage. She is noble minded, and Christian in all her deportment.

CHILDREN.

1363 I.   CYNTHIA, born 27 Aug., 1829; died infant.
1364 II.   JULIA ANNA, born 2 Oct., 1831; died 19 April, 1858.
1365 III. CHARLES THOMAS, born 11 Sept., 1834.
1366 IV.   CYNTHIA MARIA, born 22 Dec., 1837.

---

578 (I) POLLY, DAUGHTER OF OBADIAH.

Polly Janes married Joel Doolittle, resides in Vermont.

CHILDREN.

1368 I.   GEORGE (twin), born ......;
1369 II.   MELINDA (twin), born ......; died infant.
1370 III.   JOEL, born ......; married Ann Russ.
1371 IV.   AARON, born ......;
1372 V.   HARRISON, born ......; married Susanna Cable.
1373 VI.   ALONZO JAMES, born ......; married Martha Ely.
1374 VII.   SARAH, born ......;
1375 VIII. JULIUS, born ......;
1376 IX.   JOHN, born ......;
1377 X.   ELIZA, born ......; married Robert Crawford.

---

581 (IV) OLIVER, SON OF OBADIAH.

Oliver Janes married Hannah Clement, 1821. He was born in Bridport, Vt., and spent most of his days in East Cleveland, Ohio, where he died 1867.

34

'CHILDREN.

1378 I.　LORENZO, born 5 June, 1822; married Abigail
　　　　Nichols, 1855.

1379 II.　HARMONY, born 14 Feb., 1825.

1380 III.　MARY P., born 6 Aug., 1827; married Isaac E.
　　　　Warren; died 12 Aug., 1833.

1381 IV.　OLIVER, born 13 July, 1829.

1382 V.　HANNAH, born 14 Nov., 1831; died 11 Aug,
　　　　1832.

1383 VI.　STEPHENS, born 13 May, 1833; died 12 Sept.,
　　　　1834.

1384 VII.　HARRIS, born 9 July, 1835; married Celia DeWolf.

1385 VIII.　LUCRETIA, born 28 Dec., 1837; died 18 Oct., 1855.

1386 IX.　ANDREW, born 13 July, 1840.

1387 X.　ANTOINETTE, born 7 Jan., 1846; died 12 May,
　　　　1850.

---

582 (V) HARMONY, DAUGHTER OF OBADIAH.

Harmony Janes married Adolphus Hosley.

CHILDREN.

1388 I.　LUCINA S., born 30 March, 1815.

1389 II.　JABEZ J., born 13 April, 1817.

1390 III.　HARMONY M., born 9 May, 1819.

1391 IV.　ADOLPHUS J., born 7 January, 1821.

---

583 (IV) NAOMI, DAUGHTER OF OBADIAH.

Naomi Janes married William Mitchell.

CHILDREN.

1392 I.　ZYPORAH, born ......, 1818.

1393 II.　OBADIAH, born ......, 1820.

1394 III. WILLIAM, born ......, 1822.
1395 IV. LUCRETIA, born ......; married Mr. Ford.
1396 V. MILTON, born ......;
1397 VI. GEORGE, born ......;
1398 VII. HENRY, born ......; married Ann Lee.
1399 VIII. ABNER, born ......;
1400 IX. OLIVER, born ......;
1401 X. MARY, born ......; married Salmon Veasy.

585 (VIII) ALONZO, SON OF OBADIAH.

Alonzo Janes married (1) Mary Ann Disbrow, and lived in East Cleveland. He raised up a large family; lost his first wife after she had presented him with nine children.

CHILDREN.

1402 I. WILLIAM, born ......;
1403 II. MARY ANN, born ......;
1404 III. JULIA ANN, born ......;
1405 IV. HARRIET E., born ......;
1406 V. LAURA L., born ......;
1407 VI. HENRY H., born ......;
1408 VII. ALONZO, born ......;
1409 VIII. ALVINZA F., born ......;
1410 IX. CAROLINE, born ......;

Alonzo married (2) Harriet Convers, 14 March, 1852.

CHILDREN.

1411 I. FRANKLIN, born ......;
1412 II. IDA, born ..... ;
1413 III. CAREY, born ......;
1414 IV. FREDERIC, born ......;

587 (X) SOPHIA, DAUGHTER OF OBADIAH.

Sophia Janes married Asbury Sabines.

CHILDREN.

1415 I. HOMER, born ......;
1416 II. MARY, born ......;

---

588 (XI) LUCRETIA, DAUGHTER OF OBADIAH.

Lucretia Janes married Solomon Dunton.

CHILDREN.

1417 I. BURTON, born ......;
1418 II. SARAH S., born ......;

---

589 (XII) HARRIS, SON OF OBADIAH.

Harris Janes married Julia King.

CHILDREN.

1419 I.   HENRY, born ......;
1420 II. ELIZABETH, born ......;
1421 III. JULIA, born ......;
1422 IV. DIADAMY, born ......;

598 (I) HARRIS, SON OF SAMUEL.

Harris Janes married Harriet W. Mason, 1812.

CHILDREN.

1423 I. MASON, born 3 June, 1813.
1424 II. SAMUEL MERRIMAN, born 2 August, 1815; married Catharine E. Miller.
1425 III. JULIA ANN, born ......;
1426 IV. FREDERIC HARRISON, born ......;
1427 V. ALVAH, born ......;
1428 VI. ISABEL, born ......;

602 (V) SALLY, DAUGHTER OF SAMUEL.

Sally Janes married Eliphas Chapin, 1813.

CHILDREN.

1429 I. HENRY HARRISON, born 15 April, 1814.
1430 II. ELIPHAS, born 8 September, 1815.
1431 III. MARTHA, born 20 September, 1816.

605 (VIII) SYLVANUS, SON OF SAMUEL.

Sylvanus Janes, who married Eunice Moore in 1830, was a very strongly built and finely formed man. In physical strength he excelled his father, and almost every man he ever met with. He would lift timber so large and roll granite blocks so heavy, as to astonish his fellow comrades. He was modest, humble, peaceable, and kind to all. He lived the most of his life in Gill. He spent a few years in Boston and New York,

at work in trimming granite stone, and returning to
Gill, he finally moved to Iowa city, Iowa. He died
in the year 1865.

CHILDREN.

1432 I.   SUSAN M., born 5 Oct., 1832; married Eugene E.
Brown.
1433 II. MARY E., born 16 April, 1834; married Oliver
Phillips.
1434 III. SAMUEL M., born 10 Nov., 1836.
1435 IV. EUGENE A., born 27 March, 1846. He died a
patriot soldier at St. Louis, 14 Oct., 1861.

606 (IX) SAMUEL, SON OF SAMUEL.

Samuel Janes married Eveline Ballard of Gill, 1833.

CHILDREN.

1436 I.   SARAH C., born 23 June, 1834; married George
Simonds.
1437 II. ELLEN A., born 28 Feb., 1837; married George S.
Graves.
1438 III. MARTHA E., born 4 May, 1839; died young.
1439 IV. MARY ISABEL, born 25 July, 1841; married Edward E. Graves.
1440 V.   HARRIS, born 28 Feb., 1844; died infant.

607 (X) ALEXANDER, SON OF SAMUEL.

Alexander Janes married Martha Moody, in 1831. He was remarkably well built; very athletic, a match for two or three common men, as was sometimes proved by *their* rashness when living in Boston.

CHILDREN.

1441 I. JULIANNA, born 1 Nov., 1832; married William Darling.
1442 II. EZEKIEL WOOD, born ... Sept., 1841.

608 (I) MEHITABLE, DAUGHTER OF XENO-PHON.

Mehitable Janes married Medad Alexander, who was a son of Colonel Medad, son of Thomas, son of Ebenezer Alexander, the great-great-grandfather of my sister Mehitable, whom he married. He was four and she was five generations distant from the same Ebenezer Alexander, who was formerly one of the leading men in Northfield, in its early days, after its permanent settlement, and who was one of the most active men during Rev. Benjamin Doolittle's ministry. Mehitable Janes's marriage to Medad Alexander is the second of the intermarriages of the Alexanders and Janeses. She died 30 January, 1857.

CHILDREN.

1443 I. LUCIUS, born ......, 1820; died æ. 16.
1444 II. SARAH P., born 8 June, 1822; married David Wilder, died 1865.

1446 III.   ANGELINA, born ... April, 1823; married John
Thompson; 1860.

1447 IV.   FREDERIC JANES, born ......;

1448 V.   LYDIA, born 16 April, 1829; married Lieutenant
Dwight Newberry.

1449 VI.   MARY ANN, born 21 Nov., 1831; married James
Mattoon.

1450 VII.   LUCRETIA, born 16 May, 1833.

1451 VIII.   LUCIUS, born 16 Sept., 1835.

----

600 (III) ISABEL, DAUGHTER OF XENO-PHON.

Isabel Janes married John Howland, October, 1820.
They moved to Walton, Delaware county, N. Y., and
soon purchased and built a house and shop in Cannons-
ville, the adjoining town, where they lived some 18
years, and then the western fever swept the family to
Michigan, where they now reside.   Mr. Howland,
being in the line of John, direct from the John Howland of the Mayflower, who brought with him a
calabash or dried gourd full of powder, had bequeathed
to him the same *heir loom*, which is to go down to a
John of the family, till Johns or this curiosity are no
more.

CHILDREN.

1452 I.   MARY ANN, born 4 Nov., 1823; married Mr. Wilson, of Fayetteville, Arkansas.

1453 II.   CORINNA, born 17 Dec., 1826; married Lucien Kief.

----

[1] Mr. Wilson was a captain in the service of the Southern con-
federacy, so called.

1454 III. CORNELIA, born 7 Aug., 1828; married Edwin Mills.
· 1455 IV. JOHN NEWTON, born 13 Sept., 1830; married
     Sarah P. Stebbins.
1456 V.   ISABELLA, born 21 Oct., 1836; died 25 Aug., 1638.
1457 VI. SON (twin), born ..., Sept., 1844; died infant.
1458 VII. SON, (twin), born ..., Sept., 1844; died infant.

611 (IV) PASCHAL P., SON OF XENOPHON.

Paschal Peoly Janes served his father faithfully till he was twenty-one years of age, and then left home to live a few months in the vicinity of Boston. He then thought it would be fine to go to China on board a ship, which he could do only by becoming a common seaman, and go before the mast. He was gone from the country some sixteen months, and returned to visit Northfield, and related to his friends what he had seen, and what he had experienced. The sights he beheld on the Chinese waters, and in the city of Canton; women in small shoes, and carried in sedan chairs; and the strange and curious manner of life among the Chinese, hardly compensated for the cold and suffering on the ocean during the winter months, and the chase from pirates, which put them in apparent jeopardy.

He afterward settled down in New York city.

In 1853, he went to California, having lost his wife two years previously; but not realizing his expectations, he returned to the Atlantic states from the golden Eldorado, and died in 1867 in his native place.

Paschal P. Janes married Jane Eliza Hiller, 1827, in the city of New York.

CHILDREN.

1459 I.   ALDEN, born 23 November, 1828; married Hattie Cantrall.
1460 II.   SARAH, born 6 January, 1830; married (1) William Solomon, (2) W. Hart.
1461 III.   JANE ELIZA, born ......;
1462 IV.   MARTHA, born ......; died infant
1463 V.   JOHN, born ......;
1464 VI.   JULIA SYRENA, born 2 September, 1840.
1465 VII.   PASCHAL P., born 31 December, 1842; a patriot soldier, killed in battle 18 June, 1864, near Petersburg, Va.
1466 VIII.   FREDERIC, born 9 October, 1845.
1467 IX.   DU TILLA, born 5 August, 1848.

612 (V) SAMUEL, SON OF XENOPHON.

Samuel Patric Janes, married 1 September, 1824, Sarah Parsons of Northampton, Mass., where they have continued to reside, and had ample opportunity to show their hospitality.

CHILDREN.

1468 I.   MARTHA ANN, born 7 October, 1825; married William Trusdell, a lawyer of Janesville, Wis.; she died 31 March, 1859.
1469 II.   XENOPHON, born 17 September, 1827; died infant.
1470 III.   NATHANIEL P., born 22 August, 1828; married (1) Sarah A. Heath, 22 September, 1864, (2) Emma Overton, 1860.
1471 IV.   SAMUEL P., born 8 November, 1830; unmarried.

1472 v. SARAH M., born 2 October, 1832; married Rufus Suckett.

1473 vi. MARY, born 24 October, 1834; died 22 December, 1835.

1474 vii. EDWARD L., born 19 August, 1837.

1475 viii. ISABEL PATRIC, born 7 December, 1840; married Harry Dingman.

613 (VI) SARAH, DAUGHTER OF XENOPHON.

Sarah Janes married Wait Cannon, a merchant of Masonville, N. Y.

CHILDREN.

1476 i. EDWARD E., born 24 March, 1827; married ......

1477 ii. ANTOINETTE H., born ......, 1828; married Joseph Dimick.

1478 iii. CLARK, born ......, 1830; died 1838.

1479 iv. MARY ANN, born ......, 1834; married Henry Fuller.

1480 v. GEORGE W., born ......, 1837.

1481 vi. BENJAMIN J., born 7 May, 1839.

1482 vii. C. HOMER, born 5 February, 1841.

1483 viii. FREDERIC M., born 7 April, 1843.

1484 ix. ARTHUR E., born 2 June, 1845; married ......

1485 x. F. EUGENE, born 15 June, 1846.

1486 xi. CLARENA W., born 25 December, 1850.

614 (VII) EBENEZER, SON OF XENOPHON.

Ebenezer Janes after losing his wife and being unfortunate in his property, went to California to find a mine of gold. He returned, and went a second time, and still remains there, now in poor health.

It was expected he would remain at the old homestead, and keep the family name there; but after the death of grandmother and father, leaving the maiden sister in charge of his two sons, he went abroad to gratify his curiosity and pocket gold. But time brings reverses, and golden visions prove substanceless.

Ebenezer married January, 1836, Martha Billings. Martha died in 1845.

CHILDREN.

1487 I.   CHARLES X., born 4 October, 1837.
1488 II. WILLIAM B., born 16 August, 1842.

These two sons were patriot soldiers, serving quite a part of the time during the war of the rebellion. Charles was wounded, and recovered; was sick, and discharged; but afterward enlisted in the navy, and was active and greatly exposed in the famous naval attack upon Fort Fisher, which was brilliantly captured by our army and navy.

William was wounded and recovered; was twice privileged with free board at the notorious Libby Prison at Richmond; saw many severe battles and conflicts of arms, saw numerous comrades struggling with horrid wounds and grim death. Like others, returned to enjoy the fruit of untold suffering, and leaving many behind who died gloriously for their country.

----

615 (VIII) FREDERIC, SON OF XENOPHON.

The writer, Rev. Frederic Janes, was early impressed with the sentiments of divine truth, and the importance of vital piety. That godly woman (see page 109) who felt the love of mother, in the absence of one who left us for another world, exerted her sweet influence, breathing around us an atmosphere of winning and ardent piety, producing conviction and a childlike trust in the Saviour, and accomplished that gracious work, instrumentally, which is hereby gratefully acknowledged. He spent the boyhood of life in school, and portions of the summer months on the farm, so common with farmers' boys in the busy season. When about seventeen years of age he commenced the cabinet trade in Northampton. While there under the ministry of Mark Tucker, D. D., convictions were ripened into piety, and at the end of two years a yearning desire sprung up for an education to prepare for another sphere of action and usefulness. Preliminary studies at Hadley and Amherst, and a season with the celebrated classical teacher, Garfield, at Middletown, Conn., opened the way for an honorable entrance into Yale College, and a finishing at Amherst previous to a four years' course of teaching in Massachusetts, in Virginia, and in New York. During this period he pursued theology privately, with settled pastors; and spent a year in the service of the New York City Tract Society, previous to taking a pastoral charge for three years in the state of New York. Afterward he was settled in Bernardston, in 1841, near his native home, remaining nearly four years, amid arduous labors; seeing the work of God revived, many souls brought into the fold of the church, and the faith of all the members strengthened. He asked a dismission, and engaged for a season in parochial labors at Pelham, and then commenced a course of financial labors for

the Evangelical Society and kindred labors, for a
number of years. At an interval he supplied a
church in Lima, Mich., and afterward returned east,
to New York, and there labored for some different benevolent societies, edited the *Christian Parlor
Magazine*, and supplied occasionally some vacant pulpit. After spending some seventeen years in the city,
he returned to his native state, Massachusetts, by invitation, to resume the pastoral office, and build up the
cause of the Redeemer in his dear old Massachusetts.

Frederic Janes married (1) Paulina Burnell,[1] 15 September, 1833, Dr. Joseph Penney of Northampton, officiating. She died 20 November, 1851.

---

[1] *First Generation.* John Burnell married Mehitable Edwards of
pilgrim origin, born about 1692; died about 1742. Mehitable Edwards
was born 1695. Their children were: John, born 16 March, 1750.
Methitable, born 6 October, 1753; died 15 February, 1769. Joseph, born
13 December, 1756; died 23 September, 1807. Mary, born 16 October, 1757. Ephraim and Manassah, born 27 July, 1860.

Joseph married Hannah Tucker, 15 February, 1794. Hannah died
1797.

Second Generation. John married Mary Banister, 25 March, 1772.
Mary Banister was born 15 April, 1752. Their children were: Sereno,
born 11 March, 1773; Joseph, born 15 December, 1775; Melzer,
born ...., 1777; John, born 15 Oct., 1778; Luther, born 20 March, 1780;
Mary, born 7 April, 1782; Hannah, born 3 June, 1784; Calvin, born 5
July, 1786; Catharine, born 2 November, 1790; daughter, born ....,
1792; Mehitable, born 30 October, 1794.

Third Generation. Joseph married Lucy Kingsley. Their children
were: Paulina, Calvin, Lucy M., and Daniel K.

Fourth Generation. Paulina, born 1810; married Rev. Frederic
Janes, in 1833.

CHILDREN.

. 1489 I.   MARGARET PAULINA, born 17 September, 1834.

1490 II.   MARY SOPHIA, born 28 June, 1836.

1491 III.   JOHN CALVIN, born 6 July, 1839; died a patriot soldier, 18 June, 1862.

1492 IV.   LUCY AMELIA, born 10 June, 1841; married Albert Lefler, her father officiating, in Broadway Tabernacle, New York.

Frederic married (2) Rachel Brown Trusdell,[1] 18 January, 1853, Dr. George Fisher of New York, officiating.

CHILDREN.

1493 V.   FREDERIC, born 23 November, 1853; died 28 October, 1856.

1494 VI.   JOSEPHINE AMANDA, born 10 December, 1854.

1495 VII.   WILLIAM AUGUSTUS, born 11 November, 1856.

1496 VIII.   ANNA FREDERICA, born 3 April, 1858.

1497 IX.   ISABELLA, born 10 July, 1861; died 9 May, 1864.

1498 X.   CHARLES HERBERT, born 23 October, 1865.

---

[1] Mr. Gregory came from England, and settled in or near Salem, Mass. His son Joseph was a good Methodist, and freed his slaves which he owned while living in Dutchess county, N. Y. He married Anna Brundridge, and had Joseph, Nathaniel, Elijah, David, John, Benjamin, Charles, Alvah, and Mary who married Stephen Trusdell, whose parents were from New Jersey, and the latter had the following children : Ann Maria, Sarah Jane, Lucinda, Amanda, Rachel Brown who married Rev F. Janes 1853, Henry, and the Hon. and Rev. Charles G., and John Harvey.

616 (IX) MARY ANN, DAUGHTER OF XENO-PHON.

Mary Ann Janes, the youngest sister, taught school after the example of her two next older sisters, that is, by teaching found a husband. She was the early playmate and companion of childhood and youth, the trustful and confiding friend, the patient, intelligent, even tempered and discreet mother. She married 8 January, 1834, Augustine Stebbins, formerly of Granby, Mass., and moved to Masonville, Delaware county, N. Y. He was a farmer and carpenter, always ambitious and industrious. In December, 1866, they moved to East Cleveland, Ohio, where some of their children had settled, and in a community where they could enjoy more of the comforts of refined, social, and religious society, than in Masonville.

CHILDREN.

1499 I.   GEORGE J., born 11 March, 1835.
1500 II.   SARAH P., born 4 Nov., 1836; married Newton Howland.
1501 III. DWIGHT P., born 4 Sept., 1839; married Mary Ann Bennett.
1502 IV.   DEWITT CLINTON, born 22 Dec., 1840.
1503 V.   AUGUSTINE JEROME, born 1 July, 1843; married Eliza Skinner.
1504 VI.   CLARK LUCAS, born 29 Dec., 1844.
1505 VII. HERBERT HOWLAND, 25 Oct., 1847.

Five of the sons served in the army, two or three of them as musicians, as helpers or nurses to the wounded. A. Jerome was a brave and distinguished artillerist in the western army. He won honors, and more, he won a beautiful lady of Marrietta, Ohio, with whom he became acquainted at the hospital, where the prompt attention of ladies was always regarded a patriotic duty.

---

618 (II) EBENEZER, SON OF CAPT. EBENEZER.

Ebenezer Smith Janes was the oldest son of Capt. Ebenezer. He was a clerk for many years in New York city; went to Michigan by the persuasions of his next younger brother; was there as a farmer a number of years, and returned to New York from want of health to endure a bilious climate, and the hardships of a new country.

He has enjoyed some prosperity in business, and purchased a small farm a few miles out of the city near Paterson, where may be enjoyed the comforts of life. Death has frequently entered the family circle, and four of their seven children they have yielded to God who gave them. He married on the 27 of November, 1842, Mary Ann Odell, who was born in New York city, 27 September, 1820.

CHILDREN.

1506 I. WILLIAM EDWARD, born 22 Aug., 1843.
1507 II. MARY LUCRETIA, born 10 Nov., 1845.
1508 III. HANNAH EVELINE, born 27 Oct., 1848 ; died 11 Jan., 1853.
1509 IV. JAMES ODELL, born 26 July, 1852; died 16 Sept., 1852.
1510 V. JULIA ISABELLA, born 23 Aug., 1853; died 1 Aug., 1855.
1511 VI. GEORGE NEWTON, born 25 Aug., 1856.
1512 VII. ANNIE, born 16 Oct., 1858 ; died 11 Dec., 1867.

619 (III) JOSEPH, SON OF CAPT. EBENEZER.

Joseph Janes, son of Captain Ebenezer, married Hannah Holton of Northfield, who died in Penfield, Mich., in 1848. He returned to the east, and afterwards went to California; then after getting some of the shining dust came back to the Atlantic states, settled in New York, and married 2 July, 1853, Sarah Portlock, who was born in England, 28 July, 1829. She was an accomplished teacher, and after they had raised up a large family, she commenced teaching again, which seems to be a more congenial mode of life for her temperament than the duties of a farmer's housewife.

CHILDREN.

1513　i.　ALBERT LE CAAN, born 26 May, 1854; died 1861.
1514　ii.　ELIZABETH MARIA, born 7 Aug., 1855.
1515　iii.　GEORGE PORTLOCK, born 9 Nov., 1856.
1516　iv.　JOSEPH, born 18 May, 1858.
1517　v.　JESSIE LE CAAN, born 17 Feb., 1861.
1518　vi.　SARAH LUCRETIA, born 19 May, 1863.

206 (IV) EDWARD H., SON OF CAPT. EBENEZER.

Edward Houghton Janes lost his mother while quite a youth, and struggled with adverse currents till finally he triumphed over many discouragements, and graduated in medicine at the Berkshire Medical Institute, in the year 1847. After some preliminary practice, and considerable reading on the subject, he commenced practice in the city of New York, where he is now in full employ. He married 14 October, 1860, Jane M. Yates, who was born in Boston, 22 August, 1832.

Dr. E. H. Janes has been under appointment as inspector by the sanitary board, and has proved himself thorough and capable in bringing before the public the sanitary condition of the large district under his charge, giving it a minute and careful observation.

CHILD.

1519 I. MARTHA RIDGWAY, born 18 Dec., 1862.

621 (V) JULIANNA, DAUGHTER OF CAPT. EBENEZER.

Julianna Janes, a teacher in New York, married in New York city, Daniel Sanford, formerly of Connecticut, who moved to Independent, Iowa, where he engaged in trade, and was postmaster, and they both made themselves useful, and thus happy, in their new and enterprising state.

CHILDREN.

1520 I. HARRIET, born ......, 1861.
1521 II. EDWARD, born ......, 1863.

SEVENTH GENERATION.

636 (I) HEMAN, SON OF HEMAN.

Heman Janes married Olive Piper, and lives in township of Ingersoll, Canada.   Olive died 16 February, 1833.

CHILDREN.

1522 I.   LOIS, born 15 October, 1810; married David Reynolds.

1523 II. ABIGAIL, born 25 July, 1812; married Isaac Dygert.

1524 III. RUBY, born 22 April, 1814; married Herkimer Dygert.

1525 IV. LUCY, born 26 April, 1816; married Warren Harris.

1526 V.   LAURA,[1] born 14 September, 1819; married Abner Lewis.

Heman married (2) Mrs. Mary Tolman (Askins) in 1834.

CHILDREN.

1526a VI. SARAH LOUISA, born 21 January, 1835; married Robert McDonald.

1527 VII. REUBEN ASKINS, born 26 November, 1837; married Sarah Galloway.

1528 VIII. SIMEON HEMAN, born 5 February, 1843.

---

[1] Killed by lightning, 9 June, 1850.

638 (III) ELIJAH, SON OF HEMAN.

Elijah Janes, son of Heman and Abigail, married Mary Clark 14 December, 1817. She lived to raise up a large family of children, and died 14 December, 1837.

CHILDREN.

1529 I.   LAURA, born ......, 1818; (?) married Mr. Reynolds.
1530 II. NELSON, born ......, 1820; (?) married Philena Baker.
1531 III. MATILDA, born ......, 1822; (?) died 15 April, 1823.
1532 IV. ADALINE, born ......, 1824; married Mr. Mabie.
1533 V.   ANN ELIZA, born ......, 1826; (?) married Mr. Hall.
1534 VI. SARAH, born ......, 1828; (?) married Mr. Quartermass.
1535 VII. ABIGAIL, born ......, 1830; (?) died May, 1836.
1536 VIII. WILLIAM, born ......, 1832; (?) married Nellie McKay.
1537 IX. CAROLINE, born ... .., 1834; (?) died May, 1838.

` Elijah married (2) and (3) names are not at hand.

639 (IV) JAMES, SON OF HEMAN.

James Janes, son of Heman and Abigail Janes, married Lucena Sage, in Bloomfield, Vt., 18 February, 1791. We know not their history to record it.

CHILDREN.

1538 I.   LUCENA, born ......;
1539 II. HAPPYLONA, born ......;
1540 III. REUBEN, born ......;

1541 IV.   JAMES, born ......;
1542 V.   HEMAN, born ......;
1543 VI.   SALLY, born ......;
1544 VII. MARY, born ......;
1545 VIII. ABIGAIL, born ......; married George A. Clark, 1845.
1546 IX.   ALLEN S., born ......;
1547 X.   REBECCA, born ......;

651 (I) HIRAM, SON OF HUMPHREY.

Hiram Janes married 1813, Hannah Andrus, lived with his young family, at South Hero, till 1816, when he moved from the place of his nativity to Wolcott, Wayne county, N. Y. He again moved to Clarkson, Monroe county. He was the honored father of a large and affectionate family. In 1838, the western fever took him and his family to Johnstown, Wis., where he died 25 September, 1847. She died 18 March, 1833, in Clarkson, Monroe county, N. Y.

CHILDREN.

1548 I.   HIRAM, born 16 March, 1814; married Phebe A. Carpenter.
1549 II.   HORACE, born 2 Oct., 1815; married Emeline Johnson.
1550 III. JOHN E., born 9 Aug., 1817; married Esther Bagley.
1551 IV.   WILLIAM C., born 2 Feb., 1819; married Sophronia Eastman.
1552 V.   THANKFUL M., born 22 Aug., 1820 : married Ebenezer Bullock.
1553 VI.   BETSEY Ann, born 15 July, 1823; married William P. Ferris.

1554 VII. JANE ELIZA, born 2 Jan., 1825; married Lucius Bingham.

Hiram married (2) Sarah Bedient, 17 October, 1833, in Monroe county, N. Y.

CHILDREN.

1555 VIII. MARY C., born 16 Aug., 1834.

1556 IX. HANNAH M., born 5 Dec., 1836; married Harvey Pember.

1557 X. HENRY D., born 11 March, 1839; married Thomas Griggs.

1558 XI. DEFOREST, born 28 Dec., 1841; married Maria Colwell.

1559 XII. ADELIA, born 23 Jan., 1844.

---

652 (II) ANNA, DAUGHTER OF HUMPHREY.

Anna Janes married Martin Ruggles, and resides in Lockport, N. Y. Her father, Humphrey, died in Johnstown, Wis., 16 November, 1845.

CHILDREN.

1560 I. WILLIAM, born ......;

1561 II. LOUISA, born ......;

1562 III. HORACE, born ......;

1563 IV. SEYMOUR, born ......;

1564 V. CYRUS, born ......;

1565 VI. MARTHA, born ......;

---

655 (V) SEYMOUR, SON OF HUMPHREY.

Seymour Janes married Polly Eastman 15 October, 1818. He died 14 October, 1845. We have not their history particularly.

CHILDREN.

1566 I.   ALBERT, born 25 November, 1819; married Catha-
           rine Tanner.
1567 II.   CHESTER, born 15 November, 1821.
1568 III. SEYMOUR, born 14 August, 1825; married Frances
           E. Babcock; died 15 September, 1858.
1569 IV.   MARY J., born 5 October, 1827; died 7 October,
           1860.
1570 V.   HUMPHREY, born 14 October, 1828; married
           Alvin Bigelow; died 2 October, 1860.
1571 VI.   TIRZA A., born 8 January, 1830.
1572 VII. ELIJAH, born 28 September, 1832.
1573 VIII. ANNA, born 12 July, 1838.

---

656 (VI) OLIVER, SON OF HUMPHREY.

Oliver Janes married Emily Lee, daughter of Rev.
Joseph Lee, A. M., of Northeast Pennsylvania.

Oliver was a large, powerful man, weighing 325 lbs,
yet perfectly formed, and as nimble as any youth; and
his athletic qualities and Herculean strength were
never matched. He once carried nine bushels of corn
upstairs at one load, and threw an ordinary man over
a fence with perfect ease. Sitting upon the floor and
pulling sticks he threw a boasting sea captain over
his head. He was an amiable, good natured man,
and a kind husband and father. He died 21 October,
1852. She died 17 October, 1855.

CHILDREN.

1574 I. THANKFUL MARIA, born 2 November, 1820; unmarried.
1575 II. WILLIAM H., born 7 September, 1822; married Nancy Goldsmith.
1576 III. HORACE, born 23 August, 1825; married Mary Rogers.
1577 IV. ORRIN, born 13 July, 1827.
1578 V. OLIVER, born 18 May, 1829; married Ellen Phillips.
1579 VI. ELIZABETH ANN, born 22 August, 1831; married Alexander Goodrich.
1580 VII. HIRAM, born 27 or 22 August, 1833; married Elmira Tidd.
1581 VIII. LYDIA AMELIA, born 16 July, 1835.
1582 IX. HANNAH, born 21 December, 1838; married Moses Barnard.
1583 X. EMILY, born 20 February, 1840.
1584 XI. SETH, born 8 December, 1842.

657 (VII) ORRIN, SON OF HUMPHREY.

Orrin Janes married Clarissa Whitman of Canada.

CHILDREN.

1585 I. MARTHA, born 25 February, 1829; married (1) Wilder Bowers of Swanton, Vt. He died in Maquoketa, Iowa, 1858; (2) Harlow French of Maquoketa.
1586 II. MARY, born 3 March, 183..; married George Hyde of Swanton, Vt.
1587 III. A. ELIZABETH, born 21 December, 1833; married Perkins Hatfield.
1588 IV. ALBERT, born 23 August, 1837; married Harriet E. Berley.

37

1589 v.   WILLIAM, born 15 September, 1839; married
           Calista Wheelock.
1590 vi.   LAURA, born 15 November, 1842; married Elea-
           zer Jewett, of Georgia, Vt.
1591 vii. HELLEN M., born 23 June, 1844.
1592 viii. JUDSON, born 10 February, 1847.
1593 ix.   CARRY, born 15 June, 1849; died 1853.
1594 x.   FRANCES BELL, born 1 July, 1855; died 1860.

658 (VIII) SUSAN, DAUGHTER OF HUMPHREY.

Susan Janes married Cyrus Chambers.

CHILDREN.

1595 i.   WILLIAM, born ......;
1596 ii.   LOUISA, born ......;
1597 iii. MARY, born ......;
1598 iv.   HORACE, born ......;
1599 v.   SEYMOUR, born ......;
1600 vi.   CARRY, born ......;
1601 vii. MARY, born ......;

659 (IX) ELI, SON OF HUMPHREY.

Eli Janes married widow Sarah ....

CHILDREN.

1602 i.   MARTHA, born ......;
1603 ii.   ELI, born ......;

660 (X) WILLIAM, SON OF HUMPHREY.

William Janes moved from his native state, Vermont, and the town of South Hero, Grand Isle county, to try his fortune beyond the great lakes, and in the wheat growing country of the west, not far from Janesville.

William married Catharine Brace, 3 June, 1828. He resides in Wisconsin, and is a justice of the peace and a prominent citizen in the town of West Milton, Rock county, Wis. He is always interested in the history of the family, and in the welfare of his friends.

CHILDREN.

1604 I. SUSAN, born 6 December, 1828; married Chapin Aldrich.

1605 II. LOIS, born 5 May, 1833; married Zeno P. Tilton; died 22 January, 1866.

1606 III. LUTHER, born 13 December, 1841; married Clarinda Wright.

1607 IV. ELLEN, born 20 December, 1850.

662 (XII) ELIJAH, SON OF HUMPHREY.

Elijah Janes, born on Grand Isle, Vt., with other friends, emigrated to Wisconsin. He married S. Burwell, 13 October, 1836, and had the following family.

CHILDREN.

1608 I. MARY E., born 13 December, 1838; died 24 November, 1860.

1609 II. ALMIRA B., born 1 April, 1841.

1610 III.   HOMER H., born 24 May, 1843; married Minnie
             McConnell, 22 November, 1851.
1611 IV.   NATHAN A., born 2 December, 1845.
1612 V.   ELEANOR T., born 16 January, 1848.
1613 VI.   ALICE A., born 3 August, 1850.
1614 VII.   FRANCIS A., born 30 July, 1853.
1615 VIII. SETH ADEBERTH, born 21 February, 1856.

---

666 (III) PERMELIA, DAUGHTER OF JOHN.

Permelia Janes married Lemuel Rust, March, 1819.
She died 5 December, 1822.

CHILD.

1616 I.   AURELIA, born 20 April, 1822.

Phebe, her oldest sister, married Lemuel Rust, May,
1824.   He died 25 December, 1833.

CHILD.

1617 II.   HENRY S., born 30 March, 1828.

---

667 (IV) LAVINA, DAUGHTER OF JOHN.

Lavina Janes married Hiram Nettleton, 22 February,
1822.   He died 15 August, 1864.

CHILDREN.

1618 I.   JANE ANN, born 10 Dec., 1822.
1619 II.   PERMELIA, born 9 March, 1825.
1620 III.   SARAH MARIA, born 15 Sept., 1826.
1621 IV.   FANNIE, born 16 Oct., 1828.

1622 v.   DANIEL LEDOIT, born 20 Sept., 1830.
1623 vi.   HIRAM FLANDEFFA, born 9 March, 1832.
1624 vii. STILES RUST, born 7 April, 1834.
1625 viii. ELBEN, born 22 Jan., 1836.
1626 ix.   ALLURED BLISS, 14 Nov., 1838.

668 (V) HARRY, SON OF JOHN.

Harry Janes married Elizabeth A. Dickerman.   He
died 12 February, 1865.   She died July, 1866.

CHILDREN.

1627 i.   MARY HULL, born 6 Dec., 1825.
1628 ii.   HANNAH ROCKWELL, born 21 April, 1828.
1629 iii. ROSELIA, born 16 June, 1831.
1630 iv.   MARY ELLEN, born 11 Sept., 1834; married Mr.
           Steward.
1631 v.   DANIEL BENONI, born 30 Nov., 1837.

669 (VI) JOHN, SON OF JOHN.

Rev. John Janes was born at Grand Isle, South Hero,
Vt., January 4, 1802, died at Norwalk, Ohio, 8 February, 1843.

At the age of seventeen he emigrated to Ohio,
and at twenty entered the itinerant connection of
the Methodist Episcopal church. His ministry was
within the states of Ohio, Indiana, and Michigan; and,
as a pioneer preacher, traversed many a swamp and
wilderness.

He was a man of great energy and force; of genial temperament, and noted among his peers for brilliant conversational powers, endowed with wit and aptness in repartee. Bishop Thomson thus speaks of him in a published biographical sketch:

" His abilities in the pulpit were by no means of an inferior order. In his early days he was fond of polemical divinity; and, as he possessed sprightly wit, a warm fancy, an active intellect, and a dauntless heart, he was no mean antagonist. Unsparing to the strong, he was merciful to the prostrate, and courteous toward both. In his prime he was truly eloquent, though generally argumentative, he was at times exceedingly pathetic. He did not seek, like the giants of fable, by piling mountain upon mountain, to make a path from earth to heaven; rather like Apollos, he was wont, relying upon the aid of the divine spirit, to bring down heaven to earth by the melting strains of his subduing eloquence."

The companion whom he married 21 May, 1828, was Hannah Brown, born at Plymouth, Vt., 16 January, 1808. Her family emigrated to Michigan in 1827, and herself and sister, young ladies of seventeen and nineteen, formed the first Methodist society, at Ann Arbor. Her present residence is Berea, Ohio.

CHILDREN.

1632 I. MARY B., born 10 March, 1832; married W. A. Ingham, Esq., of Cleveland, Ohio. She was a teacher of belles lettres, at McGregor, Iowa.

1633 II. ELIZA R., born 27 June, 1834; died 24 Nov., 1858.

1634 III. EMMA, born 10 Sept., 1837; is teacher of Latin,
French, and belles lettres, at Cleveland, Ohio.
1635 IV. FRANK, born 25 Jan., 1840; married Tillie Ward
of Newark, Ohio.
1636 V. JOHN HENRY, born 23 Dec., 1842; died 24 May,
1847.

---

672 (IX) HORACE, SON OF JOHN.

Horace Janes married Minerva Andrus, February,
1832.

CHILD.

1637 I. SEYMOUR, born 26 Jan., 1839.

Horace married (2) Jane Rose, 15 July, 1849.

CHILD.

1638 II. MINERVA, born 1 Oct., 1850.

---

673 (X) ALLURED, SON OF JOHN.

Rev. Allured Janes (M.) married Caroline Caulkins,
November, 1831.   She died 4 March, 1865.

CHILDREN.

1639 I. HUBERT ALLEN, born ..., Dec., 1832.
1640 II. CHARLES CARROLL, born ..., Oct., 1838.
1641 III. LUCIA MARIA, born 25 Jan., 1846.

674 (XI) EMILY A., DAUGHTER OF JOHN.

Emily A. Janes married Perry Kenyon, May, 1858.

CHILDREN.

1642 I. FRANCES OLIVE, born 18 Jan., 1862.
1643 II. CHARLES PERRY, born 1 Jan., 1864.

---

677 (II) SETH, SON OF ELIJAH.

Seth Janes, from one account, married Clara Loomis, 1827. This may be right, and she might have been a first wife without issue. Another account says Seth Janes married Jerusha Ruby Fenton, 18 March, 1837. She died 23 March, 1860.

CHILDREN.

1644 I. FREDERIC MORTIMER, born 2 May, 1838 ; married Zeruah Potter, 31 July, 1860.
1645 II. EUGENIA AGNES AUGUSTA, born 4 Aug., 1842 ; married James J. McClung, 30 Aug., 1859.
1646 III. FERNANDO ALBERTUS, born 17 Nov., 1843.

---

678 (III) CHESTER, SON OF ELIJAH.

Chester Janes married Eliza Dee of Georgia, Vt.

CHILDREN.

1647 I. HOMER W., born ......, 1830.
1648 III. WILLIAM H., born ......, 1832.
1649 III. EZRA E., born ......, 1834.
1650 IV. HALBERT, born ......, 1836; married Lucy Paine, ..., 1860.

1651 v. CHARLOTTE M., born ......, 1837; married E. E. Hurlbut, ..., 1858.
1652 VI. SARAH A., born ......, 1840; married H. G. Williams, ..., 1857.
1653 VII. ADDISON B., born ......, 1843.
1654 VIII. HELEN M., born ......, 1845.
1655 IX. ADELAIDE E., born ......, 1849.

680 (V) CYRUS, SON OF ELIJAH.

Cyrus Janes married Louisa Bliss.

CHILD.

1656 I. EDWIN, born ...... ;

681 (VI) MELVIN T., SON OF ELIJAH.

Melvin T. Janes married Marcia Caulkins, 13 November, 1833. She was born 1812.

CHILDREN.

1657 I. ALVIN SABIN, born 11 September, 1834; died 10 March, 1846.
1658 II. ELBERT FERDINAND, born 4 January, 1836; killed by falling of a tree.
1659 III. CHARLES MORTIMER, born 22 May, 1838; married Harriet M. Hoadly.
1660 IV. ALFRED THOMAS, born 15 December, 1842.
1661 V. GEORGE LESTER, born 9 May, 1845.
1662 VI. WILLIS G. CLARK, born 28 December, 1849.

38

682 (VII) DANIÉL M., SON OF ELIJAH.

Daniel Mortimer Janes married Charlotte Himrod (Caulkins). She died 10 March, 1856.

CHILDREN.

1663 I.   JOHN L. CASSELLS, born ......, 1842 ; died 20 September, 1850.
1664 II. CELSUS, born ......, 1846 ; died 2 February, 1848.
1665 III. LEONARD, born ......, 1850 ; died 21 March, 1851.

Daniel M. married 19 October, 1860, (2) Sarah E. Law (born 1838).

CHILD.

1666 IV. EMMA, born 26 November, 1861 ; died 19 January, 1863.

––––––

685 (II) LORENZO, SON OF OLIVER.

Lorenzo Janes was born at South Hero, Vt., received a common school education and lived with his father till twenty-one years of age. He married in 1832, Lucina M. Post of Georgia, Vt., and resided there for a time, but afterwards went into mercantile business in St. Albans, and accumulated some property, and has retired from active business.

CHILDREN.

1668 I.   WILLIAM P., born ......, 1833 ; married Ann Crilley,
1669 II. CHARLOTTE G., born ......, 1836.
1670 III. CHARLES H., born ......, 1838 ; married Mary Banta.
1671 IV. LUCINA ANN, born ......, 1840 ; married Marshall Mason.

686 (III) ORPHA, DAUGHTER OF OLIVER.

Orpha Janes married D. Bull, about 1830. She died 1835.

CHILD.

1672 I. CLARISSA, born ......, 1831.

---

687 (IV) LUCY, DAUGHTER OF OLIVER.

Lucy Janes married H. E. Dunton, and resides near Enosburgh.

CHILDREN.

1673 I.   CAROLINE C., born ......, 1832.
1674 II.   HIRAM W., born ......, 1833.
1675 III.   WILLIAM T., born ......, 1835.
1676 IV.   HARRIET E., born ......, 1837.
1677 V.   CHARLES D., born ......, 1839.
1678 VI.   HENRY L., born ......, 1841.
1679 VII.   CHARLOTTE M., born ......, 1842.
1680 VIII. CLARISSA F., born ......, 1844.
1681 IX.   EMMA C., born ......, 1849.
1682 X.   ISABEL M., born ......, 1855.

---

690 (VII) HENRIETTA, DAUGHTER OF OLIVER.

Henrietta Janes married Abram C. Brown, who removed to San Francisco.

CHILDREN.

1683 I. CHARLES, born ...... ;
1684 II. LUCY, born ...... ;

691 (I) LUCINDA, DAUGHTER OF DAVID.

Lucinda Janes married Thomas Dockum, 10 October, 1826. He was born 26 September, 1806. He died 21 December, 1852. Daughter Charlotte died unmarried, 21 September, 1846. They lived in ...., Mo. Some of the sons reside in Atlanta, Ga.

CHILDREN.

1685 I.   ORRIN, born 29 August, 1827; married (1) Martha A. Fickly; (2) Nancy H. Harper.
1686 II.   LOVINA, born 27 June, 1829.
1687 III.   MARTHA M., born 24 June, 1830; married Daniel S. Beers.
1688 IV.   CHARLES, born 4 March, 1832; married Mrs. Sarah Harper.
1689 V.   LESTER, born 31 June, 1834; married Mary J. Reyboum.
1690 VI.   HENRY, born 10 August, 1836; married Martha Ann Homer.
1691 VII.   CHARLOTTE M., born 26 May, 1838.
1692 VIII. MARY E., born 26 September, 1840; married Lewis Reville.
1693 IX.   SARAH L., born 24 May, 1844; married William Reyboum.

692 (II) LESTER, SON OF DAVID.

Rev. Lester Janes married Sarah H. Smith of South Hadley, Mass., 1838. He is a bold, faithful preacher of the gospel, in the Methodist Episcopal church; has labored in Vermont, and in the state of New York, with great acceptance. He once spent a sabbath with the writer, when settled in Bernardston, and his preaching was much enjoyed. He went to Texas to have charge of a seminary there, and there he was engaged in the labors of the ministry. He returned north, and labored in the state of Illinois, and when the war broke out he went as chaplain to one of the Missouri regiments, and acquitted himself with honor, and returned to his adopted state to resume his pastoral duties there.

CHILDREN.

1694 I.   DAVID RODNEY, born 12 September, 1839.
1695 II.   SARAH MARTHA, born 2 December, 1840.
1696 III.   DAVID R., born 30 July, 1842.
1697 IV.   GEORGE M., born 14 December, 1844.
1698 V.   JOHN LESTER, born 24 January, 1847.
1699 VI.   PLINEY SMITH, born 13 February, 1849.
1700 VII.   WILLIE R., born 23 November, 1850.
1701 VIII.   R. KENNEDY, born 30 June, 1853.
1702 IX.   EDMUND S., born 29 January, 1858.

693 (III) OLIVER, SON OF DAVID.

Oliver Janes married Dinah Dewitt in Ohio.

CHILDREN.

1703 I.   LORIN, born ...... ;
1704 II.   ORLANDO, born ...... ;
1705 III.   LOVINA, born ...... ;

694 (IV) MARSHALL D., SON OF DAVID.

Marshall D. Janes married Lucinda Andrus of Ohio, and lives in Berlin, Ohio.

CHILDREN.

1706 I.   LUCINDA, born ...... ;
1707 II. SABINA JOSEPHINE, born ...... ;
1708 III. LAURA ELLEN, born ...... ;
1709 IV. SON, born ...... ; a patriot soldier who died in the army.
1710 V.   ORRIN, born ...... ;

---

695 (V) CHARLOTTE, DAUGHTER OF DAVID.

Charlotte Janes married Blake Barrows then in Ohio. Since moved to Iowa.

CHILDREN.

1711 I.   ANNA, born 5 February, 1841; married George Messenger.
1712 II. NELLIE B., born 21 October, 1843.
1713 III. HARRIET B., born 19 January, 1859.

---

696 (VI) HEMAN, SON OF DAVID.

Heman Janes married Martha Jones, and lives in Canada West.

CHILDREN.

1714 I.   JAMES DAVID, born ...... ;
1715 II. HEMAN ORLANDO, born ...... ;
1716 III. DAUGHTER, born ...... ;
1717 IV. SON, born ...... ;

702 (I) CHAUNCEY W., SON OF CHAUNCEY.

Chauncey W. Janes married Mrs. Mary Hall (Field), June, 1858.

CHILDREN.

1718 I. BYRON, born 29 March, 1859.
1719 II. MARY GERTRUDE, born 3 Sept., 1864.

---

703 (II) LEONARD T., SON OF CHAUNCEY.

Leonard T. Janes married Sophronia Shaffer. He was a patriot soldier, and endured so much hardship that his health is some impaired.

CHILD.

1720 I. CARRIE E., born 28 Nov., 1860.

---

705 (IV) LAURA ANN, DAUGHTER OF CHAUNCEY.

Laura Ann married John Gray.

CHILDREN.

1721 I. ALBERT THEODORE, born ... Oct., 1859.
1722 II. IDA, born ..., Sept., 1862.

710 (IV) LAVINA, DAUGHTER OF WILLIAM.

Lavina Janes, Pittsfield branch, married Dr. William Edgar of St. Louis, 1839.

CHILDREN.

1723 I.   WILLIAM HENRY, born ......;
1724·II.   CHARLES, born ......;
1725 III. EDMUND, born ...... ;
1726 IV.   FRANK, born ......;
1727 V.   IDA, born ......;

------

712 (I) MARY E., DAUGHTER OF COL. ETHAN.

Mary E. Janes of Pittsfield married William W. Goodman, 25 October, 1841.   He died 31 May, 1861. They have an intelligent and interesting family of daughters, and well educated under the influence of prosperous female seminaries.

CHILDREN.

1728 I.   CHARLOTTE, born 10 Oct., 1843.
1729 II.   KATE LOUISA, born 8 Aug., 1845.
1730 III. ALICE MARY, born 28 Dec., 1847.
1731 IV.   ELLA JANE, born 16 June, 1850.
1732 V.   SARAH PEASE, born 25 Aug., 1855.

------

727 (II) EMILY P., DAUGHTER OF ROGER.

Emily Pitkin Janes married David Parsons, 24 December, 1820.

CHILDREN.

1733 I. ELIZABETH, born 1 Feb., 1822.
1734 II. CHANDLER J., born 8 March, 1823; married Harriet A. Blinn.
1735 III. DAVID P., born 15 Nov., 1824.

729 (IV) WILLIAM W., SON OF ROGER.

William Warner Janes married Nancy Webb of Meriden, Conn.

CHILDREN.

1736 I. MARY E., born ......; married C. Bush.
1737 II. WILLIAM McDONALD, born ......; run over and killed.
1738 III. MARTHA C., born ......;
1739 IV. FANNY, born ......;

730 (V) ELISHA, SON OF ROGER.

Elisha Janes married Elizabeth Cryder, and resides in New Philadelphia, Ohio.

CHILDREN.

1740 I. WILLIAM W., born 30 March, 1834; married Julia Chapin.
1741 II. LEROY LANSING, born 27 March, 1837; is a teacher at West Point.
1742 III. ELLEN M., born 2 Dec., 1838; married L. A. Anderman.
1743 IV. MARY, born 22 Oct., 1844.

731 (VI) ELIZA, DAUGHTER OF ROGER.

Eliza Janes married Richard Warner of Lima, N. Y.

CHILDREN.

1744 I.   ELIZABETH, born ......; married Mr. Camp.
1745 II. ELISHA W., born ......; married Miss Warner.
1746 III. ABIGAIL, born ......; married Mr. Howes.

---

743 (II) ALANSON, SON OF DANIEL.

Alanson Janes married Betsey Beman.

CHILDREN.

1747 I.   AUGUSTUS D., born 15 March, 1820; married Julia
           Van Alstine, died 30 May, 1846.
1748 II.   ERASTUS A., born 24 Jan., 1824; married Eliza-
           beth W. Moon, 16 Oct., 1848.
1749 III. HORACE L., born 21 March, 1826; married Emily
           Richmond, 1862.
1750 IV.   DESTAMONY E., born 28 Dec., 1827; died 4 July,
           1838.
1751 V.   CLARISSA H., born 6 Dec., 1829; married R. B.
           Wightman, 27 April, 1853.
1752 VI.   HENRY M., born 10 May, 1832.
1753 VII. EMILY M., born 17 Aug., 1836; married J. S.
           Goodyear, 19 Dec., 1867.
1754 VIII. WILLIAM S., born 15 June, 1838; married Lelia
           Pixley, 17 Oct., 1862.
1755 IX.   MARY A. E., born 28 Nov., 1841; died 16 July,
           1858.

747 (VI) MARTIN W., SON OF DANIEL.

Martin Wilson Janes married Miss Kelleman. He was a teacher of penmanship.

CHILDREN.

1756 I. WINFIELD SCOTT, born 4 March, 1840; married Eliza Irvin.
1757 II. RICHARD M. J., born 8 Jan., 1843.

751 (IV) CHANCELLOR, SON OF ELISHAMA.

Chancellor Janes married Margaret Soop, 1823. She died 3 April, 1859, æ. 60.

CHILDREN.

1758 I. DAVID, born 25 Sept., 1825; married Elizabeth Bennett of Ashland.
1759 II. WILLIAM, born ...... 1827; ... a noble patriot soldier.
1760 III. RICHARD, born ......, 1830;
1761 IV. ELIZABETH, born 22 July, 1833.
1762 V. TUNIS, born ......, 1837;
1763 VI. FANNY, born ......, 1839;
1764 VII. FRANCIS, born ......, 1841; killed at battle of Cedar Mountain, æ. 22. See letter in Appendix.

752 (V) DESIRE, DAUGHTER OF ELISHAMA.

Desire Janes married Darius Buck, 1832, and resides in Albany.

CHILDREN.

1765 I. ADELIA, born ... April, 1835.
1766 II. WILLIAM, born ... April, 1839; ... died ......, 1857·

753 (VI) WILLIAM, SON OF ELISHAMA.

William Janes married Mary Ann Hawley, and resides in Albany. He has been a merchant at Albany.

CHILDREN.

1767 I.   CHANCELLOR, born 8 Feb., 1844; died 17 Aug., 1844.
1768 II.   JULIA MARIA, born 20 Sept., 1845.
1769 III.   WILLIAM GOMER, born 22 Feb., 1847.
1770 IV.   MARY, born 10 Aug., 1848; died 8 Oct., 1848.
1771 V.   CHARLES HENRY, born 17 Aug., 1849.
1772 VI.   JAMES EDWARD, born 2 June, 1851.
1773 VII.   FRANKLIN HAWLEY, born 19 Aug., 1853.
1774 VIII.   JOSEPH LEONARD, born 26 Aug., 1854; died 12 Oct., 1854.
1775 IX.   ALFRED EVERETT, born 28 July, 1857; died 23 Aug., 1857.
1776 X.   EMMA MONTGOMERY, born 2 Sept., 1861.

754 (VII) ADALINE, DAUGHTER OF ELISHAMA.

Adaline Janes married Reuben B. Stiles, in Bethlehem, N. Y., 2 Oct., 1830.

CHILDREN.

1777 I.   EDWARD, born 18 Dec., 1831; died 25 July, 1833.
1778 II.   WILLIAM EDWARD, born 12 Sept., 1833; married Martha A. Corning, of Palmyra, N. Y.
1779 III.   ELISHAMA JANES, born 2 June, 1837; drowned 16 July, 1845.
1780 IV.   DeWITT CLINTON, born 12 March, 1842; married Mrs. Elizabeth Curtis (Van Zandt).
1781 V.   CHARLES AUGUSTUS, born 4 Sept., 1843; died 28 Aug., 1844.
1782 VI.   ANNA MARIA, born 9 April, 1847.
1783 VII.   CHARLES A., born 9 April, 1850.

756 (IX) HANNAH, DAUGHTER OF ELISHAMA.

Hannah Janes married Isaac Ten Eyck of Bethle-
ham, N, Y.

CHILDREN.

1784 I. ANTHONY, born ......;
1785 II. ELIZABETH, born ......; married William Stannis,
of Hartford.
1786 III. DAVID, born ......; a patriot soldier, killed at
Gettysburgh.
1787 IV. CHARLES, born ......;
1788 V. ISAAC, born ......;

759 (I) ELISHA B., SON OF NATHANIEL.

Elisha Barnes Janes was a very popular professor and teacher at Albany, N. Y., where he suddenly
died 22 May, 1837. He married Fanny B. Lord,
daughter of Joseph Lord of Canaan.

CHILDREN.

1789 I. SAMUEL B., born 22 June, 1827; married Charlotte
House.
1790 II. HENRY W., born 20 June, 1830; married Elizabeth
Deming.
1791 III. JOHN J., born 10 Jan., 1833.

762 (IV) WALTER R., SON OF NATHANIEL.

Walter Raleigh Janes married (1) Anna Maria
Adams, 21 July, 1831. She died 31 July, 1845.
Walter R. has resided in New York.

CHILDREN.

1792 I.   WILLIAM VAN BUREN, born 27 June, 1832.
1793 II.   CHRISTINA ELIZA, born 18 Aug., 1835.
1794 III.   ANNA MARIA, born 16 June, 1840.

Walter R. married (2) Margaret Beardsley, 14 July, 1846. She died 26 January, 1850.

CHILDREN.

1796 IV.   WALTER B., born 7 Sept., 1848; died Oct., 1848.
1797 V.   WALTER J., born 18 Jan., 1850.

Walter R. married (3) Amanda Kelsey, 19 May, 1853.

CHILD.

1798 VI.   CHARLES KELSEY, born 31 Dec., 1853; died 10 March, 1861.

———

763 (V) ELIZA W., DAUGHTER OF NATHANIEL.

Eliza Wright Janes married Norman Williams, 15 February, 1832.

CHILDREN.

1799 I.   HARRIET, born 13 Dec., 1833.
1800 II.   SIDNEY, born 19 April, 1834.
1801 III.   CAROLINE, born 11 Aug., 1840; died ......
1802 IV.   HENRIETTA, born 10 Oct., 1847.

760 (II) LAURA W., DAUGHTER OF NA-
THANIEL.

Laura Wolcott Janes married Sylvester Curtis, 14 June, 1824.

CHILDREN.

1803 I. LYDIA, born ... Sept., 1825.
1804 II. WILLIAM HENRY, born ......, 1832.
1805 III. LAURA JANES, born ......, 1837.
• 1806 IV. EDWIN S. J. born ......, 1842.

764 (VI) HARRIET W., DAUGHTER OF NA-
THANIEL.

Harriet Wilson Janes married William Lawrence of Canaan, N. Y., 17 February, 1835. He died September, 1865.

CHILDREN.

1807 I. JOHN, born 14 Jan., 1840.
1808 II. WALTER, born 26 May, 1841.

768 (I) HOWELL W., SON OF JESSE.

Howell W. Janes married Lucy Hall of Canaan, N. Y. Children all born in Lima, N. Y.

CHILDREN.

1809 I. LYMAN H., born ......;
1810 II. DELIA S., born ......;
1811 III. GEORGE F., born ......;
1812 IV. LAURA ANN, born ......;

Howell W., married (2) Polly Hutchins.

CHILD.

1813 v. SPENCER, born ...... ;

---

769 (II) DAVID, SON OF JESSE.

David Janes married Emily Hutchins of Junius, N. Y., 24 October, 1828. He died 5 April, 1860.

CHILDREN.

1814 I. DEFOREST, born ...... ;
1815 II. OLIVE, born ...... ;
1816 III. CLARA, born ...... ;
1817 IV. DAVID, born ...... ;
1818 v. JESSE, born ...... ;
1819 VI. MARY, born ...... ;

---

770 (III) HARRIET G., DAUGHTER OF JESSE.

Harriet G. married William N. Saunders from Nova Scotia.

CHILDREN.

1820 I. WILLIAM EVANDER, born 6 Aug., 1839.
1821 II. JULIA M., born 3 Oct., 1841.
1822 III. WINFIELD SCOTT, born 12 March, 1844.
1823 IV. DAVID E., born 7 April, 1846.
1824 v. HARRIET E., born 19 July, 1848.
1825 VI. TERESEA J., born 13 March, 1852.
1826 VII. CHARLES J., born 9 Oct., 1856.

771 (IV) CHARLES S., SON OF JESSE.

Charles S. Janes married Emily Peckham of Ontario,
March, 1830.

CHILDREN.

1827 i.   MARGARET, born ...... ;
1828 ii. CHARLES, born ...... ;
1829 iii. THERON, born ...... ;
1830 iv. CAROLINE, born ...... ;
1831 v.   VOLNEY, born ...... ;
1832 vi. WILLIE, born ...... ;
1833 vii. EDWARD, born ...... ;
1834 viii. GEORGE, born ..... ;

772 (V) JULIA W., DAUGHTER OF JESSE.

Julia W. Janes, a most estimable woman, married
Joseph W. Corning[1] of Nova Scotia. They reside at
Palmyra, N. Y.

[1] JOSEPH W. CORNING was a member of the New York Assembly
in 1861, from Wayne county; and promptly and energetically aided
in every measure tending to check or to aid the government in suppres-
sing the rebellion then threatening the overthrow of the government.

On returning to Wayne county the 18th of April, the day after the
adjournment of the legislature, he at once commenced enrolling
men for a company of volunteers, under the then call for seventy-five
thousand. The company was soon organized, and he commissioned
captain, and was subsequently assigned as Company B, 33d Regiment
N. Y. Infantry. This regiment was assigned to Third brigade,
Second division, Sixth corps of the army of the Potomac, and partici-
pated in nearly all the battles, marches and retreats of the army up
to May 18th, 1863, the time for which the regiment was organized
(two years) expiring on the 22d of May, and were mustered out at
Geneva, N. Y., June 2d, 1863. In October, 1861, Capt. Corning was
promoted to the lieut. colonelcy of his regiment.

It was to Col. Corning (he then commanding the picket line near Lee's

- CHILDREN.

1835 I. MARTHA ALTHEA, born 18 August, 1839; married
William Edward Stiles.

1836 II. JOHN WALKER, born 18 September, 1841; married Catharine Drake of Palmyra.

1837 III. JOSEPH H., born 31 July, 1846; died 9 June, 1849.

1838 IV. JULIA MARIA, born 3 April, 1849.

1839 V. JOSEPH LATHAM, born 21 April, 1850; died 20
June, 1866.

Mills near the left of the enemy's lines of fortifications of Yorktown),
that the first information of the evacuation of their works by the
rebels was communicated by two Alabama negroes, just after day-
dawn on the morning of the 4th of May (Sunday). They said that
the rebels began to go on Thursday night, and that on Friday night
they took away all the wagons and most all the big guns, and most
all the soldiers went, and last night they all went. They put stove
pipes in the forts to make the Yankees think they were cannon.
Col. Corning went with these men to Gen. Hancock's quarters
(he then being in command of Third Brigade), and had him waked up,
and informed him of what these men reported. Believing the report
to be correct, Col. Corning took 60 men of his picket guard, and went
to Lee's Mills and in full view of the enemy's works, and could
readily see the stove pipes protruding from the embrasures of the
forts (five of them) as represented by the negroes; and, in addition,
there were stuffed representations of men fastened to stakes in the
parapets, with muskets and bayonets fixed to represent sentinels.
By eight o'clock the Sixth corps was in motion and crossing the
Warwick creek.

At the battle of Williamsburg, the next day, May 5th, Col. Corning commanding a portion of the 33d Regiment (and in Gen. Hancock's command on the left of the enemy) as the enemy's line un-
checked had advanced within fifteen rods of his position, ordered his
command to charge. With one loud long shout, which was taken
up and repeated by the rest of the troops, on he rushed with his
command, and before reaching the enemy they broke in confusion
and fled. This was the beginning, and all of what has been called the
great charge of Williamsburg.

Col. Corning was constantly with his regiment, and commanded

775 (VIII) LOVINA P., DAUGHTER OF JESSE.

Lovina P. Janes married Jeremiah Mabie, 1856.

CHILDREN.

1840 I. TRUMAN, born ......;

1841 II. JULIA, born ......;

---

the advanced guard at Mechanicsville, May 24th, at which time Howell Cobb's brigade was driven out of that place.

On the 28th of June, Col. Corning was detached from the 33d and assigned to command the 77th Regiment N. Y. Volunteers, and commanded that regiment during the remainder of the seven days fighting, in falling back to Harrison's landing. At Harrison's landing he commanded the brigade; also at the time of returning to Alexandria, was at the battle of the second Bull Run; being now in command of the 33d Regiment, was through the Maryland campaign; at the battle of South Mountain, and Antietam. In the later battle his horse was hit four times, and he lost about one-fifth of his regiment; was at the first Fredericksburg battle, Dec. 11th, 12th, and 13th, 1862; and again at second Fredericksburg, May 3d, 1863, in the assault and carrying the heights, in which the 33d suffered heavily, and Col. Corning's horse was killed under him on the heights. The next day, May 4th, the enemy attacked the Sixth corps three times and were repulsed, but at a fearful loss to that corps, being about one-third of the whole available force, and the 33rd lost one-half of its members in the two days. About two weeks from this, the regiment had orders to proceed to Elmira, N. Y., to be mustered out, the two years ending on the 22d of May, 1863.

In the fall of 1864, Col. Corning again recruited a number of volunteers, and joined the 111th Regiment in the Second corps at the siege of Petersburg.

January 27th, 1865, he received orders from the adjutant general of the state of New York, to organize a new regiment (194th), which was the last regiment organized in the state; and just upon the eve of departure for the army, Lee surrendered, and the 194th was mustered out at Elmira.

John W. Corning, son of Col. Corning, joined the 33rd Regiment in Sept., 1861; was appointed 2d lieutenant in December following,

794 (I) ERASTUS, SON OF BENJAMIN.

Erastus Janes moved from Coventry, Conn., to the central part of the state when a young man, and braved all the difficulties of the pioneer life, and from small beginnings made a comfortable home for himself and family. The church of God with which he has been long connected, feels his goodly influence. He is a worthy officer in the Presbyterian church and his many virtues are well known and highly esteemed. He married Lydia Woodruff of Connecticut.

CHILDREN.

1842 I. JOHN M., born 6 February, 1823; married Rosanna Van Netter.

1843 II. ELEAZER F., born 6 January, 1825; married Gertrude Van Netter.

1844 III. ASA W., born 7 May, 1829; died 12 April, 1852.

1845 IV. WILLIAM D., born 20 March, 1835; married Lizzie Louise Fenno, of Charlestown, Mass.

795 (II) ELEAZER, SON OF BENJAMIN.

Eleazer Janes married Elizabeth Hempstead, and moved to Michigan. He died January, 1847.

---

and 1st lieutenant in May, 1862; and adjutant in Nov., 1862; was engaged in most of the battles in which the 33d took part.

During the seven days fighting on the Peninsula, he was alone in command of his company, and acquitted himself bravely, and received high commendation from his superiors. As adjutant of the regiment he was active, prompt, efficient, and a brave officer.

CHILDREN.

1846 I.   ROBERT, born ... July, 1821; married ....
1847 II. IRENA, born ... Oct., 1824.
1848 III. MARY, born ......, 1825.
1849 IV. HARRIET, born ......, 1828.
1850 V.   JOHN, born ......, 1829; died 1849.
1851 VI. HENRY, born ......, 1831.

---

797 (IV) DAVID, SON OF BENJAMIN.

David Janes married Nancy Bacon, 14 January, 1829, at Lima, N. Y.   They moved to Michigan.

CHILDREN.

1852 I.   LYDIA, born 28 Jan., 1831.
1853 II.   WILLIAM B., born 29 April, 1833.
1854 III. THOMAS, born 20 July, 1835.
1855 IV.   EMILY, born 20 Aug., 1838.
1856 V.   ELIPHALET, born 4 Nov., 1840.
1857 VI.   CELIA, born 14 Oct., 1842.
1858 VII. CHLOE W., born 31 May, 1845.

---

799 (VI) HUNTINGTON, SON OF BENJAMIN.

Huntington Janes married Chloe Woodruff, 1834. They live in Michigan.

CHILDREN.

1859 I.   DANIEL, born ......, 1835.
1860 II. SARAH, born ......, 1837.
1861 III. ELIZA, born ......, 1839.
1862 IV. HENRY, born ......, 1843.

802 (IX) BENJAMIN F., SON OF BENJAMIN.

Benjamin F. married ....

CHILDREN.

1863 I.   LEWIS, born ......;
1864 II. MARIA, born ......;
1865 III. BEULAH, born ...... ;

EIGHTH GENERATION.

LINE OF ABEL.

829 (I) ELIZA, DAUGHTER OF ALFRED.

Eliza Janes married Joseph Church, 9 Sept., 1819. He is a worthy, prosperous and wealthy citizen of Hartford, Conn.

CHILDREN.

1866 I.   EDWARD, born 22 July, 1820; died 16 Nov., 1820.
1867 II. EDWIN, born 8 January, 1822; died 10 August, 1822.
1869 III. ELIZABETH MARY, born 10 March, 1824.
1870 IV. FREDERIC E., born 4 May, 1826; married Isabel M. Cares.
1871 V.   CHARLOTTE E., born 25 August, 1832; died 15 January, 1867.

830 (II) ADRIAN, SON OF ALFRED.

Adrian Janes married Adaline Root, 1823. He moved from Hartford to New York, and has accumulated some wealth.

CHILDREN.

1872 I.   JULIA E., born 6 July, 1824 ; married Giles White, 22 Nov., 1849.

1873 II.   HENRY, born 1 September, 1826 ; married Caroline Hyde, 4 June, 1850.

1874 III.   EDWARD R., born 3 May, 1829 ; married Elizabeth B. Ingalls, 4 Dec., 1854.

1875 IV.   GEORGE, born 21 May, 1831 ; married Louisa P. Entz, 17 June, 1857.

1876 V.   CHARLES B., born 30 December, 18...

1877 VI.   MARY E., born 20 August, 1837.

---

831 (III) BENJAMIN F., SON OF ALFRED.

Benjamin F. Janes, married (1) Nancy Mulks, 8 April, 1828. She died 1834. He married (2) Hopey Cook Wheaton, 4 January, 1839.

CHILD.

1878 I.   HENRY, born 5 Aug., 1833; married ....

Benjamin F. married (2) Hopey Cook.

CHILDREN.

1879 II.   WHEATON B., born 17 Dec , 1840.

1880 III.   LEWIS ALMARIN, born 23 Oct., 1843.

832 (IV) ALVIN, SON OF ALFRED.

Alvin Janes is an enterprising citizen of Rochester, N. Y. He married Irene Watkins, 11 April, 1833, who was born 22 April, 1810.

CHILDREN.

1881 I.   ELIZABETH, born 24 Feb., 1834; married Selden Oviatt.
1882 II.   ADRIAN, born 25 Dec., 1835.
1883 III. ALVIN, born 25 April, 1837.
1884 IV.   MARCUS JULIUS, born 11 July, 1839; died 9 Jan., 1840.
1885 V.   HARRIET E., born 6 July, 1841.
1886 VI.   ADALINE IRENE, born 20 March, 1847.
1887 VII. ROBERT WRAY, born 27 Oct., 1853.

---

833 (V) ALFRED, SON OF ALFRED.

Alfred Janes married (1) Susan Stottle, 24 Dec., 1835, (2) Sally Demunn, 3 July, 1842.

CHILDREN.

1887a I.   WALTER, born ......, 1836.
1888 II.   ELLA, born ......, 1843.

---

834 (VI) ADALINE, DAUGHTER OF ALFRED.

Adaline Janes married Lewis Graves, M. D., 15 May, 1833. They reside in Brooklyn, N. Y.

CHILDREN.

1889 I. ELIZA A., born ......;
1890 II. CHANDLER F., born 1 January, 1836.
1891 III. BENJAMIN F., born ......, 1838.
1892 IV. THOMAS, born ......; died ......
1893 V. ELLEN L., born ......;

---

835 (I) MARIA T., DAUGHTER OF WALTER.

Maria T. Janes married Calvin Whitney, 29 May, 1822.

CHILDREN.

1894 I. MARIA, born 23 June, 1823; married Luther Webster, 1 Oct., 1848.
1895 II. EDWARD, born 21 April, 1825; died 8 Oct., 1826.
1896 III. ELLEN, born 31 July, 1827; married J. Edwin Child, 21 Oct., 1857.
1897 IV. ANNA T., born 22 Aug., 1833.

---

836 (II) ALPHONZO, SON OF WALTER.

CHILDREN.

1898 I. MARY T., born 8 April, 1842; died 5 May, 1843.
1899 II. LEWIS GEORGE, born 19 Feb., 1844.
1900 III. MARCUS TAFT, born 13 April, 1846.
1901 IV. CHARLES FREMONT, born 5 Oct., 1848.
1902 V. WILLIAM FREDERIC, born 13 Oct., 1852.

842 (I) ELFLEDA, DAUGHTER OF ALMARIN.

Elfleda Janes married Peter Wormwood, April, 1826. He was born 7 March, 1800.

CHILDREN.

1903 I.   Son, born 12 June, 1828; died 7 July, 1828.
1904 II.   Marion E., born 21 Aug., 1829; married Alexander Campbell.
1905 III. William W., born 26 Aug., 1831; married Mary A. Kenyon.
1906 IV.   Alfred, born 3 March, 1833; died 10 Aug., 1826.
1907 V.   Lauretta, born 27 June, 1835; died 3 Aug., 1836.
1908 VI.   Catharine, born 27 May, 1837; died 12 Oct., 1838.
1909 VII. Norman, born 25 Oct., 1839.
1910 VIII. Emma Gertrude, born 12 Feb., 1849.

---

843 (II) EMELINE, DAUGHTER OF ALMARIN.

Emeline Janes married Ward Munroe of Manlius, and resides at Seneca Falls.

CHILDREN.

1911 I.   Caroline, born ......, 1829.
1912 II.   Ann Eliza, born 13 February, 1831; married Mr. Burton.
1913 III. Sidney L., born 28 January, 1833; married Cynthia ....?
1914 IV.   Emeline, born ... April, 1835; died ......, 1853.
1915 V.   Ellen F., born ... March, 1841.
1916 VI.   Eugene W., born ... February, 1844; died 1863.

844 (III) MARY, DAUGHTER OF ALMARIN.

Mary Janes married Henry Phillips, about 1829.

CHILDREN.

1917 I.   LOISA, born ......; married King Preston.
1918 II. CHARLES HENRY, born ......;
1919 III. JULIUS, born ......;
1920 IV. SILAS, born ......;
1921 V.   WARREN, born ......; a patriot soldier, killed at battle of Bull Run.

---

845 (IV) DIANTHA, DAUGHTER OF ALMARIN.

Diantha Janes married William Jackson. He died. She remains a widow at Syracuse.

CHILDREN.

1922 I.   SAMUEL ALMARIN, born 28 May, 1832; married (1) Augusta Green, (2) Catharine Hibbard.
1923 II. JEREMIAH J., born 7 Nov., 1835; died infant.
1924 III. WILLIAM M., born 22 Feb., 1838; married Matilda Gray.
1925 IV. HARRIET, born 2 Sept., 1844.
1926 V.   MARY JANE, born 16 Jan., 1846.
1927 VI. CHARLES R., born 1 Jan., 1849.

---

847 (I) IRVING, SON OF BRADFORD.

Irving Janes married (1) Nancy M. Day, 10 May, 1833. She was born 22 May, 1814.

CHILDREN.

1928 I.   ARMINDA N., born 3 April, 1838; married William
          Burdick, and resides in South Bend, Ill.
1929 II. ISIDORE F., born 1 Sept., 1840.
1930 III. LUCINDA E., born 3 Sept., 1842.
1931 IV. ALBERT L., born 26 April, 1844.

Irving married (2) Harriet Carpenter, born 20 June,
1822, and resides in Olatha, Kansas.

CHILD.

1932- V. MARY E., born 3 July, 1855.

---

849 (III) NANCY, DAUGHTER OF BRADFORD.

Nancy Janes married J. W. Childs, 30 December,
1830, and they reside in Freedom, Ill.

CHILDREN.

1933 I. MARY, born 23 June, 1838; married James Bye, 20
         June, 1861.
1934 II. LUCY, born 12 Sept., 1845; married Anson Beers, 17
         Dec., 1865.

---

851 (V) ERON, SON OF BRADFORD.

Eron Janes married Betsey Warren of Maine.

CHILDREN.

1935 I.   LYDIA MARIA, born ......, 1846.
1936 II. ELLEN FRANCES, born ......, 1848.
1937 III. ELIZABETH ANNA, born ......, 1857.
1938 IV. GEORGE W. HARD, born ......, 1864.

852 (VI) SARAH ANN, DAUGHTER OF BRADFORD.

Sarah Ann Janes married Luther A. Billings, and died 3 April, 1863.

CHILDREN.

1939 I.   SABRA, born 19 May, 1842; married Hiram Rice.
1940 II.   AMANDA, born 19 Dec., 1844; married Joseph Woodland.
1941 III.   L. BRADFORD, born 8 Dec., 1846.
1942 IV.   E. EUGENE, born 12 Nov., 1848; died ... Sept., 1865.
1943 V.   S. NANCY, born 10 Aug., 1850.
1944 VI.   E. ALBURTUS, born 15 April, 1853.
1945 VII.   EMMA J., born 23 Jan., 1855.
1946 VIII. HENRY E., born 6 March, 1857.
1947 IX.   PLINY M., born 28 Jan., 1859.
1948 X.   JOHN, born 10 April, 1863; died infant.

853 (VII) MARY ANN, DAUGHTER OF BRADFORD.

Mary Ann Janes married Stanislaus Belanski. She died March, 1858.

CHILD.

1949 I. CHARLES B., born 19 Jan., 1842; died a patriot soldier.

854 (VIII) EDWARD, SON OF BRADFORD.

Edward Janes married Anna A. Smith of Guilford, 20 November, 1838. They reside in New Haven, Conn. He works at painting, and is a very industrious and worthy citizen. Mrs. Janes was a very indefatigable nurse and helper in the hospitals among the sick soldiers, for whom she exercised a motherly care, and wrote for them many letters to comfort and alleviate the aching hearts of fond parents. They have lived in Worcester and Springfield.

CHILDREN.

1950 I.   ANN ELIZA, born 17 Nov., 1839; died 23 March, 1841.
1951 II. EDWARD RIPLEY, born 6 July, 1843; died 6 Sept., 1843.
1952 III. E. BRADFORD, born ......, 1849.
1953 IV. GEORGIANNA S., born ......, 1855.

855 (IX) EDGAR, SON OF BRADFORD.

Edgar Janes married 10 March, 1850, Sarah Moore, and resides in Rockford, Ill. He died November, 1856.

CHILDREN.

1954 I.   HELLEN, born ... Jan., 1851.
1955 II. HATTIE, born ... Oct., 1853.
1956 III. BRADFORD W., born ... Jan., 1856.

863 (I) EMELINE C., DAUGHTER OF LORENZO.

Emeline Cooper Janes married Charles C. Crail of Cleveland, Ohio.

CHILD.

1957 I. CHILD, born ......; died infant.

---

866 (IV) ELVENAH C., DAUGHTER OF LORENZO.

Elvenah Crosby Janes married 25 April, 1861, John Harris Kinzie of Chicago, an officer of a United States gunboat, Mound City, and was killed by the blowing up of that boat at the taking of St. Charles, Ark., 18 June, 1862. A daughter born after his tragic death.

CHILD.

1958 I. LAURA MAGILL, born 30 Aug., 1862.

---

902 (III) DANIEL W., SON OF IRA.

Daniel W. Janes married 22 February, 1844, Susan L. Bosworth, who was born at Ashford, 7 July, 1820. She died 17 July, 1857.

CHILDREN.

1959 I.   LAURA A., born 18 Dec., 1844, in Springfield, Mass.
1960 II   MARY F., born 7 April, 1847.
1961 III. GEORGIANNA, born 17 Nov, 1851, in Boston.
1962 IV. GEORGE HERBERT, born 29 May, 1853.

1963 v. HELEN L., born 1 March, 1855.
1964 vi. CHARLES L., born 10 July, 1857.
1965 vii. PRECINDA, born ......;

Daniel W. married (2) Caroline N. Taylor, November, 1857. She died 20 December, 1859; (3) married Helen Louisa Comstock, 11 September, 1862, and they reside in Boston.

911 (VII) HORACE P., SON OF HORACE.

Horace P. Janes fell dead in the streets of San Francisco, 5 October, 1862, by supposed disease of the heart.

He was a senior partner in a well known law firm. He was a graduate at the University of Vermont, in 1844, and admitted to the bar in New York, where he remained a few years before he went to California. He had gained a very lucrative practice. His father died suddenly 15 March, 1834; his mother resides in California. He left a wife and three children. He was considered a kind hearted and noble gentleman, and a devoted member of the Episcopal church. In the prime of manhood and in the height of usefulness he was cut down by the hand of Providence, demonstrating the common fact that death is no respecter of persons. His wife was Julia Hall of Burlington, Vt.

CHILDREN.

1966 i. LUCY HALL, born ......;
1967 ii. JOSEPH LYMAN, born ......;
1968 iii. LEWIS DWIGHT, born ......;

932 (I) JONATHAN, SON OF HENRY N.

Jonathan Janes married Abigail H. Webb, daughter of William H. Webb, shipbuilder in New York. They were married in All Saints church, by Rev. Caleb Clapp, 5 June, 1859. She was born 15 July, 1821, Sunday, in New York city. Mr. Janes is a stationer, and engaged very industriously and successfully in his professional trade.

CHILDREN.

1969 I. ECKFORD J., born 27 April, 1851; died 11 July, 1851.

1970 II. WILLIAM HENRY, born 30 April, 1852.

1971 III. EDWARD W., born 10 Aug., 1854; died 29 Aug., 1854.

1972 IV. HENRIETTA E., born 2 February, 1861; died 25 Oct., 1851.

1973 V. CHARLES HOBART, born 10 Jan., 1865; died 14 July, 1865.

---

949 (I) THOMAS M., SON OF LEWIS MARCY.

Thomas Mumford Janes married Cornelia R. Livingston, at Cleveland, Ohio. He was engaged for sometime in the express business in New York, and honorably retired in 1866.

CHILD.

1974 I. CATHARINE, born ... Oct., 1848; married by Dr. Washburn, to Charles W. Thompson, 15 Oct., 1866.

42

985 (V) EDWIN, SON OF AUGUSTUS.

Edwin Janes married Mrs. Carrie Moore Wallace of Holland.

CHILD.

1975 I. GEORGE H., born 6 Dec., 1862.

---

994 (II) WILLIAM C., SON OF TIMOTHY.

William C. Janes married (1) Julia Tyler of Warren, (2) Martha H. Bliss, of Brimfield, Mass.

CHILDREN.

1976 I.   WILLIAM B., born ......; died ....
1977 II. MARTHA B., born ......;
1978 III SALLY B., born ......; died ....
1979 IV. HARRY B., born ......; died ....
1980 V.   NETTIE B., born ......; died ....

1013 (II) ANNA C., DAUGHTER OF HORACE.

Anna C. Janes married Henry Kingsley of Middlebury, Vt.   She died 1864.

CHILDREN.

1981 I.   JENNIE, born ......;
1982 II. LILLIE, born ......;
1983 III. WILLIE, born ......;

1015 (IV) SARAH, DAUGHTER OF HORACE.

Sarah Janes married L. R. Bolton of Middlebury, Vt.

CHILD.

1983a I. CHILD, born ...... ;

1016 (V) CHAMPION M., SON OF HORACE.

Deacon Champion Marsh Janes married Fidelia A. Holcomb, 19 June, 1856. He is a very worthy, pious and good citizen of Cornwall, Vt., inheriting many of the good traits of his noble ancestors, and possessing the same beautiful estate where his father and grandfather lived.

CHILDREN.

1984 I. MARTHA LOUISA, born 7 Dec,, 1857.
1985 II. HORACE WHITNEY, born 30 Sept., 1861.

1017 (VI) BETSEY, DAUGHTER OF HORACE.

Betsey Janes married Josiah W. Parker of New Haven.

CHILD.

1985a I. ELIZA, born ...... ;

1042 (I) DAVID W., SON OF ALVAN.

David W. Janes married Jeannette Hitchcock of Westfield.

CHILDREN.

1986 I.   FRANK AUGUSTUS, born ......; died young.
1987 II. JEANNETTE ALICE, born 19 Dec., 1857.
1988 III. ANNA FRANCES, born 19 Aug., 1860.
1989 IV. FREDERIC HOMER, born ......; died young.

1043 (II) CATHARINE P., DAUGHTER OF ALVAN.

Catharine P. Janes married 16 April, 1856, Charles A. Clark of Worcester.

CHILDREN.

1990 I. MARY JANES, born 22 Oct., 1859.
1991 II. FRANK EDWARD, born 30 Jan., 1861.

EIGHTH GENERATION.

LINE OF WILLIAM.

1069 (I) WILLIAM H., SON OF EDWARD.

William H. Janes, through some mistake, is mentioned on page 220, as dying young, and the middle initial H. is omitted, inadvertently.

He married ....

CHILDREN.

1993 I. SUSAN ROLLO, born ......; 1828.
1994 II. EDWARD, born ......; 1829.
1995 III. HENRY C., born ......; 1831.
1996 IV. JOSEPH, born ......, 1834; died ......
1997 V. ELIZABETH, born ......, 1838; died in Missouri.
1998 VI. WILLIAM P., born ......, 1840; died ......
1999 VII. JOHN W., born ...... 1843; a patriot soldier, killed.

1070 (II) HENRY F., SON OF EDWARD.

Henry F. Janes has a very remarkable history. He says of himself: "I am and all my life, from my boyhood, have been a backwoodsman in the strictest sense of that word. You will no doubt think it strange that a man could live to turn his sixty-third year in the United States, and never see a rail road or a telegraph; but there is just such a man in California, and I am the man. I was born in Pendleton county, Virginia, on the head waters of the Potomac, in the Alleghany mountains, and in 1819 my father emigrated to Ohio, and I soon after left the parental roof, and from that time to the present, the western wilds have been my home; and nature, clothed in all her virgin beauty, has been the book that I ever read. I have been in the front ranks of pioneers in Indiana, Wisconsin, Iowa, Illinois and Missouri, and, in 1849, I crossed the plains to California, and my western career was cut short only by the Pacific; but for that I know not how far or where I should have been by this time. I have one

thing to comfort myself with at least, that is, the
county of Humboldt, the one I live in, is the furthest
west of any land in the United States, and I am within
a few miles of the western end of it."

He was married to Keziah Ann Talbot, 15 March,
1827, near the famous Tippecanoe battle ground.

CHILDREN.

2000 I. THOMAS J., born 5 Aug., 1828; married Ellen
         Fleisher. He was a patriot soldier.
2001 II. JAMES S., born 20 Nov., 1830.
2002 III. ELIZABETH, born 4 June, 1833; married T. M.
         Ward.
2003 IV. JOHN W., born 1 Aug., 1835; a patriot soldier.
2004 V. JASPER N., born 15 May, 1838.
2005 VI. WILLIAM H. H., born 15 July, 1841.
2006 VII. THEODORE F., born 8 July, 1844.
2007 VIII. JOSEPH T., born 22 Aug., 1848.

1071 (II) ANN, DAUGHTER OF EDWARD.

Ann Janes married H. W. Arbogast. She died, and
Henry T., her brother, adopted all the children.

CHILDREN.

2008 I. TRYPHENA, born 10 March, 1833.
2009 II. MINERVA, born ... July, 1835.
2010 III, HENRY W., born 6 March, 1836.
2011 IV. SON, born ......;
2012 V. SON, born ......;
2013 VI. DAUGHTER, born ......;

1073 (V) JOHN S., SON OF EDWARD.

John S. Janes married ....

CHILDREN.

2014 I.   PETER, born ......, 1833.
2015 II.   MARTHA, born ......, 1834.
2016 III.   ELIZA, born ......, 1836.

1074 (VI) EDWARD P., SON OF EDWARD.

Edward P. Janes married (1) ...., (2) ....

CHILDREN.

2017 I.   JOHN E., born ......, 1836.
2018 II.   FRANK, born ......, 1838.
2019 III.   ALMIRA, born ......, 1842.
2020 IV.   IDA, born ......, 1851.
2021 V.   EDDIE, born ......, 1853.
2022 VI.   JEANNETTE, born ......, 1855.
2023 VII.   HENRY, born ......, 1857.
2024 VIII. BYRON, born ......, 1859.
2025 IX.   JASPER, born ......, 1860.
2026 X.   ANN, born ...... ;
2027 XI.   MARY, born ...... ;

1075 (VII) JOSEPH T., SON OF EDWARD.

Joseph T. Janes resides in Kansas. He married ....

CHILDREN.

2028 I.   WINFIELD SCOTT, born ......, 1842.
2029 II.   HENRY C., born ......, 1844; wounded at Vicksburgh, July, 1863.

2030 III. ELIZABETH, born ......, 1846.
2031 IV. THOMAS, born ......, 1848.
2032 V. ANNA, born ......, 1851.
2033 VI. JOSEPH, born ......, 1853.
2034 VII. WILLIAM, born ......, 1855.

1076 (VIII) ELIZABETH, DAUGHTER OF EDWARD.

Elizabeth Janes married Mr. McMullen.

CHILDREN.

2035 I. DANIEL, born ......, 1840.
2036 II. ANN, born ......, 1842.
2037 III. JOHN, born ......, 1843; a patriot soldier.
2038 IV. WILLIAM, born ......, 1845; a patriot soldier.

1078 (I) THOMAS G., SON OF WILLIAM.

Dr. Thomas Gresham Janes was an eminent physician, and lived and died in Green county, Ga. He was several times elected senator to the legislature. He was a pious member of the Baptist church.

He married three times: Miss West, Miss West, and Miss Sanford.

The names of his children are not at hand.

CHILDREN.

2039 I. SON, born ......;
2040 II. SON, born ......;
2041 III. DAUGHTER, born ......;
2042 IV. DAUGHTER, born ......;
2043 V. DAUGHTER, born ......;

1079 (II) ABSALOM, SON OF WILLIAM.

Absalom Janes married Cordelia Calloway, 1816.
He died 25 September, 1847.

CHILDREN.

2044 I.   PALEMON L., born 5 Oct., 1818 ; unmarried ; died
12 Sept., 1838.

2045 II.   CORNELIA M., born 26 Sept., 1820 ; married James
R. Sanders.

2046 III.   THOMAS P., born 11 Sept., 1823 ; married Emily
Eliza Fish.

2047 IV.   NANCY W., born 18 June, 1826; married Robert
L. McWharton ; died 18 June, 1847.

2048 V.   MARY E., born 15 June, 1828 ; married Rev. J. G.
Ryals.

2049 VI.   ANN M., born 21 July, 1830; unmarried; died
24 July, 1832.

2050 VII.   MARTHA E., born 17 May, 1833 ; unmarried;
died 28 July, 1834.

2051 VIII. FELIX WILLIAM, born 11 Dec., 1836; unmarried;
died 5 April, 1853.

2052 IX.   SUSAN H., born 19 Nov., 1839; married Professor
W. G. Woodfin.

2053 X.   CORDELIA F., born 19 Feb., 1842 ; married W.
H. Pritchett.

2054 XI.   ABSALOM M., born 15 Dec., 1844; died 3 July,
1845.

Colonel Absalom Janes was a successful planter and
merchant. The *Augusta Constitutionalist* (a paper published in Augusta, Ga.), a short while after his death,
says :

" *Death of Col. Absalom Janes.*—The life and character of this distinguished individual seems to demand a passing notice. Col. Janes was born in the county of Wilkes, in this state, 8 June, 1796. He removed to the eastern part of Greene county (now Taliafero) in 1816, and resided there until 1839, when he removed to Penfield, where he terminated his earthly existence, 25 September, 1847, having just entered upon the fifty-second year of his age.

" In this dispensation of Providence, the community in which he resided for the last eight years of his life, has been bereft of one of its most active and useful citizens. He was several times elected by the people of Taliafero county, as senator to the state legislature, in which capacity he faithfully and ably sustained the views and wishes of his constituents. He was also a prominent, consistent and efficient member of the Baptist church from 1828, to the time of his death. He was treasurer of the Georgia Baptist State Convention, for eleven years. Colonel Janes had talents of a high order, with a strong, active, discriminating mind; and possessed an energy of character, that enabled him to decide and act with promptness upon all practical questions that were presented to his consideration. He reasoned from analogy; and, although his conclusions were quickly drawn, yet they were seldom, if ever, found to be incorrect. In practical financial affairs, his judgment was inferior to none. He possessed a public spirit of benevolence, and was liberal in his donations upon every worthy object that presented itself. He also possessed a philanthropic heart, and could feel for the wants of others. The poor and destitute of his neighborhood ever claimed his attention, and he always showed a willingness cheerfully to relieve them of their wants and distresses. As a parent, he was affectionate, kind and indulgent. As a neighbor, he was courteous, peaceable, beneficent and obliging.

" In 1844, the democratic party nominated him as candidate for congress in the seventh congressional district, in opposition to the Hon. Alexander H. Stephens, and although Mr. Stephens was elected, his accustomed majority was greatly reduced. Mr. Stephens was then a whig. He was a states' rights democrat, and received a larger vote than any candidate who ever run in opposition to the Hon. A. H. Stephens."

EIGHTH GENERATION.

LINE OF SAMUEL.

1244 (I) JONATHAN E., SON OF LOWELL.

Jonathan Edwards Janes married Harriet Ann Lyman.

CHILDREN.

2055 I. BERTHA ANN, born 2 July, 1858.
2056 II. EDWARD L., born 9 Dec., 1860.
2057 III. FRANKLIN S., born 9 May, 1864.

1253 (I) EDWIN S., SON OF SPENCER.

Edwin S. Janes married Sarah Strong, daughter of Elisha Strong of Northampton, 10 May, 1855. She was born 6 June, 1834.

CHILDREN.

2058 I. JENNETTE CASSENDANA, born 6 March, 1856.
2059 II. LEWIS STRONG, born 15 March, 1857.
2060 III. CHARLES EDWIN, born 17 Nov., 1860.

1256 (1) LEGH RICHMOND), SON OF REV. FRANCIS.

Rev. Legh Richmond Janes married Flora W. Smith of Syracuse, daughter of Rev. Vinal Smith and granddaughter of Rev. A. Bassett. The latter, born in Derby, Conn., about 1770, graduated at Yale College, with the highest honors, settled first in Winchester, Conn., afterwards in Walton, Delaware county, N. Y., where he preached for a time and retired in feeble health. He died in Walton, 1859. Her father, Vinal Smith, was born near Boston, 1801, and graduated at Union College in 1829; spent a year and a half in Union Theological Seminary, Prince Edward, Virginia, and a year and a half in Andover Theological Seminary.

Bronchial difficulty prevented his enjoying a continued pastorate. He was for a long time an agent for the Bible and tract cause.

Rev. Legh R. Janes was chaplain of the 99th Pennsylvania Veteran Volunteers, for the winter of 1864 and 1865. His colonel, Edwin R. Biles, was an old untamed soldier, served in Mexican war, and in Walker's filibustering expedition, serving as adjutant general. He was an infidel, with some redeeming traits of character. The regiment was engaged in all the prominent battles of the Potomac. It was also stationed in the front of Petersburg, and for a number of weeks in Fort Sedgwick, popularly known as "Fort Hell." They were in the Weldon raid, in the Thatcher Run fights at the final breaking up of the lines, and at the surrender of Gen. R. E. Lee.

Rev. L. R. Janes's first letter from home contained the news of the death of their first-born. He received it when marching to battle, in the rain, at a momentary halt.

The following lines express the mother's feelings, who penned them in her loneliness:

A CHANGE.

Happy father, loving mother,
Toddling prattler, baby brother,
Every day is sunny weather
While we all are here together.
  What delight
  Is ours to-night!   ˎ
  Happy little family!

A MONTH LATER.

Father on the field of battle,
Hushed at home the witching prattle;
First-born sleeping in the ground.
Four we were — now two are found.
  Sitting silent
  In the twilight,
  Only baby dear and I.

Father, faint not in thy duties;
Mother, mourn not buried beauties.
Faithful labor, uncomplaining,
Yield thy child to higher training.
  God bereft you,
  But has left you,
  Still a work for Him to do.

The following, written a month later, is of similar attractive interest for insertion :

SEPTEMBER.

I.

The tenth of September, we'll ever remember,
  As being the day, my heart first gave its love
Into the dear keeping of him who is sleeping
  Beside the camp-fire, with the blue sky above ;
And thought treasures up each endearing enjoyment—
  Betrothal and bridal, mid roses of May —
Our busy young life, with its hallowed employment,
  Our home, by the babe's merry laughter made gay.

II.

Another September, full well we remember,
  From home to "the front," went my husband so dear ;
Its days yet unnumbered, our first-born had slumbered
  To waken above, and the cottage was drear.
Of all sad Septembers!   My heart to the embers
  I liken, while gazing upon them alone ;
The warmth of love's blessing, light the prattler's caressing,
  Its life and its sweet sunshine has flown.

III.

How many, this autumn, sit sorrowing, sighing,
  With sick hearts more heavy, more hopeless then mine ;
Our country's strong sons in their manhood are dying,
  God grant that her daughters may never repine !
While sitting afar from the tumult of war,
  I think of the wounded, the dying, the dead.—
My own loved one there ; hear, oh Father, this prayer,
  May many, by him, to the Saviour be led !

IV.

And mother, dear mother, what if he should never
    Come back to my home, to my heart come no more?
What if I should list for his footstep forever
    In vain — never hear his dear voice as before?
Could nature endure it, the heart never breaking,
    To live on, without his dear love, precious prize —
The babe on my bosom, half-orphaned, awaking?
    Oh! terrible thought! burning tears blind my eyes.

V.

Not soldiers alone, mid the cannon's loud rattle,
    Must cheerfully struggle, their country to save;
But woman, when dear ones are falling in battle —
    Yes woman at home must be hopeful and brave,
And patient endure it, nor faith ever falter,
    Though weeping the maiden, and widowed the wife—
For dear country's sake, lay our all on her altar,
    Our heart's holy loves for the nation's dear life!

VI.

The fatherless babe, and the sad sonless sire,
    The mother, whose darling did "fall in the fight,"
Shall reap their reward, at the call, "Come up higher,"
    For these hallowed off'rings to God and the right.

Shortsville, N. Y., Nov., 1864.   F.

He lived through more exposures than usually fall
to the lot of a chaplain, but returned to his church
near Geneva, and resumed his pastoral labors.

CHILDREN.

2061 I.   CLARENCE SMITH, born 5 April, 1862; died 26 Sept.,
        1864.
2062 II. ALFRED RICHMOND, born 13 Feb., 1864.

G. M. Janes, brother of Legh Richmond, was born in Otego, 14 October, 1843. Entered Hamilton College (Clinton, N. Y.), 1 September, 1862; left at end of second year to become principal of Seneca Falls Academy, for two years; reentered college and graduated with the class of 1866; is now principal of Rural Seminary, in Pembroke near Rochester.

1319 (II) CHARLES, SON OF ELIHU.

Charles Janes married his cousin Sarah Ann Cook, daughter of Arnold and Sally (Janes) Cook, 2 August, 1836. They are active, and devoted to good works. Mrs. Janes is a very efficient sabbath school teacher.

CHILDREN.

2063 I.   LAURA, born 10 Jan., 1838.

2064 II.   ARNOLD C., born 16 Nov , 1841; died æ. 2 years.

2065 III. SARAH JARVIS, born 19 Sept., 1843.

2066 IV.   A. COOK, born 23 Aug , 1845; died 16 Sept., 1847.

2067 V.   ARNOLD C., born 10 Aug., 1849; died 10 April, 1857.

2068 VI.   CHARLES B. (twin), born 13 June, 1854; died 4 Aug., 1855.

2069 VII. MARY GRAY (twin), born 13 June, 1854; died 8 Aug., 1855.

1321 (IV) ELIHU, SON OF ELIHU.

Elihu Janes married Emily Foster, 29 October, 1835.

CHILDREN.

2070 I. EMILY A., born 23 Oct., 1836; died 8 March, 1857.
2071 II. ELIZABETH J., born 16 Dec., 1838.
2072 III. BENJAMIN F., born 8 May, 1841.
2073 IV. ELIHU II., born 16 April, 1844; died 21 February, 1849.
2074 V. CHARLES A., born 14 Dec., 1847.
2075 VI. ELLA A., born 23 May, 1850; died 8 Sept., 1850.

1322 (V) F. MORTIMER, SON OF ELIHU.

F. Mortimer Janes married Lucinda Hinks.

CHILDREN.

2076 I. MARY HELLEN, born ......;
2077 II. ALBERT HENRY, born ......;

1323 (VI) F. PRESCOTT, SON OF ELIHU.

F. Prescott Janes married Lucilla Chickering. She died 6 September, 1863.

CHILDREN.

2078 I. EDWIN PRESCOTT, born ......;
2079 II. MARY AUGUSTA, born ......;
2080 III. EMMA, born ......;
2081 IV FRANKLIN, born ......;
2082 V. CLARA COOK, born ......;
2083 VI. ELIZABETH WALKER, born ......;
2084 VII. GEORGE, born ......;

1325 (VIII) CALEB J., SON OF ELIHU.

Caleb Jarvis Janes married Mary Hannegan.

CHILD.

2085 I. SETH WALKER, born ...... ;

1349 (I) MARY, DAUGHTER OF JONATHAN.

Mary Janes married Robert Creighton of New York. Now resides in Brooklyn, a worthy and faithful mother and Christian.

CHILDREN.

2086 I.   DAVID, born ...... ;
2087 II. SUSAN, born ...... ;
2088 III. ROBERT, born ...... ;

Mary married (2) George Bolton.

CHILDREN.

2089 IV. SAMUEL, born ...... ;
2090 V. WILLIAM, born ...... ;
2091 VI. ISABELLA, born ...... ;

1350 (II) WILLIAM, SON OF JONATHAN.

William Janes married Ann Creighton of New York. He was a very ingenious mechanic; died in middle life.

CHILDREN.

2092 I. EUGENE, born ...... ;
2093 II. MARY GRAY, born ...... ;
2094 III. GEORGIANNA, born ...... ;
2095 IV. JAMES, born ...... ;
2096 V. MARY E., born ...... ;

1378 (I) LORENZO, SON OF OLIVER.

Lorenzo Janes married ...... Nichols, 17 June, 1855.
They live in East Cleveland, Ohio.

CHILDREN.

2098 I. HYLAS SABINE, born 1 March, 1856.
2099 II. ANDREW OLIVER, born 27 Dec., 1857.
2100 III. MILTON MITCHELL, born 12 Aug., 1864.

1380 (III) MARY P., DAUGHTER OF OLIVER.

Mary P. Janes married Isaac E. Warren, March,
1848.

CHILDREN.

2101 I. CHARLES OLIVER, born 30 April, 1851.
2102 II. ANDREW E., born ......, 1855.

1384 (VII) HARRIS, SON OF OLIVER.

Harris Janes married Celia DeWolf.

CHILD.

2103 I. ARTHUR DEWOLF, born 2 Nov., 1864.

1407 (VI) HENRY H., SON OF ALONZO.

Henry H. Janes married Clara Fenton, 16 March, 1865.

CHILD.

2104 I. CARRIE BELLE, born 29 Jan., 1866.

1419 (I) HENRY, SON OF HARRIS.

Henry Janes married Samantha Convers.

CHILDREN.

2105 I. ......;
2106 II. ......;
2107 III. ......;

1424 (II) SAMUEL M., SON OF HARRIS.

Samuel Merriman Janes is a thorough and efficient business man (going to the city like many poor country boys, penniless, and determined to make their genius tell on their thrift); has risen to a good fortune and competence. He married Catharine E. Miller, and is surrounded with quite a family of children, one of whom is well married.

CHILDREN.

2108 I.   JULIA A., born 25 October, 1841; married ....
2109 II. BENJAMIN A., born 22 January, 1844.
2110 III. MARY L., born 10 Dec., 1849.
2111 IV. FREDERIC H., born 15 June, 1852.
2112 V.   ISABEL, born 10 May, 1854.
2113 VI. EMILY, born 20 February, 1857.
2114 VII. HENRY A., born 2 March, 1859.

1432 (I) SUSAN M., DAUGHTER OF SYLVANUS.

Susan M. Janes married Joel Brown, 14 October, 1856.

CHILD.

2115 I. EUGENE E. BROWN, born 8 April, 1862.

1437 (II) ELLEN, DAUGHTER OF SAMUEL.

Ellen Janes married George S. Graves of Williamsburgh, Mass.

CHILDREN.

2116 I. FRANKLIN HERBERT, born 10 March, 1859.
2117 II. LILLIAN BELLE, born 3 May, 1862.

1441 (I) JULIANNA, DAUGHTER OF ALEXANDER.

Julianna Janes married William Darling.

CHILD.

2118 I. WILLIAM, born ...... ;

1459 (I) ALDEN S., SON OF PASCHAL P.

Alden Spooner Janes married Hattie Cantrall, daughter of Col. Cantrall of Kenton, Ohio, who was killed at second Bull Run battle.

CHILD.

2119 I. CHILD, born 28 May, 1866.

1460 (II) SARAH, DAUGHTER OF PASCHAL P.

Sarah Janes married (1) William Solomon, (2) William Hart. She was a noble minded young mother: died early, greatly neglected by one who is supposed to have deceived her and abused her sisters.

CHILDREN.

2120 I. INFANT, born 12 Feb., 1853; died ....
2121 II. FRANKLIN, born 4 May, 1858.

1468 (I) MARTHA ANN, DAUGHTER OF SAMUEL.

Martha Ann Janes was educated at Mt. Holyoke Seminary, and was a successful teacher. She married William Trusdell, for a time a lawyer, but he gave himself too much to speculation, and failed in business.

CHILDREN.

2122 I.   CATHARINE J., born 3 June, 1851.
2123 II. MARY H., born 14 April, 1853.
2124 III. FRANKLIN HUDSON, born 25 Nov., 1854.
2125 IV. GUY JOHNSON, born 31 March, 1859.

1470 (III) NATHANIEL P., SON OF SAMUEL.

Nathaniel Parsons Janes was for some time engaged in the dry goods trade in Massachusetts, and in New York city. He died in middle life. He married (1) Sarah Heath, (2) Emma Overton. Sarah left a daughter.

CHILD.

2126 I. SARAH ANGELINA, born ......; died infant.

1472 (V) SARAH P., DAUGHTER OF SAMUEL.

Sarah P. Janes married Rufus Sackett, 6 May, 1851. They reside in Worcester.

CHILDREN.

2127 I. SARAH F., born 6 Jan., 1852.
2128 II. HENRY E., born 29 Aug., 1853.
2129 III. JOHN R. born 26 Aug., 1855.
2130 IV. ELIZABETH M., born 30 Dec., 1856.
2131 V. RUFUS, born 24 Aug., 1858.
2132 VI. NATHANIEL P., born 10 Sept., 1864.

1475 (VIII) ISABELLA P., DAUGHTER OF SAMUEL.

Isabella Patric Janes married Henry Dingman of New York city. She was a lovely Christian, a sweet singer of sacred song, and an affectionate wife and friend.

In the early bloom of maternal thought and joy, the angels came that convoy sister spirits away to their better home in the bright abode of heaven, and took her thence to sing joyfully in paradise. She was greatly endeared to a wide circle of friends and relatives.

> "So fades a summer cloud away,
> So sinks the gale when storms are o'er,
> So gently shuts the eye of day,
> So dies a wave along the shore."

CHILDREN.

2133 I. HENRY (twin), born 20 Feb., 1865; died infant.
2134 II. ISABELLA (twin), born 20 Feb., 1865; died infant.

EIGHTH GENERATION.

LINE OF BENJAMIN.

1522 (I) LOIS, DAUGHTER OF HEMAN.

Lois Janes married David Reynolds.

CHILDREN.

2135 I.   OLIVER, born ...... ;
2136 II.   WILLIAM E., born ...... ;
2137 III. HENRIETTA, born ...... ;
2138 IV.   SARAH, born ...... ;
2139 V.   NORMAN, born ...... ;
2140 VI.   CHARLES, born ...... ;

1523 (II) ABIGAIL M., DAUGHTER OF HEMAN.

Abigail M. Janes married Isaac Dygert.

CHILDREN.

2141 I.   WARNER, born ...... ;
2142 II.   MARTHA, born ...... ;
2143 III. MARION, born ...... ;
2144 IV.   ANNA MARIA, born ...... ;
2145 V.   ELLEN, born ...... ;
2146 VI.   LAURA, born ...... ;

1524 (III) RUBY, DAUGHTER OF HEMAN.

Ruby Janes married Herkimer Dygert.

CHILDREN.

2146a I.   JOSEPH, born ......;
2147 II.   MILLA, born ......;
2148 III.   ROSE, born ......;
2149 IV.   WILLIAM, born ......;
2150 V.   GERTRUDE, born ......;
2151 VI.   EMERSON, born ......;
2152 VII.   LUCY, born ......;
2153 VIII. CATHARINE, born ......;

1526 (V) LAURA, DAUGHTER OF HEMAN.

Laura Janes married Abner Lewis.

CHILDREN.

2154 I.   HEMAN, born ......;
2155 II.   EDGAR, born ......;
2156 III. EMERSON BRISTOL, born ......;

1529 (1) LAURA, DAUGHTER OF ELIJAH.

Laura Janes married Mr. Reynolds, and lives in Canada. They have eight children.

1530 (II) NELSON SON OF ELIJAH.

Nelson Janes married Philena Baker, and lives in Geneseo, clerk of the managers of the Gen. James Wadsworth estate, who fell gloriously in the war for the Union. As our Nelson refused information, we depend upon limited information from his obliging father and others. He has five children perhaps, Mary, Laura, Willie, etc.

1533 (V) ANN ELIZA.

Ann Eliza Janes married Mr. Hall, and has six children.

1536 (VIII) WILLIAM.

William lives in Canada and married there Nellie McKay.

1538 (I) LUCENA, DAUGHTER OF JAMES.

Lucena Janes married (1) William C. Wright, July, 1825.

CHILDREN.

2157 i.   LUCY ANN, born ......;
2158 ii. ASA, born ......;
2159 iii. EVA JANE, born ......;
2160 iv. LUCENA, born ......;

Lucena married (2) David Woodward, about 1838.

CHILDREN.

2161 v. LAURA, born 13 Jan., 1839; · married Duncan M. Wilson.
2162 vi. JAMES, born ... July, 1844.
2163 vii. MARKS, born 9 Feb., 1849.

1539 (II) HAPPYLONA, DAUGHTER OF JAMES.

Happylona Janes married Jacob Sheets, about 1837.

CHILDREN.

2164 i.   ADALINE, born ......, 1838.
2165 ii. CAROLINE, born ......, 1840.
2166 iii. MARY, born ......, 1842.
2167 iv. EDWIN, born ......, 1845.

1541 (IV) JAMES, SON OF JAMES.

James Janes married Ann Smith, of Union, Pa.

CHILDREN.

2168 i.   MARVIN E., born ......, 1838; died infant.
2169 ii. JAMES, born ......, 1840.
2170 iii. JAMES LUCIEN, born ......, 1844; a patriot soldier; died in hospital.

1542 (V) HEMAN, SON OF JAMES.

Heman Janes married Maria Rouse, daughter of
Judge Rouse of Pennsylvania, 9 October, 1838. He
is an enterprising, prosperous, wealthy and benevolent
Christian gentleman. The family live in Erie, Pa.,
and occupy a neat, durable and cheerful residence, and
welcome most cordially their friends.

CHILDREN.

2171 I.   MARGARET M., born 30 Oct., 1839; died ......, 1837.
2172 II. MELANCTHON W., born 22 July, 1841; married
          Ella M. Smith.
2173 III. CAROLINE N., born 25 Nov., 1848; died ......, 1850.
2174 IV. HEMAN D., born 1 Oct., 1850.
2175 V.   WILLIAM D., born 26 June, 1853.

1543 (VI) SALLY, DAUGHTER OF JAMES.

Sally Janes married Thomas Smith, 1839.

CHILDREN.

2176 I.   MELVIN, born ......, 1840; volunteer in the navy.
2177 II. WALLACE, born ......, 1842; died 1859.
2178 III. ALLEN, born ......, 1847.
2179 IV. ELLA, born ......, 1850.

1544 (VII) MARY, DAUGHTER OF JAMES.

Mary Janes married William P. Rathbone. She died 1864.

CHILDREN.

2180 I. LUCINA, born ......, 1843.
2181 II. WATSON, born ......, 1846.
2182 III. PHEBE JANE, born ......, 1848.

1545 (VIII) ABIGAIL, DAUGHTER OF JAMES.

Abigail Janes married George A. Clark.

CHILDREN.

2184 I. ALISON, born ......, 1847.
2185 II. ELIZA, born ......, 1849.
2186 III. SON, born ......, 1860.

1546 (IX) ALLEN, SON OF JAMES.

Allen Janes married Eliza Hackett, of Union, Pa., 1849.

CHILDREN.

2187 I. WARREN, born ......, 1851.
2188 II. DeFOREST, born ......, 1853.
2189 III. HEMAN, born ......, 1859.
2190 IV. CARRIE MELVINA, born ......, 1861.

1548 (I) HIRAM, SON OF HIRAM.

Hiram Janes married Phebe A. Carpenter, 4 March, 1847. They lived in Rock county, Mis. He died in March, 1867. Both were baptized by Rev. R. M. Cary.

CHILDREN.

2191 I.   H. LOUISA, born 10 March, 1838; married Philander Campbell.
2192 II. LYDIA A., born 6 Oct., 1839; married Elias G. Abbott.
2193 III. ELLEN A., born 1 March, 1842; married Nathan L. Drake.
2194 IV. WARREN W., born 14 Jan., 1844.
2195 V.   H. MARVIN, born 20 Feb., 1846.
2196 VI. HERBERT L., born 14 March, 1848.
2197 VII. APALONIA C., born 26 Oct., 1851.

1549 (II) HORACE L., SON OF HIRAM.

Horace L. Janes married (1) Emeline Johnson, 26 March, 1840, in Michigan. She died 23 May, 1848. He married (2) Kate C. Simmons, 1 October, 1849. Lived in Harmony, Wis.

CHILDREN.

2198 I.   JULIA M. B., born 2 April, 1847; married Nelson Delano 1866, a patriot soldier who enlisted in the U. S., army in 1864, and served through the war.
2199 II. DELLA O. B., born 18 Nov., 1856.
2200 III. EVELYN, born 12 May, 1862.

1550 (III) JOHN E., SON OF HIRAM.

John E. Janes was born in Wolcott, Wayne county, N. Y.; at the age of ten, his father moved to Clarkson, Monroe county; from thence he went to Johnstown, Rock county, Wis., in 1838. Here he married Esther Bagley, 25 November, 1841. She was born in Brookfield, Vt., 4 February, 1819. They were both baptized by Rev. R. M. Cary, in 1843, into the Free Will Baptist communion. He was chosen deacon of the church.

CHILDREN.

2201 I.   OSCAR A., born 6 July, 1843; enlisted in Fourth Michigan Infantry, in 1864; wounded before Petersburg, Va. Afterward entered Hillsdale College, Michigan; graduating June, 1868.
2202 II.   GEORGE A., born 12 Oct., 1845.
2203 III. SUSANNA U., born 30 May, 1848.
2204 IV. SARAH L., born 13 July, 1851.
2205 V.   ADAH C., born 8 May, 1854.
2206 VI. JOHN L., born 8 Oct., 1857.
2207 VII. CLARENCE E., born 3 Aug., 1863.

1551 (IV) WILLIAM C., SON OF HIRAM.

William C. Janes married Sophronia Eastman of Cambridge, Niagara county, N. Y., 7 September, 1841. She was born in Attica, N. Y., 2 February, 1819; resides in Lima, Wis.

CHILDREN.

2208 I. EDMUND W., born 22 Oct., 1844.
2209 II. B. MELISSA, born 24 Nov., 1847.

1552 (V) THANKFUL M., DAUGHTER OF HIRAM.

Thankful M. Janes married Ebenezer Bullock, 17 November, 1844. She died in Lima, Wis., 26 August, 1866. Both baptized by Rev. R. M. Cary.

CHILDREN.

2210 I. EDMUND J., born 31 June, 1850.
2211 II. EMORY L., born 9 Nov., 1855.

1553 (VI) BETSEY ANN, DAUGHTER OF HIRAM.

Betsey Ann Janes married William P. Ferris, 13 April, 1841. She died in Milton, Wis., 17 February, 1864, member of (C) church.

CHILDREN.

2212 I. AUGUSTUS, born 15 Aug., 1843; married Noyes S. Belknap.
2213 II. ISAAC L., born 2 Jan., 1846; died 11 Feb., 1856.
2214 III. HIRAM J., born 20 April, 1847.
2215 IV. ELLEN C., born 20 April, 1849.
2216 V. MARY E., born 3 July, 1853.
2217 VI. WILLIAM L., born 5 Sept., 1856.
2218 VII. CHARLEY W., born 3 July, 1858.
2219 VIII. CHARLOTTE E., born 9 June, 1862.
2220 IX. BETSEY A., born 5 Feb., 1864.

1554 (VII) JANE ELIZA, DAUGHTER OF HIRAM.

Jane Eliza Janes married Lucius Bingham, 13 April, 1842. She died in Harmony, Wis., 6 April, 1847. Both members of the Free Will Baptist church.

CHILDREN.

2221 I. AUGUSTUS J., born 6 Oct., 1843.
2222 II. ANNA ELIZA, born 28 April, 1845.
2223 III. JANE, born 22 Feb., 1847.

1555 (VIII) MARY C., DAUGHTER OF HIRAM.

Mary C. Janes married (1) Harvey Pember, (2) Orlando Griggs. She was born in Clarkson, Monroe county, N. Y.

CHILD.

2224 I. HALE, born ......;

Mary C.'s sister Hannah has two children, Minnie and Cassius. Henry D., their brother, has two, Charles and Frederic.

1567 (II) CHESTER, SON OF SEYMOUR.

Chester Janes married Mary J. Deremer, 15 November, 1851.

CHILDREN.

2225 I. ALICE, born 22 Sept., 1853.
2226 II. EVA J., born 8 July, 1855.

46

2227 III. JUDD E., born 17 Sept., 1856.
2228 IV. FLORA A., born 8 May, 1859.
2229 V. CORA MARY, born 9 Nov., 1862.
2230 VI. CARRIE E., born 15 June, 1864.

1526a (VI) SARAH LOUISA, DAUGHTER OF HEMAN.

Sarah Louisa Janes married Robert McDonald.

CHILDREN.

2231 I. MARY ADELAIDE, born ......;
2232 II. CHARLES ALEXANDER, born ......;
2233 III. ROBERT DEAN, born ...... ;

1527 (VII) REUBEN ASKINS, SON OF HEMAN.

Reuben Askins Janes married Sarah Galloway.

CHILDREN.

2234 I. FREDERIC HEMAN, born 10 Sept., 1861.
2235 II. ELMA EUGENIA, born 11 Nov., 1863.

1575 (II) WILLIAM H., SON OF OLIVER.

William H. Janes married Nancy Goldsmith, 22 February, 1852. He died 22 December, 1863.

CHILD.

2236 I. FRANKLIN, born ......, 1856.

1576 (III) HORACE, SON OF OLIVER.

Horace Janes married Mary Rogers, 27 March, 1860. He weighs 267 lbs, and is well formed and a fine looking man. He is a very strong man. He once lifted a 43 gallon pipe of liquor to the counter for a landlord who lived near him, and he intended to put it on the floor inside the bar; but teazed the man by going out unexpectedly, and moving off till called back, and importuned to save him the trouble of drawing it all out by the gallon. When he had enjoyed the joke sufficiently, he turned and helped the man out of his trouble. He lives at Northville, Pa., on the lake shore.

CHILDREN.

2237 I.   EMILY, born 17 July, 1861.
2238 II. ADDIE M., born 29 Jan., 1863.
2239 III. ARTHUR H., born 9 Jan., 1865.

1578 (V) OLIVER, SON OF OLIVER.

Oliver Janes married Ellen Phillips, 9 December, 1856. Live at Northville, Pa.

CHILDREN.

2240 I.   EDDIE, born 13 Nov., 1857.
2241 II. LESLIE, born 22 May, 1860.
2242 III. CHARLES, born 26 April, 1863.

1579 (VI) ELIZABETH ANN, DAUGHTER OF OLIVER.

Elizabeth Ann Janes married Alexander Goodrich, 31 December, 1855.

CHILD.

2243 I. HATTIE, born ...... ;

1580 (VII) HIRAM, SON OF OLIVER.

Hiram Janes married Almira Teed, 12 February, 1852.

CHILDREN.

2244 I.   CHARLES, born ... Sept., 1852.
2245 II. ELIZABETH, born ......, 1855.
2246 III. GEORGE, born 26 Sept., 1857.

1630 (IV) MARY ELLEN, DAUGHTER OF HARRY.

Mary Ellen Janes, a very intelligent and amiable woman, married Mr. Stewart, and resides in Constantia, Ohio. They have had one son and two daughters. The oldest child, their son, and the youngest child, their daughter, died in October, 1865, of diptheria. Mrs. Mary Ellen Janes Steward is credited with prompt endeavors to furnish information.

1635 (IV) FRANK, SON OF REV. JOHN.

Frank Janes married Tilla Ward of Newark, Ohio, 23 May, 1865.

CHILD.

2247 I. MARY, born ...... ;

1644 (I) FREDERIC M., SON OF SETH.

Frederic Mortimer Janes married Zeruah Potter.

CHILDREN.

2248 I. LILLIAN ZILPHA, born 30 April, 1861.
2249 II. FREDERIC RAYMOND, born 5 June, 1865.

1645 (II) EUGENIA A. A., DAUGHTER OF SETH.

Eugenia Agnes A. married James McClung.

CHILDREN.

2250 I. EVA ALICE, born 5 May, 1861.
2251 II. IONA ESTILLA, born 9 Oct., 1862.

1659 (III) CHARLES M., SON OF MELVIN T.

Charles Mortimer Janes married Harriet Munn Hoadly, 22 May, 1862.

CHILDREN.

2252 I. JULIA, born 22 July, 1863.
2253 II. ROWLAND, born 7 May, 1866.

1668 (I) WILLIAM P., SON OF LORENZO.

William P. Janes married Anna Crilley, and resided at New York city. He was secretary for the National Express company, from 1851 to 1859, and devoted himself with great energy to the work. His health failed him so, that he was obliged to seek a more quiet retreat than his office, and a more balmy climate for his impaired constitution. He died at Savannah, 1860.

CHILD.

2254 I. ANNA CRILLEY, born ...... ; died young.

1670 (III) CHARLES, SON OF LORENZO.

Charles Janes married Mary Banta, daughter of Mr. Banta of the Astor House. He was his brother's successor as secretary of the National Express company for some years.

1671 (IV) LUCINA ANN, DAUGHTER OF LORENZO.

Lucina Ann Janes married Marshall Mason. She died 3 March, 1862.

CHILDREN.

2255 I.   FLORENCE, born ...... ;
2256 II. WILLIAM P., born ...... ;
2257 III. CHARLOTTE, born ...... ;

1740 (I) WILLIAM W., SON OF ELISHA.

William W. Janes married Julia Chapin, 1861.

CHILD.

2258 I. FRANK, born ......;

1742 (III) ELLEN M., DAUGHTER OF ELISHA.

Ellen M. Janes married L. A. Anderman, and they reside in Washington, D. C.

CHILD.

2259 I. CARRIE, born ......, 1863.

1748 (II) ERASTUS A., SON OF ALANSON.

Erastus A. Janes married Elizabeth Moon.

CHILDREN.

2260 I. WILLIE P., born 10 Dec., 1849.
2261 II. JULIAN A., born 21 May, 1854.

1754 (VIII) WILLIAM S., SON OF ALANSON.

William S. Janes married Lelia Pixley.

CHILD.

2262 I. HORACE A., born 22 Dec., 1863.

1758 (I) DAVID, SON OF CHANCELLOR.

David Janes married Elizabeth Bennett, and resides at Middletown, N. Y.

CHILDREN.

2263 I.   CHANCELLOR EUGENE, born ......, 1851.
2264 II. WILLIAM A., born ......, 1853.
2265 III. FANNY L., born ......, 1855.
2266 IV. ADDIE S., born ......, 1857.
2267 V.   FRANK H., born ..... , 1864.

1789 (I) SAMUEL B., SON OF ELISHA.

Samuel Barnes Janes married Charlotte House, daughter of Orla House of Troy. He was engaged for some time, to settle up the Lillie Safe company's business, and is now a broker in the city of New York; though frequently employed in matters of reference. Their children are not on our record.

1790 (II) HENRY W., SON OF ELISHA.

Captain Henry W. Janes was a member of General Grant's staff during the war, and is now in military business at Philadelphia. Previously, while in Texas, he came near losing his life, simply because a few Texans knew he was from a land that hated slavery and loved freedom, and they thirsted for the blood of all such men. His physician interposed and aided him in leaving the country, and in token of gratitude, he named his son in part from this kind hearted Dr. Blake.

CHILD.

2268 I. HENRY BLAKE, born ......, 1861.

1792 (I) WILLIAM V. B. A., SON OF WALTER.

William Van Buren Adam Janes married Mary F. Barnum, 28 April, 1851. He died in a few years.

CHILD.

2269 I. WILLIAM A. BARNUM, born ...... ;

1843 (I) ELEAZER T., SON OF ERASTUS.

Eleazer T. Janes married Gertrude Van Netter, and resides in Meridian, N. Y., with his father.

CHILDREN.

2270 I. WARREN, born 3 July, 1849.
2171 II. JOHN M., born 9 Oct., 1852.
2272 III. HELLEN, born 7 Feb., 1854.

1845 (IV) WILLIAM DUNNING, SON OF ERASTUS.

Captain William Dunning Janes married Lizzie Louise Fenno of Boston, on Washington's birth day, 22 February, 1865.

47

Capt. W. D. Janes was a bold, active officer in the army of the Union. He rose from the ranks to an honorable position, showing wounds and scars incident to the fierce conflicts through which patriot soldiers struggle in the service of their country.

CHILD.

2273 I. MINNIE LOUISA, born 7 Sept., 1866.

1846 (I) ROBERT, SON OF ELEAZER.

Robert Janes married ...., and lives in Michigan.

CHILDREN.

2274 I.   DAVID, born ......;
2975 II. ELEAZER, born ......;
2276 III. EMELINE, born ......;

1848 (III) MARY, DAUGHTER OF ELEAZER.

Mary Janes married ...., and resides in Michigan.

CHILDREN.

2277 I.   ELIZABETH, born ......;
2278 II. MARY, born ......;
2279 III. DORCAS, born ......;

1849 (IV) HARRIET, DAUGHTER OF ELEAZER.

Harriet Janes married ...., and resides in Michigan.

CHILDREN.

2280 I.   CAROLINE, born ...... ;
2281 II. TOBIAH, born ...... ;
2282 III. EVA, born ...... ;
2283 IV. AMELIA, born ...... ;

NINTH GENERATION.

LINE OF ABEL.

1872 (I) JULIA E., DAUGHTER OF ADRIAN.

Julia E. Janes married Giles White, 22 November, 1849.

CHILDREN.

2284 I. CHARLES ADRIAN, born 23 Sept., 1850.
2285 II. ISABEL, born 23 April, 1852.

1873 (II) HENRY, SON OF ADRIAN.

Henry Janes married (1) Caroline P. Hyde of Baltimore, 4 June, 1850.

CHILDREN.

2286 I. MARY, born 11 Sept., 1855.
2287 II. EDWARD BARTHOLOMEW, born 27 Dec., 1858.

Henry married (2) Ida Hyde of Baltimore, August, 1867.

1874 (III) EDWARD R., SON OF ADRIAN.

Edward Root Janes married Elizabeth B. Ingalls, 4 December, 1854.

CHILDREN.

2288 I. REBECCA INGALLS, born 31 Oct., 1856.
2289 II. HENRY EDWARD, born 27 April, 1859.
2290 III. FRANCES MARY, born 28 Dec., 1861.
2291 IV. HERBERT, born ......, 1863.

1875 (IV) GEORGE, SON OF ADRIAN.

George Janes married Louisa P. Entz, 17 June, 1857.

CHILDREN.

2292 I. FREDERIC HENRY, born 8 April, 1858.
2293 II. JULIA WHITE, born 13 May, 1861.
2294 III. ISABEL ENTZ, born 4 May, 1862.

1878 (I) HENRY, SON OF BENJAMIN F.

Henry Janes married ....

CHILDREN.

2295 I. LUCY (?), born ......;
2296 II. BENJAMIN (?), born ......;

1881 (I) ELIZABETH, DAUGHTER OF ALVIN.

Elizabeth Janes married Selden Oviatt of Rochester.

CHILDREN.

2297 I. WATKINS, born ......;
2298 II. ANGELINE, born ......;

NINTH GENERATION.

2046 (III) THOMAS P., SON OF COL. AB-
SALOM.

Dr. Thomas P. Janes married Emily Fish, 20 December, 1842.

He is the only living son of Col. Absalom Janes, and received the degree of bachelor, and master of arts from Princeton College, New Jersey, and the degree of doctor of medicine from the University of the City of New York. He practiced medicine seven or eight years, and gave up the practice from physical disability. He has retired for a number of years from public life, and attended to his planting interest near Penfield, Ga. He has never been a candidate for any public office, although, in 1863, he was offered a commission of colonel of cavalry by the confederate government (so called), which he declined from physical disability. The war for the Union caused him to lose heavily, yet he has enough left to make himself comfortable and above board.

CHILDREN.

2299 I.   EMMA C., born 2 Jan., 1847.
2300 II. MARY F., born 14 Nov., 1848.
2301 III. THOMAS P., born 19 March, 1850.
2302 IV. LELIA H., born 14 Sept., 1851; died 16 June,
          1852.

2303 v.   FELIX WILLIAM, born 24 Nov., 1852.
2304 vi.   CHARLES P., born 19 Aug., 1854.
2305 vii. EDDIE H., born 31 Jan., 1856.
2306 viii. SARAH M., born 13 Aug., 1857.
2307 ix.   LILLA E., born 3 May, 1860; died 3 May, 1860.
2308 x.   DAVID ARTHUR, born 10 Aug., 1861.
2309 xi.   JAMES M., born 15 Oct., 1862.
2310 xii. WALTER LEE, born 25 Nov., 1863.
2311 xiii. ABSALOM E., born 4 June, 1865.

NINTH GENERATION.

LINE OF BENJAMIN.

2172 (II) MELANCTHON W., SON OF HEMAN.

Melancthon W. Janes married Ella M. Smith of Erie, Pa.

CHILDREN.

2312 i.   MARTHA M., born 9 Oct., 1863.
2313 ii. FREDDIE, born 14 Oct., 1865.

2168 (II) MARVIN E., SON OF JAMES.

Marvin E. Janes married Jeredina Stafford, 1859.

CHILDREN.

2314 i.   ANNIE, born .... ;
2315 ii. JAMES, born ...... ;

2191 (I) H. LOUISA, DAUGHTER OF HIRAM.

H. Louisa Janes married ....

CHILDREN.

2316 i.   IDA, born ......;
2317 ii. FLORA, born ......;
2318 iii. MINNIE, born ......;

———.

2192 (II) LYDIA A., DAUGHTER OF HIRAM.

Lydia A. Janes married ....

CHILD.   .

2319 i. ARTHUR EUGENE, born ......;

Children of William, son of Thomas. Concerning Nos. 1082, 1083, 1084, 1085, 1088, Dr. T. P. Janes of Penfield, writes as follows:

1082. Edward Janes, third son of my grandfather, is still living, and was born 12 July, 1802. He had some seven children living, I think, three boys and four girls. He is a very intelligent and worthy gentleman.

1084. William Janes, fifth son of my grandfather, was born 27 February, 1807, and died 28 August, 1854. He represented Lee county, Georgia, several years in the state legislature. He had eleven children, seven of whom are now living, two sons and five daughters. Dr. John William Janes, his eldest son, is an educated gentleman, and a skillful physician.

1083. Archibald Janes, fourth son of my grandfather, was an educated gentleman, born 7 October, 1804, and died 1859. He had some four sons, and four or five daughters. His sons were highly educated men.

1085. Simeon R. Janes, sixth son of my grandfather, born 10 March, 1809, and died 1834. He was a most excellent man. He left three daughters, all of whom are since dead.

1088. Daniel H. Janes, seventh son of my grandfather, born 14 March, 1815. He graduated in Franklin College, August, 1835, studied law, but never practiced it. He devoted himself to planting. He has one son and five daughters, all living.

———

The following has so far got misplaced that we cannot, at this writing, connect it with the regular line. Probably of the seventh generation:

John Janes married Dorcas Pierce, and went to Michigan, to reside in 1839.

Children:

EDWARD, born .... ;
NEWTON, born .... ;
ELIZABETH, born .... ;

APPENDIX.

A few remarks concerning the Alexander family that are connected with this genealogy may be here added. The direct line of Mehitable's descent is through George, the emigrant, John, Ebenezer, and Simeon, but others are mentioned on these pages who may or may not be descendants of George.

Grandmother Janes, Mehitable Alexander, was a descendant of a high minded stock. The name of Alexander was of considerable note in Scotland. George Alexander is the first of the Alexanders that we learn came from Scotland. He was of the number who regarded Charles I an usurper, a criminal sovereign, and all of the party felt the storm about to burst upon them when Charles II was becoming seated in power. Having sanctioned the beheading of the king, he was not a friend of the young monarch, and though not obnoxious like the regicides to the sovereign power, yet he desired a retreat from the pending troubles, and came for quiet to this new world.

He was the friend of Whally and Goffe, the regicide judges, who came over the wide ocean to escape the fury of Charles II and found such a rude concealment in the celebrated Judge's cave at New Haven, and afterward a more friendly shelter in Hadley, Mass., in the house of the minister who had been long a friend of Rev. J. Davenport, and who was willing to shield men who had faithfully performed sworn duty.

George Alexander appears to have settled first at Windsor, Conn.; afterward he settled in Northampton, and was interested with his children and grandchildren in the settlement of

48

Northfield, in 1673. He was a witness of contracts with the Indians as per record. He married probably in this country Susannah Sage.

His children were :

JOHN, born 25 July, 1645 ; died 1647.
ABIGAIL, born ...... ; married Micah Mudge.
MARY, born 20 Oct., 1648 ; married Thomas Webster.
DANIEL, born 12 Jan., 1650; unmarried ; died at Hadley.
NATHANIEL, born 29 Dec., 1652 ; married 20 Jan., 1680, Hannah Allen.
SARAH or SUSAN, born 8 Dec., 1654 ; married Samuel Curtis, 6 July, 1678.
JOHN (2), born ...... ; married Sarah Gaylord.

Nathaniel's children :

JOSEPH, born ...... ; married Margaret ....
PHILIP, born ...... ; married Abigail ....
EBENEZER, born ...... ; married Abigail ....
MEHITABLE, born ...... ; married John Holton, 7 Oct., 1731.

John, who married Sarah Gaylord, died 31 December, 1733. Sarah died 3 November, 1730.

Children of John and Sarah :

JOHN, born 24 Jan., 1673.
NATHANIEL, born ... March, 1676.
SAMUEL, born 6 Nov., 1678.
JOSEPH, born 10 Oct., 1681.
EBENEZER, born 11 Oct., 1684.
SARAH, born 7 Feb., 1688 ; married John Meacham.
THANKFUL, born 20 March, 1689.
ELIZABETH, born ......
ELIAS, born ...... ; married Ruth ....

Another Nathaniel married ...., and

Children were :

HANNAH, born 27 Oct., 1680.
HANNAH (2), born 24 Sept., 1681.
RUTH, born 22 Feb., 1691.

THANKFUL, born 9 Jan., 1694.
THOMAS, born 9 April, 1696; drowned.
DAVID, born 14 Jan., 1699.
MINDWELL, born ......;
SARAH, born ......;
ABIGAIL, born ......;

Philip married Abigail ....

Children:

ABIGAIL, born 10 Jan., 1744.
AARON, born 6 April, 1746.
RHODA, born 18 April, 1747.
LUCY, born 11 March, 1749.

Ruth Alexander was the second wife of Benjamin Burt, married 17 January, 1743. He was born September, 1695. Son of Deborah Burt (Stebbins) born in Northampton, 5 March, 1672. Daughter of John and Abigail Stebbins (Bartlett) born in England 1626, and resided in Springfield and Northampton, and granddaughter of Rowland Stebbins of Ipswich county, England, came over in ship Francis, 1634, and then aged 40 per record of custom house.

Joseph Alexander married Margaret ....

Children:

ELIZABETH, born 8 Feb., 1717.
THANKFUL, born 10 Oct., 1719.
EXPERIENCE, born 3 Feb., 1721.
AMOS, born 5 April, 1724.

Then (2) marriage, Mary's children:

MIGHILL, born ...., 1737.
MARY, born ...., 1741.

Elias Alexander married Ruth ....

Children:

ELIJAH, born ...., 1733.
ELISHA, born ...., 1735; and others.

Philip Alexander married Abigail ....

Children :

ABIGAIL, born 10 Jan., 1744.
AARON, born 6 April, 1746.
RHODA, born 18 April, 1747.
LUCY, born 11 March, 1749.

Ebenezer married Abigail ....

Children :

ABIGAIL, born 20 July, 1738.
REUBEN, born 17 Feb., 1740.

Ebenezer, son of John, resided for a time in Coventry, Conn., a companion and friend of Benjamin Janes. They were leading men, and both seem to be residents of Northfield, afterward.

Ebenezer Alexander married 10 Oct., 1709, Mehitable Buck, daughter of Henry B. of Wethersfield, Conn., and her mother was Elizabeth Kirby, daughter of John Kirby.

Children were :

ELIAS, born 25 July, 1710.
ANN, (?) born 1720 ; married Samuel Taylor, 20 Sept., 1738.
SIMEON, born 26 May, 1722 ; married Mehitable Howe.
THOMAS, born 30 May, 1727 ; married Azubah .....

Simeon Alexander married Mehitable Howe. He died 19 February, 1811.

Children :

MEHITABLE, born 22 May, 1745 ; married Ebenezer Janes.
MARTHA, born 3 Jan., 1746.
SARAH, born 20 July, 1750 ; married Samuel Holton.
ELISHA, born 8 Dec., 1753 ; married (1) Sophia Stebbins, (2)
    Martha Doolittle, granddaughter of Rev. Benjamin Doolittle.
CALEB (Rev.), born 22 July, 1755.
SIMEON, born 8 April, 1757.
ISABEL, born 2 April, 1758 ; married Samuel Patric (grandfather of the compiler).
FREEDOM, born 12 Feb., 1761 ; married Mr. Clark.

JOEL, born 1 Nov., 1762.
ELIPHAS, born 8 March, 1764.
MARTHA, born 29 April, 1766.
HANNAH, born 29 March, 1768; married Mr. Cross.

Thomas married Azubah ....

    Children were :

ELDAD, born 2 Oct., 1755.
MEDAD (Col.), born 15 July, 1757.
THOMAS, born .... ;
QUARTUS, born .... ;
LAVINA, born .... ;
SYLVIA, born .... ;
LYDIA, born .... ;
GEORGE, born .... ;
CONSIDER, born .... ;

Elisha (Major), married S. Stebbins.

    Children were :

FANNY, born .... ;
ELIJAH, born .... ;
SOPHIA, born .... ;
JOSIAH, born .... ;

Second wife's (Martha Doolittle) children :

SARAH, born .... ;
ELISHA, born .... ;
MARTHA, born .... ;
MARY, born .... ;

Josiah married Myra Lyman.

    Children were :

CATHARINE, born . .. ; married Moses Field ; died 1868.
FRANCIS L., born .... ;
EDWARD, born .... ; died 1866.
JOSIAH, born .... ;
WILLIAM D., born .... ;

George Alexander, first mentioned, and his son John took
oath of allegiance by order of " our Honored General Corte,"
1678.

Five Alexanders graduated at Yale College. Rev. Caleb Alexander of New Marlborough, of Mendon and of Cherry Valley, died 1828, æ. 73.

> "Men deemed no idlers in their Master's field,
> Whose deep research, whose science, faith and love,
> And fervent utterance of truth revealed,
> The ransomed souls, their crown shall tell above."

——

This deed is published as it contains the name of the emigrant, William Janes, and the fact of his connection with Northfield Grants:

KNOW all Men by these Presents, That I, Moses Field of Northfield in the County of Hampshire & Province of the Massachusetts Bay in New England, For and in Consideration of the Sum of Fifty Pounds, to me in Hand paid before the Delivery hereof, by Jonathan Janes of the Town County - and Province Aforeſᵈ Husbandman the receipt whereof I do hereby acknowledge, Have given, granted, bargained, and sold, and by these Presents do give, grant, bargain, sell, aliene, convey and confirm to Him the said Jonathan Janes His Heirs and Assigns, all my Right, Title, Interest, Estate, Property and Demand of in and unto One Certain percel of Land Lying in Northfield aforeſᵈ Containing Six Acres & Thirty Rods be it more or less it being part of a Grant of Land made to William Janes in the great Swamp Draught & is sixty Rods long from the East End of Said Grant & is Sixten Rods & Eight feet & three Inches wide Bounded by an highway or Comon Land East. Seth Field Eſq North [Illegible] & partly on an highway South, & on the Other parts of Said Grant West.

To have and to Hold, the said granted Premises, with the Appurtenances thereof, to Him the said Jonathan Janes His Heirs and Assigns, to his and their proper Uſe, Benefit and Behoof forever ; ſo that neither I, my Heirs or Assigns, nor any Perſon or Perſons claiming from by or under me, nor William Janes the Origenal

Grantee fhall ever have any Right, Claim, Intereft or Demand therein, by Virtue of any Act or Acts already had, done or fuffered whatfoever.

In Witnefs whereof I have hereunto fet my Hand and Seal this Third Day of April in the firft Year of His Majefty's Reign. Annq Dom. 1761.

MOSES FIELD [Seal]

Signed Sealed & Delivered
   in prefence of us
       SETH FIELD
       GEORGE FIELD
       MOSES EVANS JUN

Hampfhire ye Sept 17th 1772
Then Mofes Field fubfcribes to the foregoing Inftrument perfonally Appearing Acknowledged the fame to be his free Act & Deed
Before SETH FIELD Juft Peace.

JAMES JANES (260), *probably connected with the family.*

James may be No. 260 who married Elizabath Woodruff. He served the country in the revolution, was at the surrender of Cornwallis, was at battle of Monmouth and Long island, and was at Trenton, Lundy's lane, Queenstown, Plattsburgh, and Stony point. He afterward lived in Utica, where his children were born.

He had a son, William Janes, who lives in or near Newark, N. J., born June, 1818, married Jane Dunster, whose daughter Emma was born 1849. Alexander Janes, born 7 April, 1819, married Elizabeth Dunster. The two brothers married the two sisters on the same day at Morristown, N. J. Alexander's children : Ellen Sophia, born 29 July, 1843. Hester Elizabeth, born 18 January, 1847.

The father, James Janes, married (2) a widow, Mrs. Nancy Ball. He died 1854. He was the tallest man in his regiment, being 6 feet and 3 inches. Was very strong — once lifted 1,100 lbs.

Letter No. 1.

LIEUTENANT FRANK JANES.

Headquarters 7th Reg't, O. V. I.,
BOLIVAR HEIGHTS, VA., *Nov.* 13, 1862.

David S. Janes, Esq.,

Dear Sir : Your letter inquiring as to the fate of your brother, Lieutenant Frank Janes of company F, 7th Regiment, bearing date August 17th, has just come to hand.

Lieutenant Janes was killed at Cedar mountain, in the sanguinary battle that occurred there on the 9th of August last, and very early in the fight. He received four wounds. The first was in his right thigh, the second shattered his left ankle, the third was in his hip as he was being conveyed from the field ; and the last, which proved instantly fatal, was in the back of the head, while he was going off the field on the back of the orderly sergeant of his company. He was in command of his company until wounded, and no man on that bloody day showed more gallantry in the face of the murderous fire of the enemy than he. Recognized as among the bravest of the brave, he was beloved in life, and lamented in death by the entire regiment, and by none more than myself. If unflinching heroism in the face of death should consecrate the memory of its possessor, certainly that of Lieutenant Janes deserves a prominent place in the hearts of his countrymen.

An inventory of his effects has been made, agreeable to the articles of war, and they will be sent to you by express at once.

I am, sir, very respectfully,

Your obedient servant,

WM. R. CREIGHTON,

Col. 7th Reg't. O. V. I.

Letter No. 2.

Extract of a letter from a grandson of Obadiah Janes (230) :

EAST CLEVELAND, *Jan.* 26, 1867.

Dear Cousin Frederic :

I received yours of last month in due time * * *
Some of my grandfather's (Obadiah Janes) travels might be of
interest. He was out in the service just before the revolutionary war closed, but I think in no action ; but when about
seventy years of age he started from Darby Plains, Ohio, to go to
Washington, on foot and alone, to get a pension for a man by
the name of Jackson, for which he was to have a share of what
he got for doing so. He first came to Cleveland, thence to
state of Vermont, thence to state of Maine (to obtain testimony),
thence to the city of Washington, and on his way there, one
forenoon, a man overtook him riding on what he thought a very
smart horse. They traveled along together for half an hour or
so, found that they were going about six hundred miles on the
same road ; finally the man bid him good bye ; said he must get
along faster than he could go on foot ; said he probably would not
see him again ; so he rode on out of sight ; but when night came
they both put up at the same house. In the morning grandfather got started first. The man overtook him again about the
middle of the forenoon ; as before they traveled along together
for about an hour, then the man rode on and left him again,
after bidding him a good bye, and telling him he guessed he
would not overtake him again, and they would not stay at the
same house that night, but when night came they both stayed
at the same place again. The next morning grandfather got the
start of him again and traveled on, but the man came on and
overtook him again as before. They went along together talking
for some time as before, finally the man told him that he would
not overtake him again, so as to put up at the same place that
he did that night ; so they bid each other a good bye again the
third time, and he rode on out of sight again ; and when night

49

came grandfather put up at the same place he did again, making the third night they both stayed at the same places. The next morning grandfather started on ahead again; the man overtook him again before noon, but his horse began to show signs of being tired. They traveled along together and talked as before; but when the man stopped to feed his horse at noon, grandfather went on and left him behind again ; but the man did not overtake him again, and that was the last he saw of him. He went on to Washington, obtained the pension, then from there to Vermont, and from there back to Central Ohio; traveled all the way round on foot and averaged his forty miles or more per day. Just before he died he came from Erie, Pa., to Cleveland, Ohio, on foot, and made his forty miles per day. Another instance, perhaps, is worthy of note. One night when they or grandfather (Obadiah Janes) lived near Lake Champlain, he went some ten or fifteen miles up or down the lake (I don't remember which), on skates, and coming back late in the night, all alone, he skated into the water before he was aware of it. The weather was very cold, and the ice had cracked across the lake while he was gone, and opened so that it let him in to the water. He had an overcoat on, strapped around him, but he went across the crack in the ice, then put one arm up on to the ice, let it freeze so as to stick, then put up the other arm in the same way, then raised himself on the ice ; then he skated as fast as he could. His clothes were soon frozen stiff, but he had some ways to go before he · could get to a house, then he had quite a little distance to walk on land to get to the house from the shore, and as he could not get his skates off it made it rather hard walking; but it must be done or else he must do worse; so he finally succeeded in getting to the house.

Now I suppose I had better tell you a little about father (Oliver Janes). He enlisted once in the war of 1812, so called, to go and fight the Indians ; but before they were ordered off, peace was declared, so he did not go, and I have no war record to give for him, but he claims that he was never outrun by any person. He has also been a great traveler; thinks the hardest day's travel he ever did, was one time in January, and very cold weather up west, when the country was new. He went on foot from Fort Meggs to another fort, which were forty-six miles apart, and the snow about a foot deep with a crust on it that would nearly bear him up; but when he would go to step it would break through and let him down, so he could not walk, but he was obliged to run the whole distance. There were no settlers between the forts, so he must go through, or perish.

At another time he was going over the Green mountains, and he ran fifty miles in a day, besides stopping on the mountain and gathering a vial full of balsam fir, which took him two and a half hours. This last mentioned was performed, I think, in the spring or summer when the days were longer.

Uncle Alonzo Janes was not much of a traveler; but they say he, one time down in Vermont, mowed four acres of heavy grass in a day, on a bet of ten dollars. The man that made the bet gave him one-half of it for mowing it, and after he got that done, he went into another field and mowed one-half of an acre more; then outhopped the whole company. The next generation of Janeses about here are not so smart for work or travel; but I believe they are all true Union men. I know of no copperheads among them, although they did not go to war.

Letter No. 3.

HENRY JANES (552).

Letter to his father concerning his sudden death in April, 1805, from the physician.

These lines are to inform you that your son, Henry Janes, is no more. He was drowned at the mouth of the Genesee river, on the eve of the 17 April, 1805, in attempting to cross in a small canoe for his own diversion, with a boy about fourteen years of age. The canoe unfortunately overset. The boy swam ashore. The cry was made for help, but before it could be obtained he sunk; and before they could get him out, the spectators judged him to have been under water two hours. Every exertion to bring him to was in vain. I was called as a physician in about two hours after, but to no purpose to him, for there were no signs of life found. Deceased was buried in burying ground, four miles from mouth of Genesee river, the place of his death, in Northampton in the county of Genesee, N. Y.

By papers found in his pocket book, there was not the least dispute but that his name was Henry Janes; besides, he had said that his name was Janes, from Massachusetts; judged to be about twenty-six years of age; and by his writings, he had parents living in Northfield. He had middling good clothes, a good silver watch, which are in my care; something more than to pay his funeral charges and expenses thereof. He has some notes and receipts, etc., which will be of no use to any person except his relations. I published his death in the *Western Repository*.

[Physician's name is indistinct.]

Letter No. 4.

Minerva Brown (737), daughter of Esther Janes, and Oliver Sanford, writes concerning her family as follows:

CLINTON, *Dec.* 9, 1866.

* * * David died at the age of seven years. Charles married (1) Miss Taylor, niece of General and President Taylor; has married three times; has eight children; is a widower again, and has three children living. Mary Jane married Mr. Rutherford, lives in Illinois, on one of the largest farms. Brother Charles O. was a member of the assembly, at Jefferson city, Mo. Is president of a rail road, now resides at St. Francisville, Clark county, Mo. He lived on a plantation and owned slaves before he went to the assembly. His negroes would all have left if they had felt disposed, in his absence. But on his return he found everything well cared for, for they

knew him to be a kind master. Some time before the rebellion
he knew that trouble was coming; he gave away his cook, who
had been with him twenty-five years, and disposed of others;
and through the war was uninjured, although a Union man.
Oliver Sanford died in New Hartford, N. Y., in 1827; Esther,
his wife, died 17 January, 1844, in New York city. Adaline
married Joshua Palmer, in the year 1833, in Oneida county.
Janes and Joel were twins. Janes married (1) Mabel Green
1828 (she died 3 January, 1833, in Fayette, Miss.), died young.
He married (2) Amanda Wells, 1840, in Chambersburg, Pa.,
They had six children: Walter Zenas, Laura A., Ella, Alice
Virginia, Leonore J., Janes J. Sanford. Alden Brown married Minerva Sanford, 4 October, 1830, in New Hartford,
N. Y. Children : Lucy Minerva, born 8 June, 1833. Sarah
Amelia, born 5 July, 1835, died 1845. Alden S. Brown, born
16 August, 1836. Mary Josephine, born 6 October, 1840,
died 6 October, 1846. George Diven married Lucy M. Brown,
3 June, 1863.

Her two children (my grandchildren) are Josephine Diven,
and Eugene Diven.   *   *   *

Yours truly,
MINERVA S. BROWN.

Letter No. 5.

Alanson Janes (743) was born at Canaan, Mass. His parents
removed to the state of New York about the year 1800, and settled in what is now called Livingston county. He volunteered
in the service in the war of 1812, and took part in most of the
battles and skirmishes that took place in the western part of
the state, particularly at Buffalo, Black Rock, and was at the
storming of Fort Erie. He was severely wounded and brought
to this side ; his gallantry caused his promotion from a private
to major, under General Brown. After peace was declared,
he returned to private life and commenced farming, which calling he has followed since.

His oldest son now living, Erastus A. Janes, having completed his education, chose the profession of teacher, which he
has followed to the present time as professor of higher mathe-
matics and natural sciences. Horace L. chose the profession
of law ; he read with Hon. Judge Lord, of Geneseo, N. Y.
After being admitted to the bar, he took up his residence at Mt.
Morris, where he opened a law office, and likewise served as school
commissioner for two years. His prospects for the future were
very bright, until death suddenly stopped his career. Henry
M., from the time he was of age, until the breaking out of the
rebellion served as under sheriff of Livingston county ; but
during the last war, he served the government in several capa-
cities with marked success. Wm. S. has likewise chosen the
profession of law ; has been admitted to the bar, and is now
practicing in Mt. Morris, Livingston county, N. Y.

Additional Contents of Letters.

No. 192 William Janes, southern branch, had ten sons.
Samuel settled near Maysville, Kentucky, and John and another
brother settled in the Red River country about a century ago.
Their children are scattered over the southwest, and there is
no immediate access to their records.

A sister married Jacob Rentzell, another Henry Sybert, both of
Georgetown. Rentzell kept a public house in the times of the
revolution and entertained Washington, Jefferson, and nearly
all the statesmen and military heroes of that day. One of
his daughters married and moved to western Virginia in the
neighborhood of Henry F. Janes's father, about 1820. Her
husband was in business there, and one of the granddaughters
went back to Georgetown to visit the Rentzell family. He died
from intemperance ; and the history of that branch is rather
obscure.

THE NAME JAYNE.

JAYNE is a name not connected with the descendants of William Janes, but were doubtless connected centuries ago, on the other side of the Atlantic. We allow a small space to the following:

William Jayne, born in England 1652, had three sons. Lost his wife in England. Fled from persecution to the United States. In the year 1682, preached for the Baptist church on Long Island; married a second time, had seven sons. William, the oldest, born 1684. This second William married, had a son William, born 1712; Samuel, born 1713; Isaac, born ...... ; probably third son went to Vermont.

William's grandchildren :

William of 1712, left a numerous posterity, settled in nearly all the states. Dr. Jayne of Philadelphia is a grandson of William.

Sons of William of 1712 :

> WILLIAM, born .... ;
> TIMOTHY, born .... ;
> ISAAC, born .... ;
> JOHN, born .... ;
> DAVID, born .... ;
> EBENEZER, born .... ;

Timothy was a captain in the revolution; had forty-eight Jaynes in his company, and were all poisoned except Captain Tim., his servant, and Ebenezer, father of Dr. Jayne, who was a lieutenant in the company.

ERRATA.

Page 79, two lines from *top* for 1681, read 1661.

Page 129, John, son of Elijah who died about 1811, in South Hero, Vt., moved 1812 with his mother to Pittsfield, Mass., their former residence, and in 1816, or thereabouts, they moved to Ohio. The writer has evidence, recently, that Elijah himself did not live, to move with his children and grandchildren, back to Pittsfield, then to Ohio, to spend his last days with them, as printed.

Page 114, five lines from the *bottom*, for 47 read 74.

Page 155, nine lines from the *top*, Thibeau should read Thibou.

Page 155, six lines from the *bottom*, Janes should read Jones.

Page 167, fifteen lines from the *top*, after family, read Salima married Otis Munn, in 1783.

Page 169, five lines from the *top* for Z read X, also sixth line, etc.

Page 255, eleven lines from *top*, for May read Nov., for Frances read Flora.

Page 358, three lines from *top*, for Mis. read Wis.

Page 368, instead of Samuel Barnes, read Samuel Barstow.

No. 297, for Elma read Elam.

No. 765, for Frazy read Frazer.

No. 1231, for Louisa D. Brown, etc., read Louisa Dunham of Brown county, Ohio.

No. 1269, omit died young, and insert married . . . . .

No. 1555, opposite Mary C., read married Harvey Pember.

No. 1556, opposite Hannah M., should read married Thomas Griggs.

No. 1557, opposite Henry D., should read married Maria Colwell.

No. 1558, DeForest, unmarried; served in the army to the close of the war.

NOTICE.

Any corrections that are desirable may be written out distinctly, the page or number referred to; also any additions which are needed for completeness: as it is proposed to get up an addenda of a number of pages of matter for such additions; beside, more or less information is expected from the other side of the Atlantic, concerning the ancestry of William the emigrant, and the writer expects in due time to issue a pamphlet containing the same which will correspond in size and type so as suitably to accompany this volume.

F. JANES, care of J. H. Dingman,
654 Broadway, N. Y.

INDEX.

50

Kellogg, Capt., 84.
   Joseph, 36, 75.
King, John, 62, 75.
Kingsley, Professor, 23.
Kirby, John, 380.

Laud, Bishop, 19, 31.
Lee, Gen. R. E., 341.
Leigh, Lord, 17.
Lord, Judge, 390.
Lyman, Hannah, 37.
   Richard, 37.
Lyon, Gen., 139.
   Rev. Asa, 130.

Mather, Dr. Increase, 50.
   Rev. Richard, 47.
   Rev. M., 51.
   Rev. Eleazer, 47, 49, 50.
   Samuel, 65.
Markham, Wm., 72.
Marlboro, Earl of, 17.
Mason, Rev. James, 111.
Mason, Samuel, 39.
Matilda, Empress, 27.
Mattoon, Dr. Elihu, 164.
Maverick, Mr., 49.
McClure, Mr., 18.
   Capt. John, 111.
Meacham, John, 378.
Meggs, John, 33
Miller, James, 72.
Momaugin, 22.
Mudge, Micah, 378.

Nash, Mr., 15.
Newman, Mr., 23.

Oliver, James, 108.

Palmer, Joshua, 389.
Parsons, Joseph, 45.
   Samuel, 45.
Patric, Samuel, 75, 380.
   M. A., 170.
Partridge, Col. Samuel, 107.
Peeoke, John, 86.
Penny, Joseph, D.D., 278.
Penruddock, Sir Richard, 28.
Pepper, Robert, 72.

Pierce, Richard, 76.
   ...., 376.
Piersons, 56.
Pigot, Rev. George, 103.
Pixley, Noah, 46.
Philip, King, 92.
Pomeroy, Rev. Medad, 207.
Porter, Eleazer, 58.
Pynchon, 56.
   John, 65.
   Major, 74.

Reeves, Rev. Mr., 192.
Rentzell, Jacob, 390.
Robinson, Rev. John, 115.
Root, Ebenezer, 111.
   John, 91.
Ross, Dea. John, 219.
Rouse, Judge, 356.
Rowlandson, Mrs., 72.
Russell, Mr., 72.
   Rev. John, 74.

Sage, Susannah, 378.
Sanford, Alice V., 389.
   Ella, 389.
   J. J., 389.
   Laura A., 389.
   L. J., 389.
   Minerva, 389.
   Oliver, 389.
   W. L., 389.
Salmon, Thomas, 40.
Scarl, Elisha, 44, 45.
Shays, Daniel, 171.
Shelden, Col. Elisha, 130.
Shepherd, Gen., 172.
Southworth, Gilbert, 115.
   Sir Edward, 115.
Stanton, Thomas, 22.
Stebbins, Abigail, 379.
   Rowland, 379.
Steele, John, 80.
Stedman, T. L., 150.
Stephens, A. H., 338.
Stoddard, Hon. John, 52, 58.
   Mr., 51, 52.
   Solomon, 50, 69.
Stone, Mr., 25.
Stranahan, Hon. J. S. T., 111.
Strong, Gov. Caleb, 34.
   John, 37, 47, 51.

PART II.

FIRST OR CHRISTIAN NAMES OF THE DESCENDANTS OF JANES'S FATHERS.

PART III.

NAMES OF DESCENDANTS OF JANES'S MOTHERS.

52

PART IV.

NAMES OF PERSONS WHO HAVE INTERMARRIED WITH THE JANES FAMILY, AND THE NAMES OF THOSE WHOM THEY MARRIED.—Reference by Pages.

www.ingramcontent.com/pod-product-compliance
Lightning Source LLC
Chambersburg PA
CBHW032311280326
41932CB00009B/774